D1824520

World Christianity in
Local Context

David A. Kerr
(photo courtesy of Revd Per Håkansson)

World Christianity in Local Context

Essays in Memory of David A. Kerr
Volume 1

Edited by
Stephen R. Goodwin

continuum

Continuum International Publishing Group

The Tower Building   80 Maiden Lane
11 York Road   Suite 704, New York
London SE1 7NX   NY 10038
www.continuumbooks.com

© Stephen R. Goodwin and Contributors 2009

All rights reserved. No part of this publication may be reproduced or transmitted in any
form or by any means, electronic or mechanical, including photocopying, recording, or any
information storage or retrieval system, without prior permission in writing from the publishers.

Statement on use of Scriptures
Unless otherwise indicated, the biblical scripture quotations contained herein are from the
New Revised Standard Version Bible, copyright© 1989 by the Division of Christian Education
of the National Council of the Churches of Christ in the U.S.A., and are used by permission.
All rights reserved.

Unless otherwise indicated, Qur'ānic scripture quotations contained herein are from the
Marmaduke Pickthall English translation of the Qur'ān, available online at http://www.
al-sunnah.com/call_to_islam/quran/pickthall/.

Permission to reprint the article by David A. Kerr, 'Christian Mission and Islamic Da'wah' by
the editor of the *International Review of Mission*, Jooseop Keum, is gratefully acknowledged.

British Library Cataloguing-in-Publication Data
A catalogue record for this book is available from the British Library.

ISBN-13: PB: 978-1-4411-9358-2

Library of Congress Cataloging-in-Publication Data
World Christianity in local context: essays in memory of David A. Kerr / edited by
Stephen R. Goodwin.

  p. cm.
ISBN 978-1-4411-9358-2
  1. Christianity and culture. 2. Christianity and other religions–Islam. 3. Islam–Relations–
    Christianity. I. Kerr, David A. II. Goodwin, Stephen R.

BR115.C8W67 2009
261.2'7–dc22

2008026816

Typeset by Newgen Imaging Systems Pvt Ltd, Chennai, India
Printed and bound in the UK by the MPG Books Group

Contents

List of Contributors

Dr James L. Cox is Professor of Religious Studies in the School of Divinity, University of Edinburgh. He co-ordinated the African Christianity Project in the Centre for the Study of Christianity in the Non-Western World in the University of Edinburgh from 1993 through 1998, and thus worked closely with David Kerr after the latter's appointment as Director of the Centre in 1995.

Dr Sean M. Doyle received an MA in Religion from Gordon-Conwell Theological Seminary in 2001 and was awarded a PhD in 2005 from the University of Edinburgh. His research interest includes the history of Christian interaction with Hindu culture and spirituality. He has been Assistant Professor of Religion at Methodist University in Fayetteville, North Carolina, and is currently Assistant Professor of Non-Western History at Geneva College, Beaver Falls, PA.

Dr Kenneth Fleming is a Scottish theologian. He lived in a Japanese Buddhist order in the 1980s and also worked as a Christian missionary in Thailand in the 1990s. He completed his doctorate under Moonjang Lee and David Kerr in Edinburgh. He is the author of 'Asian Christian Theologians in Dialogue with Buddhism' (Peter Lang, 2002). His major theological interests are in inter-religious dialogue – especially Buddhist-Christian dialogue – and missiology. Until 2006 he worked for the Theological Institute of the Scottish Episcopal Church, training their priests and developing contextual theology materials. He recently moved to Freiburg in Germany with his German wife and family. He is currently learning German and working part-time as an academic assistant at the University of Heidelberg.

Revd Dr Geomon Kizhakkemalayil George is an ordained minister in the India Pentecostal Church who serves as the Pastor of the International Gospel Church of Connecticut in Norwalk, Connecticut. He earned his PhD from the Centre for Study of Christianity in the Non-Western World at New College, University of Edinburgh, under the supervision of David A. Kerr. He is also the President of the International Gospel Church, a Christian mission organization in India and the Director of the Christian Missionary Theological Seminary, Bangalore, India. He is the author of the book, *Religious Pluralism: Challenges for Pentecostalism in India.* He and his wife Reji have three children.

Dr Stephen R. Goodwin earned a Masters and PhD at New College, University of Edinburgh under the supervision of David Kerr. His interdisciplinary studies include Political Science, European History and Religious Studies. He is currently lecturer in International Relations at a university in Istanbul, Turkey, with specialties in post-communist, Balkan and Turkish studies. His book, *Fractured Land, Healing Nations* (Peter Lang, 2006) focuses on nation-building and peace-building in Bosnia-Herzegovina, and he is a contributor to the book series of the European Academy of Sciences and Arts entitled, *Religion and European Integration: Religion as a Factor of Stability and Development in South Eastern Europe* (Edition Weimar, 2007).

Dr Klaus Hock has been a professor of *History of Religions – Religion and Society* at the University of Rostock since 1996. Before that, he had worked as a research fellow and lecturer at several universities and in Northern Nigeria, where he also served as a consultant to the Programme for Christian Muslim Relations in Africa (PROCMURA). His research focuses on Islam and Christian-Muslim relations (with emphasis on sub-Saharan Africa), African religions/religions in Africa, and transculturation.

Revd Dr James L. Hopkins studied at New College, University of Edinburgh, earning his doctorate at the Centre for the Study of Christianity in the Non-Western World under the supervision of David Kerr. He has worked in Eastern and Southeastern Europe for over twenty years. He is a former National Director of the Bulgarian Christian Student Movement. He was ordained in Blagavest Evangelical Church, Sofia, Bulgaria and he lectures in Contemporary Theology, Contextual Theology and Church History at United Theological Faculty, Sofia. He is presently engaged in writing and research in the areas of Church History, Eastern Orthodox Theology and Mission and Unity, and is a participant in a UK Evangelical-Orthodox dialogue process based in Oxford University.

Rev Dr Jooseop Keum is Programme Executive on Mission and Evangelism of World Council of Churches based in Geneva, Switzerland. He is also the editor of *International Review of Mission* published by the Commission of World Mission and Evangelism. He is an ordained minister of the Presbyterian Church of Korea. He received his PhD at New College, University of Edinburgh under the supervision of David A. Kerr. He served the Council for World Mission in London as the Executive Secretary of Mission Programme. Dr Keum's main task at the WCC is the development of ecumenical missiology in the twenty-first century.

Dr Ábrahám Kovács earned masters degrees at Lajos Kossuth University and Reformed Theological University, both in Debrecen, Hungary. He has also studied at Princeton University and Tübingen University, Germany. In 2003 he completed his PhD thesis at New College, University of Edinburgh. Since 2005 he holds the position of Associate Professor in the Department of Systematic Theology at Debrecen Reformed Theological University, and is a part-time lecturer in the Faculty of Art at Debrecen University. His teaching interests are in Church History and Historical Theology, and he is recognized for his work with the Jewish religious question in Hungary in the nineteenth and twentieth centuries. Among his recent publications are *The History of the Free Church of Scotland's Mission to the Jews and Its Impact on the Revival of The Reformed Church of Hungary (Vienna: Peter Lang AG, 2006)* and *The History of the German-Speaking Reformed Affiliated Church of Budapest (1858-1869)* (Debrecen: Fábián Nyomda, 2004).

Revd Dr Sophia Marriage earned her first degree at Cambridge University, and for her PhD went to the University of Edinburgh where she was supervised by David Kerr. After some post-doctoral work, including co-editing *Mediating Religion: Conversations in Media, Religion and Culture,* (with Jolyon Mitchell, T&T Clark Continuum 2003) she worked in Public Relations in both the academic and voluntary sectors for a few years, before training as a priest in the Scottish Episcopal Church. She is currently a curate in the Diocese of Edinburgh. She is married with three young daughters.

Revd Dr Misheck Nyirenda is Zambian and ordained with the Pentecostal Assemblies of God (Zambia) since 1995. He has taught hermeneutics among other courses at Trans-Africa Theological College, Zambia (1994–97), and has studied and researched various aspects of biblical hermeneutics and epistemological presuppositions for the past ten years. He holds the following theological qualifications: Bachelor of Theology (Trans-Africa Theological College); Master of Christian Studies, Old Testament major (Regent College, Vancouver); MTh (Research) and PhD (New College, University of Edinburgh). In August 2008, he assumed a lectureship in Bible and Theology at Pan Africa Christian University, Nairobi. He and his wife Annie have two children, Janet and Benjamin.

Revd Dr Miguel A. Palomino was born in Peru, and is an ordained minister of the Christian and Missionary Alliance. He completed his PhD at the University of Edinburgh. He is currently the Director of the *Facultad Teológica Latinoamericana* (FATELA), a graduate School of Theology and World Missions working in Argentina, Brazil, Chile, Colombia, Ecuador, and Peru. He is a member of the Edinburgh 1910 Missionary Conference Centenary Planning Committee, and the LCWE Executive Council for Diasporas. He, his wife Rose Mary and daughter Ana-Claudia currently reside in Miami, where he is the pastor of the CMA Church of Pembroke Pines.

Dr Diane Stinton was born in Angola and completed her undergraduate degrees at the University of Calgary. She first went to Kenya with the Africa Inland Mission in 1984 to teach in a rural secondary school for national girls. She has earned an MTS and ThM from Regent College, Vancouver, and her PhD at the Centre for the Study of Christianity in the Non-Western World, New College, University of Edinburgh. She is currently a Senior Lecturer at Daystar University, and the Coordinator of the MTh in African Christianity program. She is the author of *Jesus of Africa: Voices of Contemporary Christology* (Orbis Books, 2004) and various articles on African Christianity, and serves as the Secretary for the Ecumenical Symposium of Eastern Africa Theologians.

Dr Maurie Sween studied under Prof. David Kerr while working on MSc and PhD degrees at the Centre for the Study of Christianity in the Non-Western World, University of Edinburgh. He has been a long-term missionary whose primary work has been with those suffering disabilities in Taiwan. He is currently teaching Theology of Christian Mission at Taiwan Theological College and Seminary.

Dr Jack Thompson succeeded David Kerr as Director of the Centre for the Study of Christianity in the Non-Western World at Edinburgh University, where he has lectured since 1993. He previously taught at the Selly Oak Colleges, Birmingham, England between 1983 and 1993, and before that worked in mission education in Malawi for thirteen years.

Revd Dr Hans Ucko was born in 1946 in Sweden and has studied in France, Sweden, Israel, and India. He is an ordained minister of the Church of Sweden. He received his PhD from the Senate of Serampore, India. His thesis seeks to facilitate a dialogue on the concept 'People' and 'People of God' between Minjung Theology, Dalit Theology and the Jewish tradition. Since 1989 he has been the Programme Executive in the Office on Interreligious Relations and Dialogue of the World Council of Churches, Geneva, Switzerland. He has published several books and an extensive number of articles and papers, covering issues such as interfaith dialogue, Jewish-Christian relations, Theology, Missiology, Liturgy in several languages. He is on the Board of Trustees of Hartford Seminary and an official observer at the International Council of Christians and Jews. He is the editor of the biannual WCC publication Current Dialogue.

Acknowledgements

It is with a good measure of delight that I take a moment to acknowledge those who have been instrumental in bringing this *Festschrift* from an idea to a reality.

Kind thanks must go to the nearly forty authors who have contributed their time and thoughts to this work as a way of honouring David Kerr, but who also have worked tirelessly under some unusual time constraints owing to David's illness. In the main, authors had only half the time they normally might for this kind of submission, and they have been uncommonly distracted from their primary responsibilities as educators and leaders.

I am also grateful to Professor Fredrik Lindström, Dean of the Centre for Theology and Religion at Lund University. He has been most helpful to provide me contact information and with the list of David's publications that constitute the Appendix of this work.

Grateful am I also to Margaret Acton, formerly of Edinburgh University and currently living in Oxford. Now as before Margaret has been of exceptional assistance in tracking down sources that from my more remote outpost have proved elusive. She also assisted me by supplying email addresses and by scanning a whole manuscript to me when the original failed to arrive in my mailbox.

Peter Ford also accommodated me by providing the Arabic transliteration for a manuscript, and returned it to me in impeccably edited form, saving me several hours of work. Thank you, Peter.

David's wife, Gun, also has assisted me with detailed information, contacts, and especially receiving me both at Lund University and in their home in February 2007 when I first proposed the idea of the *Festschrift* to David. Fondly my wife and I recall the evenings in the Kerr home in Edinburgh when – from the dishes prepared by Gun to the guests and engaging conversation – an international flavour prevailed. I trust that Gun will receive these pages on David's behalf from their many friends as the labour of love that they are.

One individual has helped in a variety of truly critical ways that include providing me with contact and background information, and for being an advocate for the *Festschrift* from the very first contact we had. I should like here to give public thanks to this person, but will respect their wish to remain anonymous and in the background.

I am also grateful to Rebecca Vaughn-Williams at *Continuum* for ably guiding me through their processes to bring these manuscripts into something others around the world can appreciate.

It is generally an unhealthy sign when weekends and national holidays are embraced by the thought of having time free of lectures to work more on the *Festschrift*. To my wife, Melinda, and two daughters, especially the one who still lives at home with us, my special thanks is reserved for your patience and understanding that has allowed this project to move forward.

A great debt is owed to David himself for his inspiration over the years. And through the *Festschrift* my own life has been enriched by the contact I have had with so many truly remarkable people from all over the world. My singular regret is that David did not witness the final product. I take some measure of satisfaction, however, in knowing he was both honoured and humbled by the essays on his behalf, and that he believed that the work would make a significant contribution to those things that matter most—the dignity and personhood of those who seek to live in relationship with God. To the memory of David, our thanks for a lesson well lived.

Stephen R. Goodwin
Istanbul
18 April 2008

Introduction

Stephen R. Goodwin

A century ago ambitious plans were already underway for what would be a watershed event for World Christianity, namely, the 1910 Edinburgh World Missionary Conference. Several decades before this event Western theologians, industrialists and philanthropists spoke and wrote with an indefatigable optimism buoyed by advances in medical science, industry and the expansion of colonies and Christianity to far-flung places of the globe. Pundits and futurists of the day identified the coming decades as the 'Christian Century' wherein the Good News and goodwill would transform the planet.

Indeed, the twentieth century would prove to be transforming, but in few ways resembling the imaginations of the nineteenth-century prognosticators. The peace envisioned for the twentieth century quickly gave way to regional conflicts, which in turn led to war of unprecedented scale. By mid-century the war machinery produced weapons of mass destruction that for the first time threatened humanity with its own annihilation. Early optimism faded to postwar, post-colonial, post-modern sobriety, even outright Angst. Utopian ideologies of promise collapsed under the weight of Cold War rhetoric, and few were willing any longer to dream about the big picture; it was enough to speak in reduced terms of détente and containment. Only after the rubble of war had been cleared away to reconstruct a living space in Europe could the task of deconstructing ideas begin, which for some was an attempt to find answers to what had gone wrong, and for others was a way of reformulating the questions.

Certain sectors of the Church also were rightly excoriated for willing complicity in these wrongs. Once thought to be the engine whose faith, message and morality would inaugurate a new world order, the Church became sullied with its easy proximity to unrestrained power. Christianity deprived of its spiritual dimension and reduced to little more than another political ideology became fused to nation- and empire-building and in the process forfeited its radical prophetic voice of transformation just when it was needed most. Civil religion, as it turned out, wasn't very civil at all.

At the same time the explosive growth of indigenous Christianity during the twentieth century in non-Western forms and locations might have surprised even the most optimistic of the nineteenth-century visionaries. Undoubtedly this will be reflected by the wide representation to the Edinburgh 2010 gathering, for which plans are now underway. There is, however, little cause for global triumphalism in this or other reflective celebrations. After all, Christianity as perceived and promulgated by those with a global objective did not translate into a panacea for the world's maladies. Further, Christianity is not the only religion to go global in the last century. Islam too has witnessed extraordinary growth across a variety of cultures, which has brought its own spectrum of dynamics, especially as related to Christianity. More appropriately Christianity might rather celebrate its presence in its local self-consciousness, not in triumph over, nor in isolation from, but in relation to its neighbour, the 'Other'. This just may be Christianity's quintessential expression because it again takes on flesh and blood, speaks, feels and is there for the needs of others.

It is this fundamental focus on others that brings us to the purpose of this two-volume work of essays dedicated to the memory of David A. Kerr by his former colleagues and PhD students. As a scholar, instructor and supervisor David epitomized this attitude and profile of being there for others.

From the beginning David was advantaged to see beyond the parochialism that often accompanies religious belief. He was the son of a minister of the English Congregational Union (Wilfred, 1915–1991) and his maternal grandparents were missionaries in China (1921–1927). In 1973 David arrived in Birmingham to Selly Oak Colleges to take up responsibilities for teaching Islamic Studies, after reading Arabic and Islamic Studies in London School of Oriental and African Studies, Theology in Oxford University and writing a doctoral thesis on religious relations between Maronite Christians and Muslims in Syria and Lebanon. His gift for succinct expression was quickly realized and for a time he also worked as a BBC correspondent.

From Birmingham David and his wife, Gun, made their way across the Atlantic in 1987 to Hartford Seminary in Connecticut, where he became the successor to Willem Bijlefeld as the Director of the Duncan Black Macdonald Center. Under his direction the Center's programme became a joint venture between Muslims and Christians. This was a critical period when conservatives in both Christianity and Islam were making their presence known in the public and political sectors and the importance of learning together and from each other was crucial.

David then moved to the University of Edinburgh where from 1996–2005 he was the Director of the Centre for the Study of Christianity in the Non-Western World at New College, the Divinity faculty. Here the scope of his work was greatly broadened to include Christian encounter not only with Islam, but all the major religions, and addressed the many challenging issues facing contemporary, global Christianity. In 2005 David was invited to take the post of Professor of Missiology and Ecumenics at Lund University, Sweden. For this last post he learned Swedish which both enabled him for his teaching and endeared him to his students. Upon soon arriving in Sweden, however, he was diagnosed with Motor Neuron Disease, or Amyotrophic Lateral Sclerosis, which increasingly debilitated him and to which he succumbed only a few days ago from this writing, on April 14th 2008.

The complete list of David's publications contained in the Appendix provides an invaluable deposit of his various forays into the written word to the benefit of future generations. It must be said, however, that David belonged to that set of scholars who saw their principle task to be the education, support and development of their students; the student subsequently would be the primary witness of the scholar's work, rather than the contemporary tendency, under the pressure of publications-based funding, to issue forth a stream of books. Christopher Lamb speaks of David's 'whole-hearted commitment to teaching, pursued at the expense of his own research and writing' and David Marshall speaks of a profound impact on students, even in a short time. The number of contributions to both parts of this Festschrift from David's former students is the best testimony to his contribution to the various fields in which he has worked. They multiply his vision and influence, which accordingly have borne a rich harvest.

Much to the surprise of the doctors who attended to his slow physical deterioration in his last months, David continued to go into Lund University every ten days or so, and students under his instructions would come to the home of David and Gun for tutorials. Even in the last week of his life the focus of conversation was not about his own circumstances, but about his students and their research. This is what gave him real purpose, and he was fortunate to continue to the very last days.

Many of the contributions to this *Festschrift* contain biographical notes and references to mutual collaboration between the respective authors and David, and his own contribution to these fields. These essays and their attribution to David were finished before his passing and their personal record is left in the original tenses to reflect his living contribution to their lives. So, for instance, David's predecessor at Selly Oak, John B. Taylor, speaks of David's passion for describing Islam both accurately and respectfully; two of the hallmarks of David's work. Jan Slomp draws attention to the seismic shift in engaging Muslim scholars on the staff at Selly Oak and the critical recruitment of Muslim students and members of the Advisory Board, which together transformed the Selly Oak Centre into a truly joint enterprise. Hasan Askari, the first Muslim member of staff, speaks of a pioneering vision to include the religious experience in the study of religions. Yusuf Qamar and Abdullah Bawhab, two of the most senior members of the Muslim communities of Birmingham, who both studied under David's direction, speak warmly of Muslims' respect for his scholarship, gentle critical guidance and willingness to journey alongside students in their path of self-discovery.

Working from the Centre in Selly Oak, David's contribution to the wider debate on Christian-Muslim relations and Christian theological reflection on Islam, is worthy of note. His ability to hold together strongly held diverse opinions in a creative way is noted by Hugh Goddard in his chapter with respect to the composition of the United Reformed Church's Study Handbook for Christians entitled, *With People of Other Faiths in Britain*. This was a pioneering time, as is highlighted by Pakistani senator Khurshid Ahmad, stressing the seminal importance of the Chambesy statement in 1976. David's work on a Christian reappraisal of the Prophethood of Muhammad would make a notable contribution to the theological literature, as noted by one of his closest collaborators, Mahmoud Ayoub.

This was no less true when David was at Hartford and Edinburgh. David's predecessor in Hartford, Willem Bijlefeld, reflects that, as the Director of the DB Macdonald Center, David was instrumental in strengthening the Center as a joint endeavour of Muslims and Christians. He was able to combine in an impressive manner his different duties – administrative and editorial responsibilities, teaching and research – with a very successful involvement in the area of public relations. But Willem Bijlefeld says that his strongest memories of David and Gun are more personal, as loyal friends and as people of care and compassion who truly recognize strangers as neighbours.

For several years while Director of the Centre for the Study of Christianity in the Non-Western World at Edinburgh University, David had direct oversight for more than 30 masters and doctoral students at one time. Although this increased David's workload enormously, he chose to take under his care especially the new students so that he could know each of them personally and to ensure that they received the kind of attention that they required so that they would make a successful transition to Edinburgh and its academic setting. David also made it clear from the beginning that even when his own personal or theological views differed from those of the student, this would not distract from his commitment to bring the best effort from the student. In the tutorials this meant tough-minded challenges, precise clarifications and multiple revisions. It never meant indoctrination, disparagement or belittling. In David's office – where tutorials took place – an interesting map conspicuously adorned one of the walls. The central focus was a body of water and its littoral regions, but because the map was in Arabic, few could immediately decipher the location depicted. Closer examination usually produced knitted brows and greater confusion. David would patiently allow the student to arrive at his or her own 'Aha!' moment when the puzzle had been solved: The body of water and land masses were indeed familiar but not immediately recognizable as the Mediterranean Sea because the orientation was that of the Arab world with South oriented to the top, that is, 'upside down' to the Western observer. Thus, North Africa was where southern Europe customarily was, and the Italian and Balkan peninsulas jutted strangely upward into the Sea from where Africa usually was at home. For new students it was among the first of many lessons in taking something familiar and looking at it from a new perspective, thereby gaining fresh insight into the viewpoint of others.

Under David's tutelage students were treated to a high level of scholarship invigorated by a spirit of conviviality. Especially memorable for their collegiality were the fortnightly 'works in progress' seminars in which doctoral students presented a portion of their research for peer review and critique. The diversity of cultural backgrounds and theological persuasions represented at these gatherings allowed students to participate in something that challenged their own views and yet did so in a vigorously healthy environment. It meant not only that our research was better for the collaboration, but that for it we were somehow better people too.

Given his commitment to fair scholarship, it came as no surprise that David sometimes became exercised in his own measured way over the 'Huntington thesis' and the broad strokes with which the 'clash of civilizations' is presented. Well before, but especially after the events of 9/11, David was keen to interject when necessary in order that the 'Other' – whichever other that may have been – was fairly and accurately characterized and challenged the notion that conflict between Christians and Muslims was in some way *inevitable*. For David there was more to fear from those driving the conflict motif either from a position of ignorance or media hysteria than from Christians and Muslims desiring to live in harmonious proximity to each other. But David had this kind of insight because he was uncommonly advantaged by his relationships within the Christian and Muslim communities. These pages bear something of a watermark where David has imprinted his life on those who were fortunate to have learned from him.

The essays follow broadly two general trajectories. The first is that of Christianity in its local and, generally, non-Western context. A wide variety of nationalities is here represented, and essays originate from both established authors and younger scholars who only now are beginning to make a difference in their particular setting. Ábrahám Kovács from Debrecen, Hungary and Korean Jooseup Keum, now the Executive Secretary for Mission and Evangelism at the World Council of Churches, address big-picture issues of Christianity. Dr Kovács examines the important issue of Christian theology in relation to the other World Religions, especially as it relates to the European post-colonial, post-Christendom era when many long-held assumptions are being challenged anew. Dr Keum is advantaged by his position to analyse the pressing concern of economic globalization, its negative effects on the world's poor and how the transforming mission of Christianity might address these planetary needs. Professor Klaus Hock of Rostock, Germany, also engages the reader on a global level with his contribution that applies post-modern critiques of anthropology and selfhood to the task of inter-religious and inter-cultural dialogue with others from non-Christian confessions. And Hans Ucko asks if Christian theological affirmations are possible in relation to other faiths, to Islam, to Hinduism, to Buddhism, to indigenous traditions. He therewith sets the stage for localized discourses to follow.

Professor James Cox of Edinburgh moves the discussion to particularized contexts by examining the globalizing effect that educating African scholars in Western universities has made. His focus is especially placed on African theologian, Kwame Bediako. Professor Jack Thompson, also of Edinburgh University, interprets for us issues of (mistaken) identity in Africa, demonstrating how the integration of land-culture and tribal identity of the Ngoni people in Malawi was largely misunderstood by British missionaries during the colonial period. Zambian theologian Misheck Nyirenda offers an authentic African voice to biblical scholarship and interpretation, placing emphasis on the continuity of the Hebrew text with a post-colonial perspective. Rounding out the African section is the essay by Diane Stinton, who looks at the very contemporary issue of prophetic ministry of Christians for peacebuilding amid conflict in Kenya.

The lone contribution from Latin America comes from Peruvian Miguel Palomino who has a wide understanding of the emergent missionary Latino Church from his position as Director of the Latin American Graduate School of Theology, which has branches in Argentina, Brazil, Chile, Colombia, Ecuador and Peru. His core thesis articulates how the growing Church in Latin America has a healthy self-consciousness as related to its responsibility in the world. Even as the Churches in Latin America are looking beyond their shores in universal categories, others are looking to recover a sense of self-identity through nationalism. James Hopkins, who is involved in inter-religious dialogue between the Orthodox and Protestants in Britain, takes us into the ecclesiastical dynamics of the Bulgarian Church in post-communist Europe. Drawing attention to the fact that a historical East–West fault line, first drawn by the Roman emperor in the third century CE, runs directly through the Balkans, Dr Hopkins suggests that similar divisions may again divide the current generation through the disparity of cultural and political values of Eastern and Western Europeans.

This volume then moves to the Asian context where Kenneth Fleming gives us an intriguing essay involving baptism, Buddhism and inter-religious dialogue. Two contributions explore issues related to the Indian subcontinent. With a heritage in both the Indian and American cultures, Geoman Kizhakkemalayil George offers a fascinating insight and comparison into the knowledge of God through the idea of immediacy of presence common to both an Indian worldview and Pentecostalism. Sean Doyle is a promising young scholar whose primary interest is in discovering the extant hermeneutical tools that may legitimately be engaged for the analysis of Hindu and Christian metaphysics. In this essay he examines the Gospel of John using the Hindu concept of *bhakti* (devotion) and the interpretive schema of Anglican Bishop A. J. Appasamy. Sophia Marriage looks at Roman Catholic models of liberation and inculturation in a local Philippine context showing both continuity and discontinuity with Rome in addressing the physical and spiritual needs of this particular diocese. Also from Asia is the contribution unique in this volume that explores pain, suffering and social responsibility. Maurie Sween is especially interested to understand the contribution of well-known Chinese author Liu Hsia to this topic. This essay is no mere academic undertaking abstracted from daily life, however. Pain and suffering are permanent residents in the Sween home, as Dr Sween's wife, Lan-Shiang, has been diagnosed with multiple cancers over the past decade, and has lost a lower leg to cancer during their sojourn in Edinburgh when Dr Sween was a PhD candidate under David Kerr. This kind of severe physical malady had a special significance for David when he was diagnosed with his terminal ailment. The dignity with which these friends have lived under the affliction of physical frailty is a testimony to the grace of God and their appreciation for life and others.

The second volume focuses on Christian-Muslim encounter with three general facets. The first looks at textual and thematic issues related to Christian-Muslim encounter. The second explores issues of dialogue from those who have been at the forefront of this ongoing conversation for decades. The third looks at specific local contexts of Christian-Muslim encounter in our world, both in its historical and contemporary dynamics. In this first element Professor Mahmoud Ayoub turns to the Qur'ān and Muslim tradition to establish the framework for encounter. Christopher Lamb examines the concept of abrogation in the Qur'ān for Muslims and in the Bible for Christians, and suggests that this theme contains importance for greater understanding between Christians and Muslims. Professor Sigvard von Sicard also examines the scriptures of Christianity and Islam to elaborate the important common elements of forgiveness and reconciliation.

The second facet explores Christian-Muslim encounter through dialogue. Christian Troll begins this section with the important question of how Christians and Muslims should relate to each other in light of their respective truth claims. From a historical perspective come two contributions. F. Peter Ford looks at the early Muslim community that was afforded asylum by Christians in Ethiopia and draws some relevant observations for today. Similarly, Professor Carole Hillenbrand looks at the ever-fascinating city of Constantinople through the eyes of travellers who documented their observations of a pluralist environment in which each community had their own unique expressions, festivals, parades and costumes. Several contributions then move the encounter facet into the contemporary era. Professor David Burrell focuses his essay on the new context of the ancient Abrahamic faiths, and Professor Hugh Goddard offers an insightful overview of where recent developments in Christian-Muslim relations have brought us. In this same vein, David Marshall takes a look at the very relevant and contentious issue of religious freedom for Christians and Muslims for today.

Three essays are diagnostic in their approach and seek to address difficulties in the Christian-Muslim encounter and understanding of each other. In his important essay entitled *Islam Hostage to Itself?*, Bishop Kenneth Cragg examines the Muslim greeting of peace to ask difficult questions about the authorization of violence arising from some interpretations of the Qur'ān, and to what extent these deviate from the original intentions of Islam's Prophet. Professor Jørgen Nielsen, an educator in both Europe and the Middle East, offers a look at the constructed myths of the 'West' and 'Islam' in the past century through the lenses of the European and the Arab worldviews. Anton Wessels creatively borrows from Babylon/Jerusalem and Mecca/Medina to construct a Dickensian typology and relates the ancient scriptures to our contemporary situation. Lessons of centuries ago have resonance today through the prophetical call for political justice. With his wide experience as professor at Cambridge and the University of Punjab (Pakistan), then with the World Council of Churches, the UN as Director of the World Conference on Religion and Peace and now with the International Association for Religion and Freedom, Dr John Taylor gives us an insider's view of some of the prominent events of these organizations, and is uniquely qualified to offer insight towards overcoming Islamophobia through education and dialogue. He was also David Kerr's predecessor at Selly Oak Colleges. In America Professor Robert Hunt gives us a splendid work on the roots of American attitudes towards Muslims and looks at some contemporary encounters with the hope of changing the mostly antagonistic discourse witnessed today between Christians and Muslims. Professor Waardenburg of Lausanne is also well-known for his involvement in and contribution to dialogue. His essay addresses the recent Open Letter from Muslim clerics, which is a response to the 2006 Regensburg remarks of Pope Benedict XVI concerning the nature of Islam. This compares nicely to the essay by Prof. Senator Khurshid Ahmad whose collaborative work with David Kerr is recalled. His essay looks at the watershed document that they co-authored on 'Islamic Da'wah and Christian Mission' (1976). At the request of Professor Ahmad, that document is here reproduced with the kind permission of the editor of *International Review of Mission*, Jooseop Keum, as an appendix to his chapter. As well, the outspoken reply by Sayyid Abul A'la Mawdūdī to the 'Message of His Holiness Pope Paul VI' concerning the institution of the Day of Peace following the 1967 Arab-Israeli War is included in that it is inherently part of what Professor Ahmad is addressing. Undoubtedly readers will find the chapter by Professor Ahmad and these two appendices to be as thought-provoking today as they were more than 35 years ago. Appropriately at this point is Chris Hewer's chapter revealing the kind of shared living community for Christians and Muslims created by David Kerr at the Centre for the Study of Islam and Christian-Muslim Relations in the Selly Oak Colleges in Birmingham. His chapter is as much a tribute to the vision of David as it is to the extraordinary circumstances that allowed so many Muslim and Christian scholars to learn both about and with each other in an accommodating environment. One can only agree with Dr Hewer that more such communities are needed.

This volume would be incomplete without the final facet exploring Christian-Muslim encounter in its local context. Philip Lewis at the Department of Peace Studies in Bradford examines efforts to restore a modicum of peace in that city after unrest spilled over into street violence in 2004. Also with a focus on Europe is my own analysis of state stability and viability in postwar Bosnia-Herzegovina, especially with the continuing presence and growth of Islamist groups in the Balkans. Bosniak Safet Bektović, once a refugee from the Balkan war in Bosnia, offers a glimpse of Muslim-Christian coexistence and possible mutual recognition in his adopted nation of Denmark. Jan Slomp, who is the National Advisor for relations with Islam for the Reformed Churches of the Netherlands, includes India and Pakistan with Europe in his presentation of how the persons of Jesus and Muhammad are viewed in these lands. Both essays by Drs Bektović and Slomp are important for their perspectives in lands where individual freedoms of expression exercised through the media are challenging religious communal norms and sensitivities over the central figures of Christianity and Islam. Two contributions come to us from the continent of Africa where Christian-Muslim encounter will prove critical in this century. Edward Riak Kajivora gives us insight into the current travail found in Sudan by tracing the trajectory of the growth of Islamists in that country, and Akintunde Akinade uses a contextual theology approach to analyse Christian-Muslim relations in Nigeria today.

The foregoing introduction serves then to bring us to the point of discovery of three discernable treasures. First, there is a rich breadth of diversity found in Christianity today. A century on from Edinburgh 1910 it is impossible to assert that Christianity is merely a Western religion with forms and idioms recognizable only to Westerners. The contrary is today the case. Christianity has expression under nearly every tongue, tribe and nation, and its diversity is Christianity's strength.

Second, these pages identify a rich encounter of Christians with others, especially with Muslim colleagues. Herein is the difficult question for the decades ahead, however. If Christianity finds it strength in its ubiquity and diversity, will it respond in a Christ-like fashion to its non-Christian neighbours? Will Christians vis-à-vis their Muslim neighbours learn from or repeat the hard lessons of history? Our century requires an appropriate response from us. Perhaps even now we are writing the first chapter of just such a report for Edinburgh 2110.

Third, these pages testify to the rich and varied friendships that David Kerr enjoyed over these many years. And because there is no effort in this Festschrift to tailor the essays to a singular persuasion, a wide continuum of voices is afforded. Of course, each voice is that speaker's own, and rightly so. Still, with these many and diverse voices the authors are univocal about David's influence on their lives. It is thus hoped that this work will create a platform through which David's ethos may be known, and that his contributions to World Christianity and engagement with Muslim communities may leave an indelible and lasting footprint in the right direction for others to follow.

Part One

Global Themes

Chapter 1

The Challenge of the Post-Christendom Era: The Relation of Christian Theology to World Religions

Ábrahám Kovács

Approaching religion in the academic life: secular and theological attempts

As the means of travel improve day by day and new media techniques are rapidly overcoming the hurdles in front of scientific researchers, ideas and thoughts between cultures and continents travel with an incredible and unforeseen speed. These developments contribute to a global society on earth, and the information coming from any direction – be it cultural or technical, religious or secular – impregnate the receiver-culture directly or indirectly. The impact and influence of the Other cannot be avoided entirely for the major part of a society, country or culture.

Our newly transformed societies in Europe, especially Central and Eastern Europe, are becoming increasingly multicultural. The realm of Christians in Europe as it was in the Middle Ages is over. Indeed, the flaws in the bastion of Christendom began to appear with the challenge of Humanism and Reformation, later the legitimacy of an exclusively Christian-based society was questioned by the Enlightenment. Finally after World War II the last underpinnings holding up what remained of the fortress of Christendom were wiped out by the secularization of Europe, both East and West.

These two forms of secularization differed in many ways but both rejected Christianity as the only basis offering ideological support for governing a society. The Western European world showed an open form of secularization in contrast to the aloof and rigidly closed world of the Soviet bloc. In the West two processes ran side by side. Secularization stemming from the Enlightenment began to change profoundly the theological–ideological tenets upon which a society was based while allowing at the same time competing worldviews, ideologies and philosophies to enter into its cultural realm. The old colonial structures gave way to the appearance of migrant communities from former colonies, and a fundamental change took place that altered the perception of the world for a Western European people. This is conspicuous in the case of Great Britain.

It is not at all uncommon today to find a black African or Asian person with a British self-identity and speaking English as fluently as their mother tongue, something that was unthinkable just two generations ago. However, this was not the case for Hungary until the collapse of communism. Of course it occurs in our society on a much smaller scale than in Britain, but now, over the last 17 years, one may encounter young people of Asian, Arabic or African origin who are also Hungarians. With EU enlargement came ethnic diversity, and Central–Eastern Europe has become even more colourful and mixed. Such a phenomenon was simply unimaginable in former times. Before 1945 races and nations maintained separate identities so that the intermingling of communities, or individuals from respective communities, was often considered to be the worst thing that could happen. Although they lived in the same geographic region, only a few stepped across the national and cultural boundaries of their community.

Today people are used to living together and finding marriage partners from cultures and ethnic groups quite different from their own. This ongoing process of change does not exclude religion and faith, since at the very heart of any culture are its religious traditions. Owing to this, people face a multitude of fascinating, weird, and strange beliefs and practices, and begin to ask questions and trace the similarities and differences with their own stances. The result of such a conscious or subconscious endeavour – one may think that it is often the part of everyday social interaction – depends greatly on a person's own intentional convictions and preconceived ideas. There is an urgent need to find ways to relate to each other with respect to these differing beliefs. This should lead us to investigate in more detail what sort of responses have emerged from our tradition, that is, the 'Christian' tradition – at least in the cultural–historical and social sense of the term.

Having briefly discussed this relevant and important issue of the impact of globalization on religion, we move on to explore how different religious traditions are regarded from a Christian perspective. In the cultural-religious context of Hungary contemporary Christianity will be used as the point of reference. I thus restrict my comments to the present and examine contemporary approaches of theology to different world religions. This cannot be done entirely without reference to the past, but I will allude to it only as necessary.

Various theological approaches to other religious traditions: a concise historical survey

The relationship between ecumenism and theology of religions

The *theologia religionum*, the 'theology of religions', is a recent discipline that evolved only since the 1940s. The name itself creates a debate because it is not really a theology, in the singular sense, of various world religions. Rather, it is what Christian theology says about other world religions, or more specifically, what the perception of religion is on the matter of salvation. Probably it is better to talk about Christian approaches to world religions, or if we really wish to be inclusive, we must speak of Christianity's relation to religious traditions. But should this take a theological, liturgical or missiological approach? Which major elements should constitute the discussion? God, salvation, the problem of evil, theological anthropology all provide interesting topics for discussion.

More challenges lurk around the corner. Other religions have varying concepts of God or 'Ultimate Reality', and use religious terminology with different meaning. So is the case with Christian salvation and Buddhist liberation. Some argue for comparability, while others find this impossible. Thus, for the sake of limiting the discussion, let us acknowledge that 'salvation' is central in many religious traditions such as Islam, Judaism, Buddhism and Hinduism. This premise also addresses a common human concern. Nonetheless, many Christians claim that their way of understanding salvation is the best or the correct belief. Since European Christians after Constantine the Great were not challenged by other faiths, multiculturalism was virtually unknown in Europe until the medieval period. The exclusive position of Christian faith and practice supported by state control effectively eliminated all competition from other belief systems. This situation changed under Enlightenment forces, but Christendom still held strong until the twentieth century. For these many centuries Christians did not need to ask how they ought to adapt to the presence of other faiths. The problems of inculturation and adaptation only emerged with the beginning of the Roman Catholic missions of Roberto de Nobili, Matteo Ricci and others like them, but these exciting debates were kept to the far and unfathomable lands of India, China and Japan. While Western European exploration brought encounter with thrilling and mysterious cultures, people and religions during the age of discovery, Central Europeans, including Hungarians, were far more isolated and had few opportunities to experience the fascinating challenges of their Western counterparts in Britain, Holland and France. The secularization process in the West reached its zenith after World War II. At the same time Central Europe remained almost entirely unaffected by other cultures and religions of Africa, Asia and the Americas. By implementing their own kind of secularism, communist regimes delayed the encounter with other faith traditions.

But today the religious map of Europe, including Hungary, has changed. A question, emerging out of the old Christendom context, enables us to come closer to the understanding of the Other in the contemporary world. David Bosch presciently observed, 'The same impetus that made adherents of a given Christian denomination ask: who are these Roman Catholics, Anglicans, Methodist, Orthodox also led to the question, who are these people of other faiths, these Hindus, Buddhists, and Muslims? At least in this formal sense then, there is a relationship between ecumenism and the theology of religions'.[1]

Hungary encountered these two different challenges simultaneously after the collapse of the communist regime. Nonetheless, there was and is often confusion at the educational level between dialogue with other Christian traditions and the interaction between Christianity and other religious traditions, in particular world religions (*theologia religionum*).

Bosch is certainly right to highlight the interrelatedness of ecumenism and theology of religions discussion since the openness to other denominations may well lead to a greater understanding of those who belong to an altogether different religious tradition. Once we are able to overcome the hurdles and hindrances posed by dogmatic and historical differences between different Christian traditions, we may be able to listen to those whose faith is different from ours. So long as creedal differences remain, there will be a need for Christian Churches to be aware, accept and tolerate the Other. However, while faith in Christ acts as a unifying element among Christian denominations, this is not true of the relationship between Christianity and other world religions. We may assume that the great world religions are very distinct, even while the tendency in scholarly circles is to trace the underlying common human concerns behind each religion. One may rightly argue for the similarities between religions, while the other seeks to point out the differences. This directs our attention to the dialectical tension in which we all live. It can be seen when theologians, secular scholars and common people endeavour to grasp what the other religious faith means by such terms as salvation, redemption and creation.

Throughout the centuries this was not a serious question for Christians who possessed the 'key to salvation'. The Catholic Church declared its own right to show people the way to salvation. During the Reformation the problem of salvation emerged again since each one of the Protestant denominations claimed to hold the truth in opposition to the Roman Catholic Church as well as to each other. Each regarded itself as the *one* and *only* Church through which a person could be saved. However, some contemporary theologians – such as John Hick – hold that this view cannot be maintained today.[2] What was believed to be true then is not necessarily the same in our age. Thus, the challenge of world religions to Christianity is impossible to ignore.

The common Western Catholic 'development'

First and foremost, we must bear in mind that all Protestant denominations and the Roman Catholic Church share the same Christian tradition. This is so even after the turmoil of the sixteenth century because they both have common roots which neither can claim exclusively as their own. The Protestant tradition often neglects its 'Catholic' origin and hardly pays attention to its roots, behaving as though true Christianity started only with the appearance of Luther and Calvin.[3] In the Roman Empire Christians regarded non-Christians as 'pagan', which is a term from the Latin *paganus* meaning the people of rural areas. People of the ancient faith of Greek and Roman culture maintained their former beliefs in villages for a longer period of time whereas the cities more quickly came under the influence of Christianity, which was fostered through the support of militant emperors such a Constantine the Great. As time passed, the life of the followers of Christ forming smaller communities was made compulsory to the society at large and this in turn transformed people and culture of the Roman Empire into Christendom. It became a society operated under the aegis of an official Christian worldview. Slowly the word pagan gained a pejorative, derogatory connotation, dividing Christian city-dwellers from village inhabitants. In most of the European countries from the 5th century forward the Roman Catholic Church condemned any religious practices and beliefs that stood outside the Christian faith and were not tolerated.

Nevertheless, Christianity did not always act from a position of power. During the first centuries Christianity was slowly fighting for a place of recognition within the tolerant and pluralist Roman Empire.[4] Early apologists not only sought to defend Christianity against such charges as atheism, denial of emperor worship and promiscuous activities, but tried also to be a voice that ran counter to these accusations.[5] Tertullian, Origen, Tatian and Justin all refuted the charges of the 'pagans' and Jews, while at the same time making the case for Christianity's superiority over other religions. Needless to say, this kind of 'impertinent' claim of superiority bothered the intellectuals of Roman society. Tertullian is a typical example of the radicalism and fundamentalism of early Christian faith. His attitude is summarized in his most oft-quoted and famous phrase: *Quid ergo Athenis at Hierosolymis?*, that is, 'What does Athens have to do with Jerusalem?'.[6] In his *Address to the Greeks* Tatian says that the best of classical literature from Homer and other Greek poets tell shameful things about the gods, such as adultery, incest, and infanticide.[7] He raised the question of how are we to worship such gods, clearly inferior to us? Likewise Justin Martyr thinks what has happened in the incarnation is that the underlying reason of the universe, the Logos or Word of God, has come in the flesh.[8] The Logos is the 'true light that enlightens' everyone. This was the view held by Justin and the second and third century Christian philosophers of Alexandria.[9] Justin also believed that

> there were also among the pagans those who knew the same Logos, however dimly . . . Whatever truth is in the writings of Plato was granted to him by the Logos of God, the same Logos who was incarnate in Jesus. Therefore, in a way Socrates, Plato and other sages of the antiquity 'were Christians,' for their wisdom came from Christ. This is not to say, that the incarnation was not needed, for those philosophers of old knew the Logos 'in part', whereas those who have seen him in his incarnation know him 'fully'.[10]

All these views reappear in contemporary Christian thinking both in the Catholic and Protestant traditions. The understanding of scripture of the Early Church Fathers was very much in line with the exclusivist claim of the New Testament based upon ancient Israelite religion. There are similarities between the pluralistic context of the Roman Empire and our 'postmodern' time, as Kwame Bediako points out.[11] However, there is a significant difference between these two worlds and times. Contemporary relativists such as John Hick and Paul Knitter offer profoundly different solutions from the Early Church Fathers and moved away from the traditional Christian doctrines to the degree that it would have been labelled non-orthodox in the past. In other words it was unacceptable by any of the mainline representatives of Christianity.

The first three centuries of the Church were very fruitful in terms of seeking out various responses to the challenge of other religions, such as Roman and Greek religions, or that of Egypt and the Middle East, which are mostly extinct today. Christians were forced to dialogue with them as part of their missionary activities. Interaction had many channels, and persecution also contributed to the need for Christians to articulate their belief in relation to other religious or non-religious people.

After Constantine declared Christianity to be the state religion Christian attitudes did not essentially change, except that they became more agitated. They loudly propagated their view of a so-called superior religion. The core of the Christian message is to proclaim the absolute truth exclusively in relation to other religions or philosophies. The inherent ideological non-tolerant nature of this faith (that is, uncompromising in the means and essence of salvation) easily shifted from the externally and internally peaceful fundamentalist stance of early Christianity to a combative and aggressive form of mission from the early Middle Ages, imposing its particular worldview as a compulsory form of belief. As time went on people began identifying the structure, that is, the outward appearance of the Christian Church, with the particular belief about salvation, the content of the 'new' official faith of Europe.

Bosch is certainly right to point out that some decades later after Constantine the Great Emperor Theodosius' decrees of 380 and 391 inevitably prepared the road for Pope Boniface's (VIII) bull, *Unam Sanctam* (1302), which proclaimed that the Catholic Church was the only institution guaranteeing salvation. A doctrine was encapsulated as '*extra ecclesiam nulla salus*', or as expanded by the Church, 'We believe in her (the Church) firmly and we confess with simplicity that outside of her there is neither salvation nor the remission of sins.'[12] During and after the Middle Ages – when great geographical discoveries excited Europe – Roman Catholic missions expanded into the areas of Asia and Africa, upholding the exclusivist idea of the Holy Roman Church. No wonder that the kingdom of God was made coterminous with the *Corpus Christianum*.[13] A later development of Christian (Roman Catholic) dogma condemned to the everlasting fires of hell all who were not attached to the Catholic Church (1442). As the tradition developed it led to claims of infallibility for the Catholic Church in *Chatechismus Romanus* (1556) and finally ended up claiming infallibility for the Pope himself in the nineteenth century.[14]

However, it would be a distortion to present the Catholic development only as it appears above, since Nicolaus Cusanus in his *De Pace Fidei* was eager to show although there are different teachings, traditions and liturgies of religions, the essence is common, so the nature of religion is universal. Thomas Aquinas also tried to build a bridge rather than starkly excluding religions different from Christianity. He distinguished between natural and revealed religion arguing that the former is the *praeambulum fidei* and *Praeparatio evangelica* which reaches its final form in the revealed religion that is Christianity.[15] These two attempts show a willingness to wrestle with the exclusivist nature of Christian religion. Later as the advancement of Christian culture extended beyond the geographical sphere of Europe the same problem occurs in different contexts.

It was only in the nineteenth and early twentieth centuries that the adaptation theory finally penetrated into Roman Catholic thinking and had a profound practical influence. However, enculturation did not simply fall from the clouds. Beyond the medieval attempt, Roman Catholic missions prior to the modern age became quite engaged with the question of intercultural relations. It is worth recalling the conflicts of Rome with Robert de Nobili in India (1577–1656) and Matteo de Ricci in China (1552–1610).[16] What were their views like? In Verkyul's opinion their

> adaptionist theory has a too optimistic view of man. It does not reckon seriously enough with man's radical rebellion against God, nor with the radical nature of the gospel of Jesus Christ. Proponents of this theory do not shout out to the heathen; 'Repent, for the kingdom of heaven is at hand!', but rather, 'Come under the wing of mother church and she will prepare you for heaven.' This is a form of Christian sublimation, an elevation of natural man into the realm of supranature. It seeks to bring about a new man by the discipline of a new law.[17]

However, The Second Vatican Council was significant for making this shift. We cannot here discuss this point in any detail, nor do we offer a critique of the aforementioned statements. However, it can be acknowledged that there is an element of truth in the fear articulated above. Verkyul's penetrating critique against a 'liberal' form of Christianity certainly points to the relevant problem of what the core of the Christian Gospel is: Christ, or the Church. Depending on the answers, christologies, or ecclesiologies come to the fore in the current debates, as we shall see. The responses took on many forms. The decrees of Vatican Council II, especially *Nostra Aetate* – approved in October 1965 – 'represent the first time in its history that the Roman Catholic Church has faced the question of how to relate to other non Christian religions in an official way'.[18] Other decrees, such as *Lumen Gentium* and *Ad Gentes*, also significantly altered the traditional Roman Catholic thinking and moved in the new direction of fulfilment. This topic will be discussed later in regard to the theologies of Karl Rahner and Hans Küng.

Early Protestant attitudes

Although Protestants had nothing comparable to papal bulls, their attitude often differed only marginally from that of Rome. Although different in form, Christian mission took place under the sword of God. Bosch argued where the Catholic model insisted that 'outside the church there is no salvation,' the Protestant model affirmed that, 'outside the word there is no salvation.'[19] He alluded to the peculiar feature of the Protestant faith that within the shaping and moulding of this new expression of Christian faith only the criterion changed; the goal and attitude did not. Moreover, a special character of the Protestant faith is that each Protestant movement tended to articulate what the proper form of Christian salvation was to the exclusion of the other. Once the debates among Protestants were settled in Europe, the Protestant powers of England, the Netherlands and Denmark began to follow expansionist policies that exploited other cultures and people. They carried out mission in the name of a worldview that often sanctified the means. Knitter argues that the old Catholic and early Pietist models of mission essentially meant conquest and displacement. These models understood Christianity to be unique, exclusive, superior, definitive, normative and absolute, and consequently the only religion worthy of the divine right to exist and extend itself. For most of the Middle Ages Christianity's archenemy was Islam. 'Mohammed was a "second Arius"; Islam was a post-Christian *imitatio diaboli*, a menace that had to be crushed before it crushed the Church. Hence the Crusades, which, on the whole, miscarried. This did not change the Christian attitudes toward Islam, however.'[20] This view can also be observed in one of the most well-known statements of the Protestant faith, the Westminster Confession. During the Middle Ages the hegemony of Christianity was unopposed by other religions except for Islam, which challenged Christianity at the political level and 'ideological' level, that is, the religious perception of how the world should be ruled. At the same time Christendom witnessed a significant challenge from within. Humanism, the Reformation and later the Enlightenment prepared the ground for changes unseen in the long, exclusivist rule of Christianity in Europe.

The ideological foundations of the modern and post-modern eras

The greatest challenge raised by the Enlightenment was the French Revolution which profoundly shook the Roman Catholic Church. By the time of Napoleon, the Roman Catholic Church was forced to accept humiliating conditions to save her position in a secular state. Bosch points out that the unshaken, aggressive and collective certitude of the Middle Ages, which existed until the eighteenth century, has vanished in Europe. As far as the world of values (to which religion was assigned) was concerned, the Enlightenment in principle adopted a relativistic attitude, as Knitter explains with the following:

In the course of time this would erode hitherto unshakable Christian certainties and slowly make the church aware of the existence of a dilemma it had never needed to recognize. With the collapse of colonialism Christianity lost its hegemony – even in the West, its traditional home – today has to compete in the open market of religions and ideologies.[21]

This relativized position was especially pronounced following the shock of World War II. People in the West turned away from traditional beliefs while in the eastern part of the European continent the secularizing force of communism appears with an unflinching impetus to 'bring peace', the only truth and justice, to all nations. This eschatological drive and intense feeling were major characteristics of early Christianity too. Many great scholars drew attention in various ways to Marxism, which sought to eliminate religion, especially Christianity, and eventually replace it.[22] This was also the context of Hungary where churches lived in a ghetto situation and were severely persecuted. The former alliance of the old establishment, which for the French disappeared with Napoleon, was cut off only after the 1940s in this region. In the states of the Communist Bloc the political elite not only completely separated religion and state, but they also asserted that the best ideology for a secularized state is atheism.[23] The Marxist states closed the doors of the churches and erected obstacles to the practice of religion. Marx attested that religion – in Europe this meant Christianity – is an opiate, but he did not realize that he offered another in its place as the single best medication to human suffering.[24] Eliade threw light on the fact that that there was an element of redemption in Marxism as there is in Christianity. While Marxism accused Christianity in different ways, it embraced similar ideals, such as possessing a unified belief of 'salvation', or the saving action of the working class people, and aimed to realize the same goals, such as sharing common goods and caring for each other.[25] Thus, the former Eastern Bloc emerged from communism and entered the last decade of the twentieth century relatively unexposed to Western influences, and isolated from the social-religious processes of the West.

Today, however, we live in a world that has changed across the 'old' continent. Hans Küng pointed out that today Christianity in Europe faces a twofold challenge: The world religions and modern Humanism. We must add another one, that is, new religious movements. As the danger of communism disappeared, new religious expressions emerged, of which the New Age is one of the strongest in Central and Eastern Europe. With the enlargement of the EU that encompassed former Communist Bloc nations, this process accelerated further. New Age believers and modern humanists claim that the Age of Christianity is waning and that a new, unified religion should replace Christianity. Christianity in this part of the world found itself on the defensive. Because nationalism interweaves religious belief with identity, traditional Christianity still has a firm grasp on the psyche of Eastern Europeans, yet the challenge of world religions, new religious movements and modern humanism has made significant inroads. This poses various questions for Christians. Philosophers and theologians of the Christian faith such as S. J. Samartha, Karl Jaspers, C. S. Lewis try to build bridges between the exclusivist nature of Christianity and the world religions, and some speak from an apologetic stance.[26]

In this context the question arises repeatedly whether Christianity is indeed something essentially different, something special from other perceptions of the world.[27] Nowadays there is an attempt to form a global theology from the side of Religious Studies and a Christian enterprise – from the side of theological faculties – to evolve a Christian *theologia religionum.* Sometimes an overlap can be seen owing to persons being involved in both of these developments. On the one hand a scholar can be a Christian, and on the other may hold beliefs about Christianity which are not in line with historic Christian doctrines.

Wilfred Cantwell Smith's attempt is the best example of such a stance from the discipline of Religious Studies. It is worth studying his position in greater detail. He viewed himself as a Protestant Christian, yet was willing to leave out most of the fundamentals of Christian doctrine.[28] Doubtless he earnestly tried to cope with the problem of how to relate to other religions, and one can learn a lot from him. He was a historian of religion, a respected Islamic historian who brought to the discussion a deep first-hand knowledge of that tradition. The point of departure for Smith's approach is his conviction that a certain unity of the world religions already exists.[29] He claimed that all religious communities are involved in such an ongoing process while at the same time dwelling in the constant presence of that transcendent power in whom we all move and have our being. Religions are beginning to converge and to form a single configuration woven out of the threads of many religious communities. All human history is salvation history. He argued that we are the first generation of Christians who are learning to recognize God's saving deeds in all the religious processes.[30] Smith insisted that no reasonable claim to theological knowledge can be made on the basis of one religious tradition alone. Therefore, when he said that all cosmic salvation is one and the same, and that 'as a Christian' he knew this on the basis of Christ, he is begging an enormous question. On what ground does one know this on anything more than a Christian conviction?

His failure to provide a clear treatment of this issue is telling. He might have argued that others know ultimately that there is one and the same cosmic salvation, but they know it 'as Muslims', 'as Buddhists', and so on. But of course, Buddhists believe that there is but one true cosmic 'salvation' and it is what the Buddha achieved; Muslims believe there is but one, and claim it is the one the Qur'ān describes. The main problem is practical as well as doctrinal. It might be that each particular religious tradition thinks and speaks of cosmic salvation, but most of them claim that their understanding of salvation is the correct one. Then comes the critique of Smith's stance: Which of these views is the correct one? Mark Heim says in his essay that it is important to Smith that 'cosmic salvation' be one and only one but just as important that it have concrete features. Otherwise that salvation would threaten to provide faith also with some determinate character and so undo all his efforts to remove it from the realm of historical contention.[31] Thus Smith questioned the historical concreteness of Christian tradition and did not allow us to define our faith exclusively as our ancestors, the reformers in faith did. One must make it clear that the understanding of Christian faith is ultimately exclusionist. Those, who follow the Reformed tradition, must confess with their forebears that Jesus is the only way to the Father and that there is no salvation besides him.

It is not surprising to find that there have always been scholars puzzled by this exclusivist claim, even among adherents within the Christian faith. The bewildering diversity of the attempts to solve the tension enhanced by the exclusionist claim of Christianity (Nurnberger lists no fewer than 27 varieties[32]) is an indication that thus far no clear direction seems to be emerging. These types have been distinguished as relativistic, dialectical and anti-dialectical. Küng differentiates four fundamental positions. We, however, will follow the six categories suggested by Whaling, namely, exclusivism, discontinuity, fulfilment, universalism, relativism and dialogue. These categories may also be chartered under three titles such as exclusivism, exclusionist inclusivialism and pluralist inclusivism. We think that this grouping will give us a different and rewarding insight into the approaches of theological attitudes towards religion.

Contemporary Christian theological approaches to different religious traditions

Exclusivism: the absolutist theological position

We have already discussed the medieval approaches which are most obviously observed in papal bulls. Conspicuously the common origin of tradition and its later developments have trends within their respective theological realms that highlight the theological uniqueness of Christian religion. Bosch's superb analysis showed us that the traditional Western Catholic and Protestant attitude towards other religions was often exclusivist, which is part of the pre-modern paradigm. Whaling points out that exclusivism has two forms, namely, institutional exclusivism as articulated through *extra ecclesiam nulla salus*, and a doctrinal form that underlines what is the true doctrine of salvation. Absolute exclusivism is represented by the medieval positions of common Western Christian heritage, and today the same is largely true of the contemporary evangelical position, which is orthodox in its theological outlook in many respects.[33] Moreover, the Fundamentalist wing of Evangelicals is typified by the so-called fundamentals articulated in 1912–1914 in the States. They stressed the inerrancy of the Scripture, the virgin birth and the deity of Jesus, his sacrificial and substitutionary atonement and penal substitution, the resurrection of Christ, and the miracles or alternatively his pre-millennial Second Coming and the Final Judgement.[34] Similar to this position is that of neo-orthodox theologian Karl Barth, who advocates a view best termed as *discontinuity*. Bosch draws attention to the fact that in his *Church Dogmatics* the Swiss theologian radicalises and outbids Luther and Calvin – his two main interlocutors – and consciously turns against the Enlightenment's evolutionary optimism and endorsement of autonomous humanity. Barth declares religion to be unbelief, a concern – indeed the one great concern – of godless human beings.[35] He wrote:

> Revelation does not link up with a human religion which is already present and practised. It contradicts it, just as religion previously contradicted revelation. It displaces it, just as religion previously displaced revelation, just as faith cannot link up with a mistaken belief, but must contradict and displace it as unbelief, as an act of contradiction.[36]

He goes on to contrast religion as a human fabrication with revelation, which is something totally different, coming directly from God. Barth's position is a form of stark exclusivism best understood in its context. First, it is vital to understand that Barth addressed a historical situation within Protestant liberal theology originating from Schleiermacher and Troeltsch who placed the concept of religion at the heart of Christian theology. Thus, Barth participated in a polemic in Protestant theology within his own context rather than addressing directly the theological question of the Christian approach to other religious traditions.[37] Second, Barth's theological departure point lay at Calvin's observation which spoke of the human being as an *idolorum fabrica* 'idol factory' and the idol thus manufactured is religion, Christian or otherwise. Nonetheless, his theological argument revolves around the idea that true religion is Christianity because of revelation. In other words there is no other revelation except the one given through Jesus Christ. Therefore, salvation is bound to the limits of the Christian faith. Two conclusions can be drawn from this. First, both Calvin and Barth asserted the absolute salvific claim of Christianity while denying other religions any place where true salvation, true religion is concerned. The conspicuous matter in both positions is that they had very little knowledge of other religions.[38] Second, their major concern arises from within the interest to clarify their own Christian theological context.

Exclusivism: the absolute socio-cultural exclusivism of secularization

A secular approach to other religions often bases its argument on socio-cultural factors rather than on theological premises. This view is less overtly theological than the former one in that regard it underlines trends in the secular world as being vital for forming a rationalist theological attitude to religions based on observation gained from the socio-cultural study of religious culture and history.

The arguments developed here seek to explain the cultural uniqueness of Christendom and its concomitant Judeo-Christian worldview that facilitated its advance. From a socio-cultural point of view they are 'exclusivist'. It is interesting to see that in spite of the sociological–historical assumptions underpinning this view, secularization, while taking a theological stance, developed a kind of attitude to religions in the modern world. Scholars such as Arend Van Leeuwen claimed that 'Judaeo-Christian thought paved the way for modern science and technology'.[39] With its stress on creation, the historical process, incarnation, prophecy, matter, the body and historical purpose, Western Christendom provided the ideological roots for the rise of modern science and technology and the process of secularization, whereas other religions would probably wither away under its onslaught. By arguing for the theocratic model versus the static ontocratic model of the East, Van Leeuwen underlines that biblical religion shaped Western civilizations, and from its theological–ideological framework stem such concepts as progress and revolution.[40] This secularist approach, which is also shared by Harvey Cox, is not very interested in the theological distinctiveness of Christianity as an internal issue but only in the outward socio-cultural features of Christianity. To that end it uses the biblical data as historical material. Van Leeuwen's ideas are echoed in liberation theology. He presupposed that Christianity is in the vanguard of the secularization process since demonstrably only this religion is capable of bringing new freedom, justice and fulfilment to humanity. Other religions are 'wedded to sacred worldviews that inhibit that from advancing naturally into the new freedom, justice and fulfilment from the birthright of humankind.'[41]

Exclusivism maintained: inclusivialism – fulfilment and universalism

Besides the two exclusivist categories, I believed that the third also retains an element of claiming absolute uniqueness, thereby being exclusivist. Fulfilment and universalist theologies make concessions but essentially subscribe to the distinctive role of salvation through Christ. Therefore, inclusivism in the Christian theology of religions is both an acceptance and rejection of other faiths at the very same time, a dialectical 'yes' and 'no'. In other words, it is best described as a stance maintaining the theological uniqueness of Christianity in a dialectical form. To be inclusive is to believe that all non-Christian religious truth ultimately belongs to Christ, the Logos, the Saviour or the Christian Church. The connection between Christian faith and other religions are established in many ways. Inclusivism arrives at confrontation, unlike Kraemer and Brunner, but seeks to discern ways by which the non-Christian faith may be integrated correctively into Christians' thinking.

Inclusivism has also its own biblical bases, such as Paul's speech in Athens (Acts 17. 22–31). Some claim that men in Athens were Christians without knowing it. I believe this is a superficial exposition of the biblical text since Paul nowhere states that he regarded them as Christians. He says, 'I perceive that in every way you are religious' (Acts 17.22b). If they were already in some way Christian, what then would be the point of inviting them to repent and for him to subsequently teach them?

The fulfilment approach suggests that other religions do have God, and truth, and spirituality, but they only have them in part through the medium of Logos. Their destiny is to be fulfilled by the perfect Logos who is Christ himself.[42] This view has its own striking parallel to the basic approach of Justin Martyr.[43] Bearing in mind that Justin tried to use Greek philosophy as a tool, he modified the concept of Logos to make his newly adopted Christian faith intelligent to his audience. The apologist speaks of Logos, employing philosophical–theological language rather than using a biblical–theological mode of expression by stressing elements, terms and concepts of Christology, such as Christ, Jesus, Son of God, Messiah. This premise, which is his starting point, allows him to arrive at the target he seeks to prove, namely, that the Logos is Christ, and the Logos is also wisdom, which is partially present in other religions and philosophies.

Besides Justin, some people argue that the medieval attempts at adaptation, indigenization, and accommodation of De Nobili, Ricci and Xavier are in the same school.[44] They all ascribed some worth to the religions and cultures where they carried out their mission work. In modern times it is not surprising to see that liberal theology saw Christianity sitting on the throne of the pyramid of religions. This idea gained sufficient acceptance that, on the eve of the twentieth century, an American theological journal gave expression to the belief in the ultimate triumph of Christianity by changing its name to the *Christian Century*. 'The liberal theology of the day accepted the validity of other religions but believed that it was still the best and was sure to outlive them.'[45] Many liberals and conservatives alike maintained that world religions could prepare the way for Christianity. Notably this view brought two otherwise fiercely fighting opponents to common ground. Many argued for this view based on the idea of progress employed by Christian theology. Such were the post-millennialist Scottish missionaries, who believed that God was fully revealed in Christ thereby implicitly allowing some place for the validity of partial knowledge about God. This pyramid kind of evolutionist picture is expressed by a different notion that highlights the superior form of Christianity – or better expressed, Christendom. Hence, we have those such as J. N. Farquhar who argued in his famous study on Hinduism that the 'crown' of Hinduism was Christianity.[46]

Modern thinkers also arrived at a similar position. Joseph Sittler argued in favour of a cosmic Christology and the unity of humankind under the new Head, the cosmic Christ. Karl Rahner's position mirrored a shift within the Roman Catholic tradition from an ecclesio-centric (*extra ecclesiam*) to a Christocentric approach to the theology of religions.[47] His point of departure is Christology whereby he never abandons the idea of Christianity as the absolute religion nor of salvation except through Christ. But he recognizes supernatural elements of grace in other religions, which have been given to human beings through Christ. There is saving grace within other religions, but this grace is Christ's. So people of other religious traditions are regarded as 'anonymous' Christians. Rahner's thesis has been modified in several aspects by H. R. Schlette, A. Camps and R. Panikkar as well as H. Küng.[48] Some argue that universalism is just a variation of fulfilment but has its own legitimacy as a separate category. Contemporary universalists have attempted to show that Christ is presently unknown in other religions of the world so that they are, so to speak, included in God's salvation as honorary Christians.[49]

These post-modern approaches share common characteristics. To varying degrees all maintain the essence of exclusivist Christian teaching. They claim that without Christ there is no salvation, revelation is given only to Christians, and it is Christianity and the Christian Church that secures salvation. Thus, all are 'exclusivist' claims in the sense that, where some leave a wider space for Christ's grace, the intercessory role of the Christian Church, and the uniqueness of revelation, others narrow the scope. However, it is an unfair comparison to only emphasize the similarities between them, as there are also striking differences between, say, Barth's extreme exclusivism and Rahner's all-encompassing exclusivism.

Crossing the Rubicon – beyond exclusivism and its variations: relativism and pluralism

So far all the models we have seen insist on the unique role of Christ or Christianity in the world of history. They emphasize theological argumentation and place stress on socio-cultural features of Judeo-Christian thought on the one hand, and on the other, struggle with the claim of absoluteness while ascribing some role and validity to other religions.

According to Bosch, exclusivism and fulfilment can be seen as models which are clearly pre-modern and modern but which show traces of a post-modern paradigm. A. Schopenhauer, G. W. Leibnitz and philosophers of similar thinking were all deeply imbued with the Enlightenment spirit which represented a decidedly modern understanding of religion. In their view, if there is such a reality to which the various religions refer, it is the same for all. The Oxford historian Arnold Toynbee used an old Indian tale to make this point. There are different names for experiencing the same reality, like the six blind Indian men who felt various parts of an elephant and described it differently depending on the part of body they had touched – a snake, a sword, a fan, a wall, a pillar and a rope. The question in each instance is the same, only the answers differ. Thus along their different paths the various religions guide us towards an identical summit.[50] It is worth paying attention to a contemporary 'liberal-evangelical' voice; this extreme relativism of the Enlightenment is hardly ever found today in Christian circles.[51] Instead modifications are the order of the day.

The first theologian of this pathway was Ernst Troeltsch.[52] An exponent of the history of religions school, he had throughout his life grappled with the issue of the so-called absoluteness of Christianity until, towards the end of his life, he underwent a shift in his thinking. In his *Der Historismus und seine Überwindung* he argued that Christianity then still held final and unconditional validity for Westerners, but only for them. For other peoples and cultures their traditional religions hold equally unconditional validity. John Hick combines Troeltsch's idea with the notion that all religions are different human answers to the one divine Reality and says that they embody different perceptions which have been formed in different historical and cultural circumstances.[53] He presses hard for a

> 'Copernican revolution' in the theology of religions, consisting in a paradigm shift from a Christianity centred or Jesus-centred to a God-centred model of the universe of faiths. One then sees the great world religions as different human responses to the one divine Reality, embodying different perceptions which have been formed in different historical and cultural circumstances.[54]

Paul Knitter in his new model for the quest for truth in faith defined truth not by exclusion but by relational terms. He says that

> [t]ruth by its very nature, needs other truth. If it cannot relate, its quality of truth must be open to question. Absoluteness is defined and established not by the ability of the religion to exclude or include others but its ability to relate to others, to speak to and listen to others in genuine dialogues.[55]

Bosch makes a good observation that the paradigm shift of Knitter and Hick is too profound for mainline Christian tradition. He reckons that they 'clearly and seriously question the finality and definitive normativity of Christ and Christianity'.[56] Knitter goes one step further than the universalist and fulfilment theologians and expresses his doubts about the reliability of much of the Christian tradition, notably its Christology, arguing that it is a later accretion and not in keeping with Jesus' own self-understanding, which was theo-centric. This interpretation allows him to dispense with Christo-centrism even for Christians, and he advises that they too should move to theo-centrism. With this view it is little wonder that he finds the positions of Rahner and Küng inadequate.[57] Hick also speaks with a similar critical tone:

> In the attempt to retain the dogma of no salvation outside the Church, or outside Christianity, we have the ideas of implicit, as distinguished from explicit, faith, of baptism by desire, as distinguished from literal baptism; and, as a Protestant equivalent, the idea of a latent Church as distinguished from the manifest Church; and, again, the suggestion that men can only come to God through

Jesus Christ but that those who have not encountered him in this life will encounter him in the life to come.[58]

He cannot accept Küng's notion that

> [a] man is to be saved within the religions that is made available to him in his historical situation. Hence, it is his right and his duty to seek God within that religion in which the hidden God has already found him. All this is until such time as he is confronted in an existential way with the revelation of Jesus Christ. The religions . . . are the way of salvation in universal history, the general way of salvation, we can even say, for the people of the world's religions: the more common, the '*ordinary*' way of salvation, as against which the salvation in the Church appears as something *very special and extraordinary*.[59]

Hick charged Küng that he 'goes on to take away with one hand what he has given with the other'.[60] Thus we see a brilliant critique from the liberal perspective of those who in my view crossed the theological Rubicon.

It is worth noting that their quest may come from the honest desire to create a place for non-Christians within the realm of Christianity, but while doing so it was necessary to depart from Christianity's long-accepted theological premises to philosophical premises. In so doing they cannot do justice to either of the two sides. Again Bosch's commentary hits the mark when he says that their endeavour 'is at least more honest in that they explicitly debunk the idea of any need for Christ and the Church'.[61]

It is clear that Hick borrowed his ideas from Wilfred Cantwell Smith's *The Meaning and End of Religion*.[62] Similarly, Knitter's model appears to be less original than he claims. It is close to Swami Vivekananda's position as it is to Toynbee's,[63] who envisions the historic religions reappearing above our horizon in a spirit of mutual charity. Yet it is a more sympathetic view than what Vivakananda holds since he advocates the idea from a Hindu stance whereas Toynbee's idea seems to be a kind of 'Hindu' inclusivist idea which is not Christian. Vivekananda declared at the World Parliament of Religions:

> The Christian is not to become a Hindu or a Buddhist, nor a Hindu or a Buddhist to become a Christian. But each must assimilate the others and yet preserve its individuality and grow according to its own law of growth.[64]

In other words, everybody should remain in his or her realm of religious tradition without giving up the main beliefs, and still have an openness towards others.

All these approaches are different reflections and responses to the challenge of other worldviews, and all of them have emerged from a mutual interaction called dialogue. In the next section I want to outline the basis on which dialogue can be done.

Dialogue and, or mission?

In its essential meaning dialogue refers to a sort of openness to the opinion of those belonging to other religions and at the same time opens a gate through which one may grasp the other person's beliefs. Dialogue is a complex notion, both in theory and in practice, and it is necessary first to begin to unravel that complexity. First, we focus on where it may occur. It may well start naturally at a grass-roots level, or may be induced by government. It could well be academic inter-religious dialogue with representatives of different religious communities involved in such a process. It is relevant for us to note that the Christian dialogue with other religions may operate with different theories, goals and forms. First, dialogue can be done with an intention to listen and try to understand the beliefs of other religions. Another goal of dialogue is more secular, inasmuch as different religious traditions are more concerned about economical, political and sociological issues rather than theological ones. The third goal brings theology and Religious Studies closely together inasmuch as both endeavour to establish the facts about other religious traditions in order to avoid overt misunderstandings. There is an overlap between Religious Studies and theology because both seek to achieve this end from different angles.[65] Finally dialogue is regarded as *mutual witnessing*. At this point we also find divisions of opinions. Martin Buber who has given a profound analysis of the nature of dialogue has made it very clear that the presupposition of genuine dialogue is not that the partners agree beforehand to relativize their own conviction but that they accept each other as persons.[66] The two polarities are the involvement of *epoché* and *Einfühlung* in dialogue on the one hand, and, on the other, the viewpoint which finds it almost impossible to put one's conviction into brackets because this would be to imply that our convictions do not matter. Whaling argues that what is most important in the dialogue is to have a humble attitude which wants to listen and is open to incorporate the enriching ideas of the other who holds onto a different yet beautiful religious tradition.

A major critique of those representing traditional Christianity is their lack of knowledge about other religions and their unwillingness to listen to the other side. It is also true that top church leaders act too quickly in formulating a common statement with leaders of other world religions. In doing so they often forget that Christianity is a missionary religion. This is indirectly underlined by Sundarara Rajan, a distinguished Hindu writer on philosophical questions and religion, who attested, 'if it is impossible to lose one's faith as a result of an encounter with another faith, then I feel that the dialogue has been made safe from all possible risks.'[67] Knowing both sides of the criticism does not exempt us from addressing the difficult challenge of a conscious encounter with peoples of other religions, either through mission or dialogue. A Christian should always proclaim the Gospel even if he or she engages in dialogue. This stems from the very nature of Christian conviction as Leslie Newbigin often characterized it. But the way it is done in dialogue especially poses a challenge for many Christians. The statement from the San Antonio Conference on World Mission and Evangelism has a position that is fair to the missional nature of the Christian Church, and it does justice to mission and dialogue at the same time. The statement says: 'We affirm that witness does not preclude dialogue but invites it, and that dialogue does not preclude witness but extends and deepens it.'[68] Whatever form Christian encounter with persons of other religions may take, it carries a creative tension that has to be learned by participants on both sides, day by day.

Notes

[1] D. J. Bosch, *Transforming Mission* (New York, Orbis Books, 1993), p. 235.

[2] J. Hick, *God Has Many Names* (London: Macmillan Press, 1980), p. 50.

[3] 'The lack of knowledge about the early church in depth is very disappointing at our theological faculties' I wrote in Princeton in 1997. Since then at least in Debrecen in Hungary, and Kolozsvár (Cluj-Napoca, now in Romania) the theological schools introduced Early Church History and History of Dogmatics. Besides this, a society was established for Patristic literature composed of scholars teaching at secular, or church-affiliated higher institutions.

[4] E. Gibbon, *The Decline and Fall of the Roman Empire* (London: J. M. Dent, 1910).

[5] R. Wilken, *The Christians as the Roman Saw Them* (New Haven: Yale Univ. Press, 1982).

[6] Tertullian, Prescription Against Heretic (De Praescriptione haereticorum) I. 7. p. 9.

[7] Tatian, *Address To the Greeks*, ch. 8.

[8] M. J. Edwards, 'Justin's Logos and the Word of God' *Journal of Early Christian Studies* 3.3 (1995), p. 261–290 and L. W. Barnard, 'The Logos Theology of St. Justin Martyr' *Downside Review* 89.295 (1971), 131–141.

[9] E. C. Dewick, *The Christian Attitude to Other Religions* (Cambridge: Cambridge University Press, 1953), p. 120. See also W. Temple, *Readings in St. John's Gospel I* (London: Macmillan, 1943), p. 10.

[10] J. L. Gonzales, *The Story of Christianity* (New York: HarperCollins, 1985), vol. 1, p. 56.

[11] K. Bediako, Theology and Identity: The Impact of Culture Upon Christian Thought in the Second Century and in Modern Africa (Oxford: Regnum Books, 1992).

[12] *Unam Sanctam*, promulgated 18 November 1302. See: www.papalencyclicals.net./Bon08/B8Unam.htm. Accessed 5 August 2008.

[13] J. Verkuyl, *Contemporary Missiology* (Grand Rapids, MI: Eerdmans), p. 343.

[14] A. B. Hasler, P. Heinegg, *How The Pope Became Infallible: Pius IX and the Politics of Persuasion* (New York: Double Day, 1981). See a book-review by Roger O'Toole in *Sociological Analysis* vol. 43. no.1. Spring 1982 pp. 86–88.

[15] *Summa Theologica*, I. II. 109, 1. ad. 1. cited by L. Liptay, *A kereszténység viszonya más vallásokhoz*, (Pozsony: Kalligram, 2005), pp. 36–37.

[16] J. D. Spence, *The Memory Palace of Matteo Ricci* (New York: Penguin Books, 1984).

[17] Verkuyl, p. 345.

[18] P. Rossano, 'Christ's Lordship and Religious Pluralism in Roman Catholic Perspective', in *Christ's Lordship and Religious Pluralism*, G. H. Anderson and T. S. Stransky, eds (Maryknoll, NY: 1981), p. 106.

[19] Bosch, p. 476.

[20] P. F. Knitter, *No Other Name?* (Maryknoll, NY: Orbis Books, 1985), p. 18.

[21] *Ibid.*, p. 475.

[22] N. Bergyajev, *A kommunizmus igazságai és hazugságai* (Budapest: Kairosz Kiadó, 2003), p.143–144.

[23] *Ibid.*, p. 74–76.

[24] A. Kee, *Marx and the Failure of Liberation Theology* (London: SCM Press, 1990), p. 30–31.

[25] M. Eliade, The Myth of the Eternal Return, or Cosmos and History (London: Arkana, 1989), pp. 148–149.

[26] S. J. Samartha, 'The Quest for Salvation and the Dialogue between Religions', *International Review of Mission*, LVII.228 (1968), p. 224.

[27] H. Küng, *On Being a Christian*, (London: Collins, 1977), p. 23.

[28] W. C. Smith, 'Vergleichende Religionswissenschaft: Wohin – Warum?' *Grundfragen der Religionswissenschaft*, pp. 75–105.

[29] S. M. Heim, *Salvations: Truth and Difference in Religion*, Faith meets Faith series (Maryknoll, Orbis Books, NY. 1991) 'Forms of faiths', p. 45.

[30] C. Smith, 'The Changing Christian Role in Other Cultures', *Occasional Bulletin of the Missionary Research Library*, 1967.

[31] Heim, p. 69.

[32] K. Nurnberger, 'Systematisch-theologische Lösungsversuche zum Problem der anderen Religionen und ihre missionsmethodischen Konsequenzen' in *Neue Zeitschrift für Theologie und Religionsphilosophie* vol. 12.1970. (13–43), p. 42.

[33] F. Whaling, The World's Religious Traditions: Current Perspective in Religious Studies (Edinburgh, T. & T. Clark, 1984), pp. 10–11.

[34] I. S. Rennie, 'Fundamentalism and the Varieties of North American Evangelicalism' in *Evangelicalism: Comparative Studies of Popular Protestantism in North America, the British Isles and Beyond, 1770–1990* M. A. Noll, D. Bebbington and G. A. Rawlyk eds (New York, Oxford University Press, 1994), pp. 333–364.

[35] K. Barth, *Church Dogmatics*, vol. I.2. (Edinburgh T. & T. Clark, 1978), p. 302.

[36] Barth, p. 303.

[37] F. Whaling, *Christian Theology and World Religions: A Global Approach* (Basingstoke: Marchal Pickering, 1986), p. 77.

[38] L. Liptay, *A kereszténység viszonya más vallásokhoz*, (Pozsony: Kalligram, 2005), p. 95.

[39] A. T. Van Leeuwen, *Christianity and World History* (London: Edinburgh house Press, 1964), p. 331.

[40] A. T. Van Leeuwen, Reply to Criticism: A Defence of Christianity in World History, (London: SCM Press, 1966), V.c.

[41] Whaling, *Christian Theology*, p. 82.

[42] Whaling, *How to Compare Religions*, p. 3.

[43] Jusztinosz, 'Apológia I.' in *A II. századi görög apologéták* transl. László Vanyó (Budapest: Ap. Szentszék Kiadó, 1984), pp. 64–120.

[44] A. Neely, *Christian Mission: A Case Study Approach* (Maryknoll, NY: Orbis Books, 1995). This book contains an excellent discussion of such topics.

[45] Bosch, p. 479.

[46] J. N. Farquhar, *The Crown of Hinduism* (London: Oxford University Press, 1913).

[47] K. Rahner, 'Das Christentum und die nichtchristlichen Religionen' in *Schriften zur Theologie* (Einsiedeln-Zürich-Köln, Benziger Verlag 1964), V. p. 139.

[48] H. H. Schlette, *Die Religionen als thema der Theologie* (Freiburg: 1964), pp. 13–14.

[49] Whaling, *How to Compare Religions*, p. 3.

[50] A. J. Toynbee, *Experiences* (London: Oxford University Press, 1968), p. 328.

[51] Bosch, p. 481.

[52] E. Troeltsch, *Die Absolutheit des Christentums und die Religionsgeschichte*, 3rd ed. (Tübingen: Siebeck, 1929), pp. 96–122.

[53] J. Hick, *An Interpretation of Religion* (London: Macmillan Press, 1989).

[54] J. Hick, *God has Many Names* (London: 1980), p. 5ff.

[55] Knitter, p. 219.

[56] Bosch, p. 483.

[57] Knitter, p. 147.

[58] Hick, *God Has Many Names*, p. 50.

[59] J. Neuer, *Christian Revelation and World Religions* (London, 1962) p. 52 ff.

[60] Hick, *God Has Many Names*, p, 50.

[61] Bosch, p. 486.

[62] N. Anderson, *Christianity and World Religions* (Leicester: IVP, 1984), p. 25.

[63] Toynbee, p. 329.

[64] J. H. Barrow, ed. *The World's Parliament of Religions*, 2 vols. (Chicago: The Parliament Pub. Co. 1983), I, p.170.

[65] Whaling, *Christian Theology*, p. 91.

[66] W. A.Vissert-Hooft, *No Other Name* (London: SCM press, 1963), pp. 117–119.

[67] Sundarara R. Rajan, 'Negotiations: An Article on Dialogue Among Religions' in *Religion and Society*. 21. no. 4, p. 74.

[68] *The San Antonio Report*, ed. F.R. Wilson (Geneva: WCC, 1990) I. 27., p. 32.

Chapter 2

'Take Home the Good News': The Mission of the Church in the Context of Neo-Liberal Economic Globalization

Jooseop Keum

Introduction

In the development of ecumenical understanding and practice of mission, it has been vital to constantly ask the question, 'What is God's mission today?' The ecumenical movement recognizes that mission is not our mission but God's mission. We are invited as partners to participate in God's life-giving works for suffering humanity and creation. In order to discern what God's mission is, it is important to carefully read the 'signs of times' today.

It will be argued in this essay that neo-liberal economic globalization and its impacts are one of the most urgent mission issues today which is threatening many lives in the contemporary world, particularly in the global south. How then can the Church understand economic globalization and missiologically respond to the challenges caused by it? It is the aim of this essay to bring a theological critique to global economic injustice and to discuss the mission of the Church in the context of neo-liberal economic globalization.

The story of the cotton seed

When I organized a training programme for the mission enablers on the theme of globalization and mission in 2004, one of the participants from India proposed a project application for training purposes, entitled, 'The Natural Seed Project'. The participants were wondering, and at the same time were surprised, about why a natural seed project for the church's mission programme was proposed.

One participant was a mission enabler in the diocese near Nagpur where agriculture is one of main industries in that part of India. The farmers in his village were widely using GMO (Genetically Modified Organism) seeds for farming, which were produced by trans-national agricultural companies. They believed that this promised more harvest and income. However, shortly afterwards they realized that the GMO seeds could not be re-cultivated. His farmer friends could not understand why the seed was so expensive and why it would only produce one crop. Moreover, because they relied heavily on GMO seeds, they had to buy chemicals and fertilizers from the same trans-national agriculture companies. Furthermore, because the farmers did not have enough money in the spring, they had to borrow money from banks to buy their seeds, chemicals and fertilizers. And this was the beginning of the tragedy that would follow. When the harvest season came, the bankers visited the harvest field and decided to take back the agreed initial loan that was used to purchase the seeds and replaced it with another loan that had an unbearably high interest rate. For his farmer friends, the remaining money from the loan was not even enough to pay for the basic education of their children, or to buy enough food. Indeed, they had to wait until the next harvest season to buy such necessities. Consequently, the farmers' debt only increased.

The hopelessness of this story is common to farmers throughout the mission enabler's province. Indeed, during the past 10 years approximately 3,000 farmers have committed suicide in the Nagpur region. The mission enabler from India said: 'In order to break this endlessly spiralling chain of injustice introduced by economic globalization, development of natural seeds is one of the mission priorities of my church.' Although natural seeds may not promise better productivity, it is the only way for farmers to escape the greedy hands of the trans-national agriculture companies and the banks. Indeed, the Natural Seed project is a life giving mission project for his rural community.

The story of the madman

The title of this essay, 'Take home the good news' is based on the parable of 'The Exorcism of the Gerasenes Demoniac', Mark 5.1–20. When Jesus arrived at the other side of the lake, the pagan land, he met a madman who was living among the tombs. This man was possessed by a powerful evil spirit. However, Jesus defeated the devil power and dramatically healed him. Although the man wanted to follow him, Jesus sent him home to his family as a witness to what Jesus had done for him.

In modern commentary, many have focused on this story with particular reference to Jesus' power to defeat the devil and on his healing ministry. From a mission perspective, mission to gentiles or home and family mission have been emphasized.[1] Some have also tried to make the connection between the notion of home and contextuality in mission. If we apply a similarly narrow interpretation, we will fail to read the deep meaning of the parable with regard to God's mission today. In order to enrich our understanding, I would like to suggest we reread the text through the eyes of an Indian cotton farmer with the following emphases.

First, let us draw our attention to the home of this madman, Gerasenes.[2] Gerasenes was one of the cities of *Decapolis*, the ten cities, which the Roman army built for a defensive purpose. We should also understand that east of the Sea of Galilee lay a gentle land and that first-century Palestine was under the occupation of the Roman Empire. Gerasenes (Gerasa) was a centre of the resistance movement against the colonial power.[3] The Romans brutally punished the people in Gerasenes because of their resistance and claimed the silence enforced by punishment as an authentic peace. The Roman imperial religion forced worship of the emperor as a living God, and proclaimed this as 'the good news of *Pax Romana.*'[4]

The Roman occupation polarized the demoniac's home. Some became collaborators, others became resistance. Some lived as normal, others withdrew.[5] Religiously, the people in Gerasenes were pagans who had no way for salvation. Economically, some people there started to worship *Mammon*, because they had learned that only money can secure their lives in such a hopeless situation. However, in reality, there was no way to climb the ladder unless they became collaborators, such as tax collectors. It is important to recognize that the demoniac became mad in this context. He was crying for some good news among the tombs, where it was possible that his beloved family and friends were massacred and buried.

Second, the name 'legion' is highly significant. The 'unclean spirit', which made him mad was the largest unit of the Roman ground army.[6] The demons threatened Jesus by saying, 'We are many.' However, the earthly power of the empire could not win over the sovereignty of God. The legion begged Jesus to allow them to move into the herd of pigs. By doing so, the devil power (Nero's persecution of the Markan community) continuously attempted to stay in Gerasenes as another form of oppressive power. In this context, the term 'herd of pigs' referred to a band of Roman military recruits.[7] In the Bible a pig is an unclean animal and a symbol of paganism. Since Antiochus Epiphanies had forced the Jews to eat pigs, it also became the byword of recently recruited imperial solders.[8] However, at the end of day, they all had to be thrown into the lake, like the Egyptian empire army in the Exodus.

Third, the people in Gerasenes asked Jesus to leave. But the healed man began to spread the good news. If the healing miracle was a narrative of merely an individual exorcism without any connection to empire, there would have been no reason for the people not to welcome Jesus, just as those on the Western shore of the lake did before he sailed. Thousands of patients were expected to crowd around him. But instead, the people asked Jesus to leave. This story certainly had socio-political implications. It provokes a fundamental transformation of the structure introduced by the empire. The people were afraid of the consequences that such a transformation would bring and they requested Jesus to leave their home. The healing of legion was not only a personal exorcism, it was also a proclaiming of the new Kingdom which is inherently different from the Empire. But the people rejected this calling of the Kingdom of God movement. And at the same time, they rejected Jesus' mission of transformation!

The healed man wanted to follow Jesus, but Jesus sent him back to his home and gave him the mission to witness to what he had done for him. When Jesus healed the Jews, he would normally ask them to keep silent, but this time he gave a mission to a gentile to proclaim the good news, namely, the coming of the Kingdom of God. When Jesus gave him the mission, 'take home the good news,' he did not simply proclaim it among his family members and home villagers. Rather, he travelled Decapolis,[9] the ten cities across the Sea of Galilee. He crossed the boundary between the Jew (west of the sea) and the Gentile (east of the sea). Where then, was the home for him? Certainly he did not understand home merely as a blood connection or a geographical concept. For him, where people were crying and needed the news of God's Kingdom, this was his missionary home.

What is happening at our home?

Globalization in its broad sense refers to the rapid growth of linkages and inter-connectedness between nations and social communities which make up the present world system.[10] However, the project which facilitates this tide is the neo-liberal mode of economic globalization which promotes the rapid growth of international trade, the vast expansion of speculative movements of financial capital internationally and the astounding spread of mass communication around the world.

The major actors of economic globalization are the institutions originating from the Bretton Woods system represented by the World Trade Organization (WTO), International Monetary Fund (IMF), World Bank, and trans-national corporations (TNCs) today. The Organization of Economic Cooperation and Development (OECD) and the G8 are those who bless this economic order and benefit from it.

Economic globalization promises to bring millions of people into active participation in the global economic life. Many people say that globalization has both positive and negative aspects. For instance, access to knowledge and information through the internet, communication through mobile phones, increased opportunities for international travel and in general lower prices for consumer goods are the positive consequences of economic globalization.

However, neo-liberalism renders national governments powerless to protect public goods and services, such as education and health. It thus places the utmost importance on private capital and so-called unfettered markets to allocate resources efficiently and to promote growth. Consequently, it cancels the welfare function of the state.[11]

Based on the analysis of Rogate Mshana, WCC Programme Executive on Economic Justice, the biggest challenge to our home today is the impact of neo-liberal economic globalization. The world economy has become the Champagne

Glass Economy in which the top 20 per cent of the population holds 83 per cent of the world's wealth, the next 20 per cent have ownership of 11 per cent of the world's wealth, and the bottom 60 per cent of the population must cope with only 6 per cent of the world's wealth.[12] Indeed, the rich are becoming richer and the poor are becoming poorer in this economic development.

The top six richest people in the world earn and spend more than all the people in sub-Sahara African countries put together. Furthermore, the people of sub-Saharan Africa spend almost half of their cash income on expensive HIV/AIDS drugs for their family at home.

The polarization of the global economy is causing extreme poverty in the global south. Furthermore, privatization of education and health is threatening basic human rights. As we listened to the story of the Indian farmer, we can see that this polarization of the global economy becomes a matter of life and death for the people of the global south.

The injustice of the global economy has been projected by neo-liberal econo-mists, who believe that if they remove the intervention of state and ethical val-ues from the market, the world economy will dramatically grow. They claim that this growth will bring the ultimate well-being and even salvation of humanity.[13] Furthermore, International Financial Institutions support and develop this neo-liberal economic model. These institutions are the new forms of global empire in the twenty-first century.

The drive of the neo-liberal economy affects other creatures as well. Efforts to preserve our earth and creation are regarded by neo-liberal economists as an inef-ficient hindrance to economic growth. Is this not a classic example of structural 'madness', a madness that is happening within our missionary home today? How then can we take the good news to the victims of this global 'madness'?

What news is good for our home?

Professor Duncan Forrester, who for many years has advocated the involvement of Christians in social action, says 'Christian contributions to the world ought to be a way of confessing the faith, as part of the mission of the Church.'[14] Chris-tians throughout the world should be able to confess our faith with regard to economic issues and we believe that this should be done through the mission and spiritual life of the Church.[15] This is especially true when life is the issue in question. The Church has to take a firm faith stance on life issues because we believe it is the most powerful action the faith community can take. The Church should adopt a faith-stance that, through mission, enables it to give life to the suffering of God's creation.

As we have learned from the Accra Confession proclaimed by the World Alli-ance of Reformed Churches (WARC) in its General Council in 2004, neo-liberal globalisation is a matter of life and death for the majority of the people that live in the global south. The aim of globalization is to integrate people's lives into a single world economy and this continues to cause much suffering. Globalization has an ideological dimension or a quasi-religious message that says, 'The global market system will save the world.'[16] Globalization has served as a vehicle of a 'universal' global culture that undermines religious and cultural plurality.[17]

One could say that this is a similar message that was proclaimed throughout the world by the Roman Empire in Jesus' time as we read in the biblical story of the madman in Gerasenes! The Empire said its policy of uniting all different systems, markets, and cultures would eventually bring prosperity and peace to all people. In the name of prosperity and peace, all nations had to be subject to the power of a mono-globalizing system that was introduced by the Empire. The emperor declared this as the good news, which would save the world but at the same time would force people into worshiping him. Is this not an echo of what neo-liberal economists are saying today?

However, it was terribly bad news for the people in Gerasenes and indeed it made their daily lives worse. People soon realized that globalization of the Roman Empire was not for the benefit of all and that it only benefited Roman citizens. In this context, Jesus had a mission to introduce an alternative to globalization of the Empire: 'The globalisation of the Kingdom of God!'

The 'Great Commission' (Mathew 28.18–20) has been the watchword for the modern missionary movement, but from a colonial perspective it has been over-emphasized. In a globalized context, reading the text with special reference to 'all nations' gives a new insight into today's Christian mission. In the text Jesus says that although the Roman Empire was only one nation that never allowed the existence of all nations through its absolute power, go to all the small nations that are subject to the Roman Empire and dignify and teach them that you are the subject of God's Kingdom, not the Empire. This is the commission that we have today in the midst of neo-liberal economic globalization as well.

This mission was first carried out by the Apostle Paul. He established the early Church as an alternative community for the Kingdom of God's movement while rejecting the globalization of the empire. It is highly important to recognize that globalization from below, or the alternative to the political–economic globalization of empire, was one of the most important missions of the Church since the beginning of Christianity.[18] Indeed, globalization of the Kingdom of God against globalization of the empire has been the core of Christian mission, the Good News!

Partnership in transforming mission

Based on the above understanding, I believe that seeking and developing alternatives to neo-liberal economic globalization is a call to God's mission for our home today. It is a prophetic calling for the world Church for our mission at this juncture of history. We need to transform the traditional concept and approach to mission. While we are busy planting churches, preaching the Gospel, managing schools and hospitals, developing projects and maintaining institutions, sometimes we forget what all these efforts are for. Going back to Jesus in the text today, it was clear that his mission was to give people the fullness of life who were suffering under the globalization of the Roman Empire. His mission was more than religious conversion. Therefore, we need to bring back this life-centred approach to the heart of Christian mission.

One of the most important tasks of the churches, based on reading the signs of the times today, is developing transforming mission for structural change. Moreover, in order to tackle this global structure, we have to empower ourselves towards a new stage of partnership in mission. Since the second half of the last century, the world Church has focused on the work to establish equal partnership in mission, overcoming the colonial pattern of world mission. But what is partnership for? Have we not increased our partnership as a family in mission to give a life for suffering humanity and creation through united efforts? Is it not our ultimate goal to develop together a global missionary movement to actualize the Kingdom of God? I believe this is the time to test the authenticity of our partnership to face the most serious mission challenges of today.

However, in reality, the efforts by the WCC and WARC to address global economic issues as a faith matter have brought controversial responses and divisions between the churches. Although the churches have in their different ways been in the struggle against poverty and economic oppression, their responses tend to be influenced by an 'us/them' dichotomy and 'subject/object' ideology of development rooted in a Western model of donor-influenced charity. Assessing this dichotomy, Roderick R. Hewitt says:

> This is undergirded by a deceptive theology of salvation and a my-evangelisation model in which being saved is presented as a personal life-transforming gift that comes from others (external source/s) without equal emphasis being placed on challenging and changing the political, social, religious and economic structures that are the root causes that keep the poor in poverty![19]

Concluding remarks: 'hope as vision'

Placing economic issues central to churches' understanding of what they are called to be and to do is a vital missiological agenda in the twentieth century. We cannot avoid anymore the issues of structural poverty in the world. We are facing a difficult journey of seeking to facilitate the conversion of churches from their reluctance to address and take tangible action on structural issues that create and maintain poverty. Indeed, it is the important task of missiologists to develop theological critique on neo-liberalism and seeking alternative globalization. This concern of has become an urgent mission in our era.

Duncan B. Forrester has said

[h]ope is resistance to a hopeless situation. Hope keeps open the horizon of the future and motivates action. Our faith in a New Heaven and a New Earth gives substance to hope, shapes and sustains hope. This hope is at its heart and throughout social. The hope is good news to the poor and all who suffer.[20]

This hope challenges the existing order of injustice and structural evil. The bankruptcy of hope never exists in Jesus and his movement for transformation of history. People in the street are shouting, 'Another world is possible!' Shall we dare to dream together an alternative to economic globalization, an alternative world?

Notes

[1] For example, see, Ben Witherington III, *The Gospel of Mark: A Socio-Rhetorical Commentary* (Grand Rapids: Eerdmans, 2001), pp. 178–84.

[2] Matthew 8.28 reads 'Gadarenes,' and some other ancient manuscripts read 'Gergesenes' and 'Gerasa', a leading city of Decapolis; John R. Donahue and Daniel J. Harrington, *Sacra Pagina: The Gospel of Mark* (Collegeville: A Michael Glazier Book, 2002), p. 163.

[3] Historian, Josephus recorded that 'a thousand of the youth' were killed by Roman solders in Gerasa because of their rebellion against the Roman Empire. *War*, 4. pp. 486–90.

[4] Duncan B. Forrester, 'Mission in the Public Square: Christian Political Discourse as Public Confession', unpublished paper, 1999, p. 2.

[5] Richard Dormandy, 'The Expulsion of Legion: A Political Reading of Mark 5.1–20', *The Expository Times*, 111, (Edinburgh: Edinburgh University Press, 2000), p. 335.

[6] Roughly 6,000 troops. John R. Donahue and Daniel J. Harrington, p. 166.

[7] Richard Dormandy, p. 335.

[8] See, J. Marcus, *Mark 1-8*, (New York: Doubleday, 1999), pp. 341–2.

[9] Mark 5.20.

[10] A. McGrew and P. G. Lewis ed., *Global Politics: Globalisation and the Nation States* (Cambridge: The Policy Press, 1992), p. 303.

[11] WCC, Alternative Globalisation, Addressing Peoples and Earth (AGAPE): A Background Document (Geneva: WCC Publications, 2005), p. 10.

[12] *Ibid.*

[13] F. A. Hayek, *Law, Legislation and Liberty*, vol. II: *The Mirage of Social Justice*, 2nd ed. (London: Routledge, 1982), pp. 63–70.

[14] Forrester, 'Mission in the Public Square', p. 1.

[15] André Biéler, *Calvin's Economic and Social Thought* (Geneva: WCC Publications, 2005), pp. 304–309.

[16] 'The People of God among All God's Peoples', Report from a Theological Round-table Sponsored by the Christian Conference of Asia and the Council for World

Mission, November 11-17,1999' Article 1.2.3; See also, Duncan B. Forrester, *Christian Justice and Public Policy* (Cambridge: Cambridge University Press, 1997), pp. 149–64.

[17] 'The People of God among All God's Peoples,' 1.2.5.

[18] See, John D. Crossan and Jonathan L. Reed, *In Search of Paul, How Jesus's Apostle Opposed Rome's Empire with God's Kingdom* (New York: Harper Collins Publishers, 2004).

[19] Roderick R. Hewitt, 'The Missiological Implications of the Accra Confession', CWM-WRAC Joint Consultation on Accra Confession and Its Implications in Mission, 15–19 May 2006, Kuala Lumpur, p. 1.

[20] Forrester, *Christian Justice and Public Policy*, pp. 246–7.

Chapter 3

Open Boundaries, or: Perspectives on 'Person' for Inter-Religious Dialogue[1]

Klaus Hock

'L'homme n'existe pas!' – *Man doesn't exist*! This was the revolutionary watchword when in the late 1970s the ideas of the renowned French philosopher Michel Foucault gradually entered the scene of intellectual discourses in Europe and beyond. The proclamation of *the death of God* by Friedrich Nietzsche[2] seemed to have found its complement, or even fulfilment, in the proclamation of *the death of man* by Michel Foucault.[3] Though this is – and always was – a wrong interpretation of Foucault's intentions, his philosophy was nevertheless regarded as a serious attack on mainline traditions of European thought. Even in traditions like, for example, those represented by the so-called Critical Theory of the 'Frankfurt School', it was held that man, despite all kinds of restrictions, flaws and distortions, and notwithstanding man's entanglement in the implications of the 'Dialectic of Enlightenment', is still the acting agent in history, a being which is constituted by his/her 'self'. And against this background, Foucault's approach seemed to imply the annihilation of what was considered the very basis of all Western thought – the idea of man as person, as the acting subject in history and society.

I shall come back to this observation, again. For the moment, it should only serve as a starting point for unfolding the perspective on our topic, a perspective that is very complex and multi-faceted, even if we focus on concepts which have developed within a context of allegedly homogeneous, or at least shared, cultural traditions – in this case, the European, Western or occidental context.

Thereby we must indeed take into consideration that European or Western concepts of anthropology are strongly moulded by Christian traditions. Furthermore, due to the venture of the modern missionary movement, European expansion, and globalization, European anthropologies rooted in Christian traditions have deeply influenced discourses on anthropological principles in other cultures and religions as well. In a first step, I would therefore like to outline some basic aspects of anthropological principles in (Western) Christian tradition, starting with some brief remarks on the category 'person' as I use it in this contribution. Then, I shall very briefly sketch some aspects of anthropological principles in various cultural and religious traditions. Finally, I will attempt to summarize this survey in a rough systematic order, before drawing some conclusions for our topic in view of its relevance for inter-religious and inter-cultural dialogue.

'Person' – a contextual category

'Person' has been one of the key categories in the dogmatic disputes in the ancient Church.[4] But it has been taken from a pre- or non-Christian usage. The meaning of the Latin term of unknown origin ('mask', 'role', 'status') derives from *per-sonare*, 'to sound through', referring to a mask which was used in the theatre as a loudspeaker for reinforcing the sound of the actor's voice – like the horn of a gramophone. However, this term – *persona* – was never used in the meaning it has received in modern thought as 'person'. What we have in mind when we talk about 'person' was in ancient times related to terms like 'self' (*se*, *ipse*), 'nature' (*natura*), 'consciousness' (*conscientia*), etc. Interestingly, in ancient philosophy the term *personae* was used for describing 'masks' covering the very nature of man, thereby specifying man by de-fining him/her both in correlation and in opposition to animals (by the *persona* of reason) and other human beings (by the *persona* of 'specifics'), etc.

As a *sociological term*, 'person' refers to someone fulfilling a social role. But the meaning of 'person' is not strictly defined. It refers to – as I may call it – an individual's 'fluid unit' of characteristics, motives, feelings, interests. These characteristics derive from a complex interplay of biological and psychological factors which are continuously adjusting to their social and physical environment. Accordingly, as a *socio-cultural phenomenon*, a person is a more or less stable arrangement of those characteristics, motives, feelings, interests that have been transformed in the course of his/her socialization, namely, by internalizing socio-cultural patterns like norms, language, cosmologies, ideologies, etc. Consequently, a person is not an isolated entity, but always and fundamentally an interrelated unit with 'open boundaries' – open boundaries towards the community, towards other beings, towards the cosmos, etc.

Religious concepts of 'person' are in a way derivatives of the cultural environment. They are, so to speak, a special case of the sociological concept of 'person', with the focus on religious ideas and notions determining the understanding of what makes a person a person. But again, religious concepts of 'person' refer to entities with 'open boundaries', entities which are dependent on a specific religious understanding of the relationship between individual and community, body and soul, man and nature, 'self' and cosmos. Accordingly, as a religious concept, a person always holds an intermediary position, as a medium, a vessel, a vehicle, of forces beyond herself/himself, of 'powers' with a religious quality.

Today we use the term 'person' synonymous with 'self', 'me', 'individual', etc. All these terms are contextual categories, as they refer to an interrelational entity that is placed into a multi-dimensional context of relations to religious forces beyond himself/herself. I would like to expand on these observations by referring to Christian anthropological principles. Here the basic relationship is between man and God, but it is unfolded in a complex network of relations between man and cosmos, man and man, man and community, etc. Fundamentally the Christian understanding of the human being is based on complementary traditions. According to the paradise narrative, the human being is primarily considered to be a sinner, on the one hand, and on the other, according to the creation story, humans are created in the image of God. Therefore we can read the history of Christian theology in view of its anthropological principles as the emergence of diverse opinions ranging from more negative and pessimistic to more positive and optimistic perceptions of the human being. In modern times there was more emphasis on positive and optimistic perceptions, combined with a focus on man's autonomy and responsibility against God and His creation. So we see that anthropological principles in one faith tradition are not necessarily homogeneous, but pluralistic and variegated, and in the course of time, they may change.

Aspects of anthropological principles in various cultural and/or religious traditions

I shall only briefly sketch some aspects of anthropological principles in various cultural and/or religious traditions, by which I can only scratch the surface of the matter.[5]

Indian traditions

I start with examples from the Indian context.[6] Looking back into ancient Indian traditions, the interrelational aspect of anthropological principles becomes very vivid. The *purusha-sukta* gives an account of the sacrifice of a cosmic being. By the sacrifice of this being, the cosmic order is established. This order comprises creatures and seasons, norms and morality, society and nature. In short, it is an overarching, universal order which includes the human beings as well. Man is put into a fundamental, eternal order, *sanatana dharma*, that carries (from skr. *dhr*) him as well as the whole cosmos. This eternal order is differentiated in various dimensions. According to its moral dimension, man is heading towards releasing himself from all lustful desires for the sake of gaining *moksha*, liberation, by living up to the virtues he is supposed to observe. According to its social dimension, man is put into a specific place in society where he has to fulfil his social obligations. In a biographical dimension, the four *ashramas* (student, head of family, hermit, saint) give a guidance for one's life. Paths of doing (*karma-yoga*), of love (*bhakti-yoga*) and of intuition (*jnana-yoga*) provide orientation and navigation in the eternal cycle of birth and death, of dying away and returning again. Generally speaking, it is not an autonomous formation of the individual that matters. Rather, it is the individual's capacity of fitting himself in his specific place into that cosmic order of *sanatana dharma*.

In this context it is not politically incorrect to use 'man' as a masculine noun. It is in line with traditional Indian anthropologies which are deeply influenced by the ideals of the Manusmriti, the so-called Laws of Manu which do not provide salvation for females and for members of the two lower castes.

The teaching (*dharma*) of the Buddha starts from the same point of departure, namely, the transitory quality of the human life which is subject to the eternal cycle of death and rebirth, the *samsara*. His analysis of this transitory quality of the human life, however, brings about new insights into the 'nature' of man. Just as anything is perishable and transitory, there is no soul, no self (*atman*), and there is no persistent substance. Man is 'non-self' (*anatta*), made up of name and form (*nama-rupa*) as transient components which temporarily constitute what we consider a person. The idea of a stable 'me' is delusive. The formation of an autonomous individual is not important. What matters is breaking the chain of eternal death and rebirth by recognizing the delusive character of a 'self' and to act 'without purpose' in order to escape the *samsara* by 'fading away'. Later developments in Buddhist thought and practice have added new perspectives. The ideal of the *arhat* who follows this path was in some traditions replaced by the ideal of the *bodhisattva* – a being full of mercy who refrains from fading away into the *nirvana* (literally, 'to cease blowing') for the sake of the 'salvation' of myriads of other beings. But the common denominator with the older Buddhist teaching is still the relational aspect that denies any anthropocentric foundation, as well as rejecting any selfish motive on the path towards salvation.

Important also is the effect of *karma*, or the consequence of one's doing, which is immediately effected by one's doing. This is the case with all religious traditions originating from India, Hinduism, Buddhism or Jainism, just to mention the great mainstream traditions. The concept of *karma* seems to implicate the totality of the human being; health or affliction, prosperity or poverty, that is, anything good or bad. However, when we scrutinize the texts and practices of these traditions, we find an amazing variety of interpretations as to the causes of good or bad befalling individuals or communities. Unlike many Hindu traditions, Jain and Buddhist traditions are very sceptical about the possibility of dealing with diseases, infertility or other calamities by the means of rituals and religious healing or divine interventions, as those misfortunes are considered to be a result of bad *karma*. However, some diseases are regarded as amenable to treatment through ritual or medical means. We can find Jain traditions reporting diseases which were caused by a curse and could be cured by a Jain monk. We also find Hindu traditions considering diseases not a result of *karma* but a sign of the *Kali Yuga*, the 'Age of Vice', which, according to most interpretation of Hindu scriptures, is the present stage of the cosmic development through which the world goes, the Dark Age where humanity is the farthest from salvation. As to the anthropological implications of these views, we can observe that the human being is neither totally determined by his/her *karma*, nor exclusively dependent on rituals or religious 'operations'.

Chinese traditions

Turning to anthropological patterns in Chinese traditions with a focus on Daoism, we start from the observation that here there is no conceptual dichotomy between body and soul, or mundane and transcendental.[7] Unlike in Western and other traditions which refer to the soul as 'the true self', Daoism focuses on the ideal *state* of the true self. Furthermore, while many religions put emphasis on salvation, Daoism is more about health, although in a holistic perspective. Consequently, healing and morality are just two aspects of the same coin, correlating human life and cosmology as part and parcel of an organic whole. If we want to apply to Daoism a religious term like salvation, we could describe it as a 'transformation' by which the prevailing individual, social and natural illnesses are healed and the order of the cosmos is restored. Again, we can observe in Dao traditions that there is no clear-cut unit that constitutes a human being. Humanity could be understood as a fluid entity, and the key question is not 'who is humanity?', but 'What is the ideal state of the true self?' Accordingly, an individual person can only be understood in relational terms, taking into consideration his 'performance' in view of the cosmic order. As a result, the individual person is not limited. Rather, she/he is made up of parameters which deal with man's condition, not with his/her being.

African traditions and ethnic religions

When we turn to anthropological patterns in African cultures and religions the picture becomes even more complex.[8] Unlike Buddhist or Hindu traditions, concepts of reincarnation in African religions point to multiple entities ('souls') of the human being. For example, a dead person can return to earth by being born as a child which may be identified as the incarnation of his own grandfather – even while this grandfather is still alive! Moreover, the same person is believed to live simultaneously in the world of the ancestors, a shadow-world of the so-called living dead behind the world, which is not strictly separated from the world of the living. Evidently reincarnation is not understood as something affecting a particular person, an individual 'soul' or a single entity. Reincarnation is a trans-personal, trans-individual incident, having an effect on the whole community and beyond.

Indeed, this trans-individual, communal concept of incarnation is in line with the communal orientation of anthropological principles in African religions: *co-existo, ergo sum* – 'I am, because we are'. In addition, many African traditions refer to the human being as having a specific share in the 'power' that runs through a hierarchy of beings. In Bantu traditions, for example, *ntu* refers to the power of life which is found in gods and spirits, ancestors and human beings, animals, plants, and even inanimate objects like stones or water. Humanity represents just one stage in this hierarchy of living power, without clear-cut borders, and placed into a network of beings comprising this world and the next.

We can observe similar ideas in other ethnic religions, which may develop specific interpretations of humanity's location in the world. For example, there is the concept of a close liaison between a particular group of people and an animal, the *totem* (from the Ojibwa term *ototeman*, 'she/he is of my family'), or there are concepts of a close relationship between humans and the cosmos.

Generally speaking, anthropological principles in ethnic religions emphasize the communal identity of human beings, their mutual interrelationship with their environment and their share in the hierarchy of a power of life running through a hierarchy of beings. Again, the human being does not appear as a clearly defined entity, distinct from other humans or any other being.

Islam

When our survey turns to Islam, we feel a bit more at home owing to the fact that Islam is part and parcel of the family of the three 'Western' religions and taps the sources of Judaism and Christianity. The anthropological principles of Islam stand in the tradition of the biblical creation stories, with slight differences in view of the sinful nature of humans.[9] According to the Qur'ānic message, the consequences of the fall are not as disastrous, as humanity retains an uncorrupted nature (*fitra*) which provides him/her with the capability of living a life in accordance with the will of God. The privilege of humans is reflected in their investiture as *khalifa* of God, that is, God's viceroy, even successor on earth. Nevertheless, the Qur'ān continually refers to humanity's weakness and wickedness, and several passages stress God's authority at the expense of human autonomy. Furthermore, emphasis is placed on humans as part and parcel of the (Muslim) community which is the acting subject in Islam (cf. S. 3:110) and is a recipient of what God has accomplished on behalf of humanity (cf. S. 5:4).

Religious parameters of the human being as a relational entity

Anthropological principles in various religions and cultures are very complex and highly variegated. I would like to systematize the variety of religious assertions about the human being by putting them into a pattern of questions dealing with origins, disposition, substance, essence and destination.[10]

Where do I come from? – origin

Most religious anthropologies refer to *a non-human origin* of humanity. This can be seen in various creation myths and stories. Man may originate from gods, animals, mythological beings, a *homunculus* or the cosmos. She/he may have emerged from pre- or proto-human species, or she/he may have been 'just there' as part and parcel of a universal order, as implication and manifestation of a cosmic equinox.

What am I made of? – substance

Frequently an identity in substance exists between humans and the universe. Many creation stories refer to humans as made from cosmic 'raw material' such as mud, clay or soil, or of seeds from various vegetables or other elements. Sometimes this material is reported to be animated by the word of god, by divine breath, by any action taken by a god or other superhuman beings. Still, sometimes there may even be a relational identity with the cosmic order (cf. Daoism). The substance of man may be conceived as a complex formation of elements or components, as may be found in the Indian teaching on the *gunas*, concepts of body and soul or even multiple souls, ideas of a divine spark in the human being, etc.

What makes me a 'Me'? – disposition

This is undoubtedly one of the most crucial questions in religious anthropologies and it takes us back to the discussion on the understanding of 'personhood' – that entity with 'open borders'. Indeed, the borders of 'Me' are not necessarily identical with the borders of my body or of my lifetime, as was shown above. What makes me a Me? Is there an identity of this Me and the cosmos (ancient Vedic tradition or Jainism)? Or of my self and the divine absolute (*atman – brahman*)? Or is this 'Me' void (Buddhism)?

Who am I? – essence

Closely related to the foregoing is the question of essence. Generally, human beings are male or female. But there are also glimpses of androgyny, often derived from an original hermaphroditic state. Because of this the differentiation of gender must be secured by ritual performance of *rites de passage* for the individual life cycle. Many religious traditions know further 'essential dispositions' making affiliation to a certain group an essential feature of one's being (secret societies, caste affiliation, etc).

Where do I go from here? – destination

Most religious traditions aim at a transformation of the human being and his/her reconstitution in a new dimension: as reborn Christian, as *jivamukti*, as *arhat* or *bodhisattva*, etc. The human being can reach a state which gives a foretaste of his/her final destination or may be regarded as anticipation of this goal. But nothing is granted with certainty. Consequently, humans seek to reassure themselves by restructuring their identity through theory (that is, mythology, cosmology, theology, eschatology) and practice (ritual, service, prayer). This constitutes specific anthropological principles in various religious and cultural contexts whereby each religious tradition claims to hold 'the truth' about what humans are and what they should be. Accordingly, the difference between anthropological principles in various religions and cultures raises a major challenge for inter-religious and inter-cultural coexistence, namely, in how far does the claim of holding the truth grant full recognition of human beings in other religious or cultural traditions?

As we have seen, there exists a variety of responses. These answers, however, relate to the same questions. Consequently, we may come to a general conclusion dealing with observations on anthropological principles in various religions and cultures.

Conclusion

When we look back on our findings and summarize our survey, our initial observation has been endorsed: A person is not an isolated entity, but always and fundamentally an interrelated unit with 'open boundaries' toward community, other beings, the cosmos, etc. As a religious concept, a person always holds an intermediary position as a medium, a vessel or a vehicle of forces beyond herself/himself, and of powers with a religious quality. There is a common denominator in all *religious* anthropological principles, namely, religions attribute to the human being limited capabilities of dealing autonomously with the conditions of his/her existence. Consequently, religions generally try to restrict man's freedom in view of his/her efforts in dealing with that matter. The rationale of this position is based on the idea that the human being must comply with his/her determination by religious forces, abide by a divide plan or conform to a cosmic order. That is to say, the human being must acknowledge the limits of his/her freedom and autonomy for the sake of his/her identity, for the aim of becoming himself/herself, of transforming oneself into a real and 'true' human being.

In view of these religious anthropological principles perhaps we need not investigate so much who man *is*, but investigate the religions' prospect for the human being in his/her relation to other human beings, to god, nature, the cosmic order, that is, his/her relationship to anything outside himself/herself. If this is the case, we might even find an analogy to modern and post-modern anthropological concepts, even to ideas like those by Michel Foucault. Similarly, Foucault is not so much interested in who man is. He thinks that dealing with this question will lead us into a cul-de-sac and that therefore this question is misdirected. In dealing with Immanuel Kant's basic questions of What can I know? What ought I to do? For what may I hope? What is the human being?, Foucault recasts these questions by investigating the conditions constituting humanity's capability to know, act and daringly hope. How have we become agents who know, who act, that is to say, exert power or submit to power, and who consider themselves to be morally responsible for their actions? The question of 'What is the human being?' is rejected by Foucault as running the risk of terminating the process of the Enlightenment. Anthropocentrism and Enlightenment are mutually exclusive. However, Foucault's concept does not proclaim 'the death of humanity' or destroy the idea of the human being as an acting subject. Rather, Foucault wants to 'de-centralize' the human being from an enslaving anthropologism and 'save' him/her as an historical, finite individual free of essentialized attributes.

When we reread what has been said about religious anthropological principles, we may discover that there is an analogy between these post-modern ideas and religious anthropologies, namely, the human being becomes an acting subject by recognizing his/her limitations, thereby understanding himself/herself as an interrelational entity which is placed into a multi-dimensional context of relations to (religious) forces beyond herself/himself. By recognizing this, the human being is empowered to rediscover himself/herself as being released from all bondages of 'anthropologism' for the sake of being capable of positively relating to anything outside himself/herself – an aim which is of fundamental significance as a topic for inter-religious and inter-cultural dialogue.

Notes

[1] This contribution is based on a paper with the title 'A Person – How to Define? Anthropological Basic Assumptions in Various Cultures and Faiths', which was given as a key lecture on the occasion of the 19th International Seminar for Intercultural Pastoral Care and Counselling, 'Truth Will Make You Free – Spaces of Exchange in Missionary Work and Pastoral Care'. This seminar was organized by the Society for International Pastoral Care and Counselling (SIPCC) and took place September 17th - 22nd, 2006 in Hamburg, Germany at the Mission Academy/University of Hamburg (http://www.ekir.de/sipcc/index_english.htm). Accessed August 2007. The paper has been revised for this publication.

[2] Friedrich Nietzsche, *The Gay Science: With a Prelude in German Rhymes and an Appendix of Songs* (Cambridge: Cambridge University Press, 2001 [1882]).

[3] The thoughts referred to are primarily developed in Michel Foucault, *The Order of Things: An Archaeology of the Human Sciences* (London: Routledge, 2002 [1966]).

[4] For the following passage generally, see *Self, Soul and Body in Religious Experience*, ed. by Albert I. Baumgarten (Leiden etc: Brill, 1998). Cf. Hubert Cancik,

'Art, Person', in *Religion in Geschichte und Gegenwart: Handwörterbuch für Theologie und Religionswissenschaft,* 8 vols., Hans D. Betz, Hans Dieter / Browning, Don S. / Janowski, Bernd / Jüngel, Eberhard. ed. (Tübingen: Mohr Siebeck 1998 [=RGG⁴]), vol. I, col. 1120–1121.

[5]   For the following chapters, cf. *Concepts of Person in Religion and Thought,* ed. by Hans G. Kippenberg (Berlin: Mouton de Gruyter, 1990).

[6]   With a focus on sociological considerations, compare David N. Gellner, *The Anthropology of Buddhism and Hinduism: Weberian Themes* (New Delhi etc.: Oxford University Press, 2001). More specifically on Advaita Vedanta philosophy see Joseph Payyappilly, *The Concept of Man in the Advaita Vedanta of Sankara: An Inquiry Into Theological Perspectives* (Frankfurt am Main etc.: Lang, 2005).

[7]   See Fu-Long Lien, Der Mensch im Tao – der Mensch vor Gott: Eine vergleichende Studie über die religiöse Anthropologie im chinesischen und im christlichen Denken (Ammersbek bei Hamburg: Verl. an der Lottbek Jensen, 1990). For more details, see Karyn Lai, *Learning from Chinese Philosophies: Ethics of Interdependent and Contextualised Self* (Aldershot etc.: Ashgate, 2006).

[8]   See Theo Sundermeier, *The Individual and Community in African Traditional Religions* (Hamburg: Lit, 1998).

[9]   Toshihiko Izutsu, *God and Man in the Koran: Semantics of the Koranic Weltanschauung* (New York: Books for Libraries, 1998, repr. Tokyo 1964).

[10] Cf. Andreas Gruenschloss, art. ,Mensch II. Religionswissenschaftlich', in: RGG⁴, vol. V, col. 1052–1054.

Chapter 4

In the Silence is a Presence

Hans Ucko

New dimensions in spirituality

In his garden in Birmingham in the summer of 1982, David Kerr introduced me
to a new dimension in inter-religious dialogue, which at that time had not been
on the map of my interfaith landscape: the contribution of Sufi mysticism
through the music of the *Mevleviye*, the Sufi order founded by Rumi. We listened
to a cassette. Although I couldn't see the whirling, I could sense it; the silent
expression of *dhikr*, the remembrance of Allah. The music opened wide all doors
in me, letting in the dimension of spirituality in my world of interfaith dialogue.
It has remained like this throughout my ministry in interfaith dialogue; a voice
as if from another world, when people of different faiths praise God in a way that
is theirs and where I am invited. In this space I grow silent. I listen to the recita-
tion of suras. I hear the chanting of sutras. I watch the small vessels of flowers
and lights slowly being carried by the waves of the sea, invited and filled with the
realization that God is here and yet I didn't know it.

   The cassette remains with me today. It has been played often; the tape is
worn. Music, prayer, liturgy, silence, symbolic actions are the necessary facets to
remember that faith and religion are not commodities, but a response to the
awe, echoing in the recesses of our souls.

Moving beyond pejoratives in early
Christian-Jewish dialogue

In those days my experience of inter-religious dialogue was limited to that between
Jews and Christians. It wasn't even called inter-religious dialogue. It was *sui
generis*. The Jewish-Christian dialogue was, at least as far as Sweden was concerned, mostly a monologue – a Jewish monologue necessary for Christian
mindsets. Christians offered space and invited Jews to talk about being Jewish
and what Judaism was all about. It was something exceptional in the history of
religion; people of one faith prepared to let a people of another faith make
known their faith. Christians heard Jews identify themselves and those who listened realized how much Jewish self-definition differed from how traditional
Christian scholarship had defined Judaism. Christian theology had disparaged

Judaism, defined it as legalistic and self-obsessed. Judaism had been portrayed as a religion of futile attempts to merit salvation, vain efforts to placate a God, who, as any Christian theologian could have told Jews, didn't dream of anything else but to offer salvation freely, as Grace beyond Grace. As Swedish Lutheran scholar Hugo Odeberg said in his book, *Pharisaism and Christianity*, published in 1943(!) and compulsory reading for students of theology as late as the 1970s: 'Pharisaism is not something that can be combined with Christianity, but something that, if it is permitted to extend its influence, will work as a deadly poison which is bound to destroy the Christian life.'[1] Odeberg expressed the same 'teaching of contempt' as so many Christian theologians had done throughout the history of Jews and Christians.[2] It is true that Odeberg tried to make distinctions between what he called Pharisaism and Judaism but such theological fine-print distinctions evaporated when Jews with pride in the dialogue with Christians defined themselves as the very followers of the Pharisees. Listening to Jews, there was consternation over how Christian scholarship had lied about Judaism. '"The Synagogue", "Jewish legalism", and all those old slogans of our theological tradition came tumbling down like the house of cards they were. In their place, actual Judaism, the living faith of this living people of God, came into view.'[3] Christians learned that the pejorative comments about Pharisees in the Christian tradition needed to be recast, not least because Christianity itself had been greatly influenced by the teachings of the Pharisees.

Christian theology has through this dialogue achieved something, realizing the wisdom of Krister Stendahl's words:

> The Ninth Commandment actually says it all: 'Thou shalt not bear false witness against thy neighbour.' For our culture in general and for the ministers, pastors and priests in particular, it is important that we do not picture 'the other,' the other person's faith, in a manner that they do not recognize as true. Yet much of religious thinking has been shaped by the thoughtless and even unintentional distortions of other persons' faith, thoughts, intentions and history.[4]

Christians amended rituals and liturgies, reworked and reworded hymns and prayers, which had expressed anti-Jewish slurs. In Germany, Landeskirchen rewrote their constitutions and pledged that their church was inextricably related to the 'covenant never revoked' that God had made with the Jews at Sinai.

The reality of antisemitism and its theological next of kin anti-Judaism were addressed in the Jewish–Christian dialogue. The dialogue affected from a Christian perspective mostly intra-church concerns, theologically dense, notwithstanding that some Christians involved themselves in the plight of Soviet Jews and opposed the United Nations General Assembly resolution (1975) 'that Zionism is a form of racism and racial discrimination'.[5] However most Christians involved in the dialogue bypassed in silence the Israeli–Palestinian conflict or cautiously addressed it by wishing peace for all.

Theological scholarship developed that sought to formulate a Christology, which did not have the spectre of anti-Judaism as its background. Instead of a theology of *adversos Judaeos*, another theology was crafted, which had learned from Jewish self-understanding and exegesis to rethink a Christian tradition, which in the words of Paul van Buren had been 'wrong about Israel, the people of God, and therefore to that extent wrong about the God of Israel'.[6]

The Jewish-Christian dialogue responded to something that was wrong in the relationship between Jews and Christians, a theological wrong which for Jews in society led to a loss of civil rights, ghettoization, Inquisition, pogroms and the Shoah. The theology in the Jewish–Christian dialogue attempted the reparation of the wrong. The theology reread the Bible; Pharisees were rediscovered as examples of faith in the New Testament; Paul in particular was reread and the Letter to the Romans got a new emphasis. The 'no' of Jews to Jesus as the Christ became providential for the grafting of the gentiles, the wild olive shoot, onto 'the rich root' of the olive tree.[7] And if one twisted the arm of Paul a little bit, one almost managed to get it all together, a salvation history, which both Jews and Christians could affirm: Christianity as a Judaism for gentiles and two covenants running parallel in salvation history until the end of times.

All this may be true; yes, we hope that Christian theology, or any theology for that matter, may affirm the other in his or her otherness. But is it only because we move around within the parameters of the Bible that it is possible to test and even launch such a theology? Both Jews and Christians are the addressees in the Bible. We should of course rejoice if theology, in spite of all difficulties, is able to acknowledge the covenant from Sinai also *post Christum*. It is remarkable. But are such theological affirmations possible also in relation to other faiths, to Islam, to Hinduism, to Buddhism, to indigenous traditions? Or is the theological generosity vis-à-vis Judaism and the Jewish people a product of specific and exceptional circumstances and possible only because the Bible provides enough openings that allow for such a move?

Krister Stendahl asked me the first time we met, 'Are you one of those theologians for whom it is Jews and Christians against the rest or do you also see all the people of other faiths within God's menagerie?'[8] One aspect of the question is that for many it is safer to theologize within the world of the Bible and for this the Jewish–Christian dialogue is particularly equipped. One does not have to leave the precincts of the Bible.[9] This dialogue as well as the ensuing theology is fully at home in the Bible – its chapters, verses, concepts, horizons.

Living together or living next to each other?

Needless to say, there is no story about Muslims, Hindus or Buddhists in the Bible and this makes relations with Muslims, Hindus or Buddhists as well as any theological reflection very different. When faced with dialogue with people of other

faiths, many feel uneasy venturing beyond the biblical narratives.[10] 'Throughout my years in the World Council of Churches, I have met so many representatives of the churches admonishing the WCC not to stray beyond what they call
'the dialogue of life.' 'All this dialogue', the argument runs, 'there is nothing
new with it: we have been in the dialogue of life with Hindus, Muslims, Buddhists since Christianity was first established here. We call it dialogue of life.'
But when you begin to press for elaboration, dialogue often means 'living
together' or maybe rather next to each other: you don't bother me and I don't
bother you. While refraining from interfering with the other is praiseworthy, it
cannot qualify as dialogue. And dialogue means more than just interacting, there
needs to be some kind of reflection as to what this encounter might mean for my
own self-understanding. It is the direct lack of explicit biblical reference material
that makes it difficult. Therefore, if one wants to pursue dialogue with Muslims,
Hindus, Buddhists, one has to look for other tools, other parameters and other
considerations that necessarily will be less precise than in the Jewish–Christian
relationship. Insisting on biblical backing forces generalizations, comparisons
and inferences. This is always a bit risky. Jews and Christians share a book, or at
least the major part of a book. Christians and Muslims do not. They may refer to
persons and events in each other's narratives but the narratives differ.[11]

Muslims and the Abrahamic heritage

Unlocking the door and somehow venturing outside, one might however at the
doorstep of the Bible meet quite a few Jewish, Christian and Muslim theologians,
all emphasizing the Abrahamic interrelationship as *raison d'être* for an extended
dialogue. Although we are not exclusively within the worldview of the Bible, they
would point to the biblical figure of Abraham for us to lean on in our theologizing. Whatever we may say about the differences in understanding Abraham among
Jews, Christians and Muslims, Abraham is loved, coveted, invoked, and commemo-
rated in all three traditions. The claim to a shared Abrahamic heritage marks in
many ways the inter-religious dialogue and encounters between Jews, Christians
and Muslims today. The reference to Abraham as a bond of unity between adherents of the three monotheistic religions is no longer exceptional.[12] The claim that
we are all sons and daughters of Abraham is often the starting-point in attempts to
extend Jewish–Christian dialogue to involve Muslims.[13]

But the relationship to Abraham is different and seems to offer more tangible returns to Jews and Christians. Christian thinking affords Christians the
prerogative of 'rocking most comfortably in the bosom of Abraham'. Paul writes
to his Christian flock:

No distrust made (Abraham) waver concerning the promise of God, but he
grew strong in his faith as he gave glory to God, being fully convinced that

God was able to do what he had promised. Therefore his faith 'was reckoned to him as righteousness.' Now the words, 'it was reckoned to him', were written not for his sake alone, but for ours also.[14]

Jewish sources meanwhile, claim that Abraham, Isaac and Jacob are both the physical and spiritual ancestors of Judaism and quote the words of the Bible:

I will establish my covenant between me and you, and your offspring after you throughout their generations, for an everlasting covenant, to be God to you and to your offspring after you. And I will give to you, and to your offspring after you, the land where you are now an alien, all the land of Canaan, for a perpetual holding; and I will be their God.[15]

The connection to the land is explicit and is used in corroborating claims on the land in the Israeli–Palestinian conflict.

But what do Muslims get out of the Abrahamic heritage seen from a Christian or Jewish reading? The Bible does not seem to provide much more than the desert to Ishmael, the 'wild ass of a man, with his hand against everyone, and everyone's hand against him; (and) at odds with all his kin.'[16] Many with me would like to ask whether the Abrahamic heritage is inclusive, inter-communal or ecumenical. Is it not rather confirming an unequal distributive sharing of the grace of Abraham? 'Christian Abrahamism pretends to reconcile but it turns into a denigration of Islamic integrity and universalism.'[17] While it certainly is true that Muslims often refer to the kinship between Jews, Christians and Muslims as having its origin in Abraham, the Qur'ānic criterion for the claim to Abraham's heritage is not to prove anything or substantiate any particular gift to the children of Abraham, such as grace or land, etc. The Qur'ān suggests above all that we emulate Abraham:

Without doubt, among men, the nearest of kin to Abraham, are those who follow him, as are also this Prophet and those who believe: And Allah is the Protector of those who have faith.[18]

The contemporary imperative to move from 'dialogue' to 'relations'

So much for theological narratives. Meanwhile in the real world, the urgency of engaging with contradicting religious contributions in the political sphere has become all the more evident. The Canberra Assembly of the World Council of Churches in 1991 took place at about the same time as the first Gulf War. Saddam Hussein's call for jihad against the infidels and President Bush's conviction that God was on the side of the United States made obvious that theology is not enough for dialogue. The Assembly delegates realized that our time needed another dialogue, one that ensured that Muslims were not pitted against Christians or the other way around.[19] 'Relations', more than 'dialogue', was the concept to capture encounters between people of different faiths. Dialogue sounded like talking endlessly about issues, not changing conditions, all while religion increasingly was becoming a tool to fuel conflict. The World Council of Churches changed the name of the dialogue programme from the 'Subunit on Dialogue with People of Living Faiths and Ideologies' to the 'Office on Inter-religious Relations'. Not a word about dialogue but a hope that the programme would contribute to establishing relations and be meaningful in the nexus of religion and conflict.

The Israeli–Palestinian conflict was soon and much more intentionally pushed into the Jewish–Christian dialogue. It had of course been there before but had then as much as possible been bypassed because of the unease of how to address it. This approach proved untenable, which has threatened and still threatens the fellowship and trust between Jews and Christians that had taken so much effort to establish. Increasingly Christians active in the dialogue with Jews were asked how exactly the Jewish–Christian dialogue dealt with the Israeli–Palestinian conflict. The issue had been there all along as the elephant in the room that everyone knew was there but no one wanted to acknowledge. Many Christians involved in this dialogue felt and feel even more so today that they are expected to locate themselves, politically or even visibly in the Palestinian refugee camp of Dahaisheh or in Katyusha-shelled Sderot. Is Jewish–Christian dialogue able to be in solidarity with the Palestinian people in their claims for a state, the return of refugees and a stake in Jerusalem? Or is Jewish–Christian dialogue in relation to the State of Israel buttressing Jewish self-understanding, that is, the State of Israel is 'the beginning of the growth of our Redemption'?[20]

Concerns regarding theological dimensions in dialogue alone are no longer sufficient. Dialogue of life is also inadequate as a remedy against an unexpected development in the interaction between religion and world. The increasing role of religion in public life and the increasing use of religion in political conflict are bringing the dialogue out of its theological ivory tower. Religion

has forced itself dramatically into the public square. In 1960 John Kennedy pleaded with Americans to treat his Catholicism as irrelevant; now a born-again Christian sits in the White House and his most likely Democrat replacement wants voters to know she prays. An Islamist party rules once-secular Turkey; Hindu nationalists may return to power in India's next election; ever more children in Israel and Palestine are attending religious schools that tell them that God granted them the whole Holy Land. . . . President Mahmoud Ahmadinejad of Iran, not usually a reliable authority on current affairs, got it right in an open letter to George Bush: 'Whether we like it or not,' he wrote, 'the world is gravitating towards faith in the Almighty.'[21]

Of course religion has always been part of conflict but maybe it is more obvious now. The way global communication goes, there is little time for more in-depth analysis and conflicts are therefore more easily portrayed in terms that make them appear to be critically about religion. And of course, religion is no *virgo intacta* and is more often than not willing to grab the banner assembling the faithful against the enemy. The conflict in Northern Ireland was overwhelmingly portrayed simply as a conflict between Catholics and Protestants. The bloodshed in the Balkans was reduced to a conflict between Orthodox Serbs, Catholic Croatians and Bosnian and Albanian Muslims. Young Muslims were behind 9/11. Dangerous God-talk became more frequent in Israel/Palestine following the Six-Day War. A bridge to Sri Lanka supposedly built by Ram may play a significant role in Indian elections. And in Sri Lanka itself, Buddhist monks have been on the barricades using a racial-nationalist language against the perceived threat to Sinhalese people and religious culture.

Interfaith understanding: not for theologians alone

The world has to deal with religion, but it doesn't seem to know how. The Oslo process collapsed, Rabbi David Rosen argues, in part because no religious people were involved. Following the London bombings of 2005, Tony Blair realized that he needed to understand home-grown terrorism not only from an economic or social perspective but also from a religious point of view. Interfaith dialogue is therefore not an issue merely for theologians but also for politicians, economists, ecologists, environmentalists. The World Economic Forum, the World Bank, development agencies and others have or want to have a stake in interfaith dialogue. The world is too dangerous to leave religion only in the hands of religionists; doing so has proved to have disastrous consequences.[22]

The new role of religion is probably the consequence of the failure of secular creeds: Religion's political comeback started during the 1970s, when faith in government everywhere was crumbling. Many of the fathers of decolonization throughout the world got their schooling in Western universities, more often than not bastions of the new secular world in opposition to antiquated religious traditions. Everyone thought that religion would fade away and that secularization would take over. But many of the secular visions crumbled and soon thereafter the last power of secular ideology, the Soviet Union, imploded and left the world in an ideological vacuum. In the absence of sustainable values in an increasingly complex world, religion is now again being sought as a solution. And inter-religious dialogue has become such a household word that its meaning is often lost amid pap and political correctness. It becomes a fad invoked without much serious thought in the hope of ticking boxes and fulfilling expectations. The participation of swamis, gurus, cardinals, sheikhs and rabbis, preferably in religious garb, adds a photo-op to the event and while such gatherings can often be valuable, there is also a need to ask some serious questions.

Is the invitation to religion to sit at the table of the World Economic Forum, albeit in a *strapontin*, the folded up chair, now flipped down for extraordinary use, an expression of co-opting religion into the discourse of economy without any consideration for what religion is all about? Is the call for religion to be part of the development agencies' discourse really respecting the integrity of religion? Is the new emphasis in the WCC for 'co-operation' an expression of the fatigue that dialogue alone is not seen to have yielded the visible fruits that one expected?[23]

> There are . . . expectations that dialogue can significantly contribute towards resolving political or communal conflicts and restoring peace, in situations where religion seems to be implicated. . . . The impact of dialogue in the context of conflicts may disappoint high expectations. When it is unable to quell conflict, its relevance is questioned.[24]

In an effort to bring the protagonists of religion around the table for dialogue and cooperation, one easily overlooks significant aspects of religion. Religion is not a corporation or company and

> interreligious dialogue is not an instrument to instantly resolve problems in emergency situations. Contacts and relations of precious trust and friendship between people of different religions, built quietly by patient dialogue during peacetime, may in times of conflict prevent religion from being used as a weapon.[25]

In all the calls for dialogue, in all these official callings upon people of religion to involve themselves in cooperation, to sign documents, to make declarations, one seems to have forgotten that it actually 'takes two to tango' and just because I happen to be ready for cooperation, doesn't necessarily mean that my partner of another faith finds him/herself in the same situation. Libyan Muslim scholar Aref Ali Nayed says, 'Dialogue is not about imposing one's views on the other side, nor deciding oneself what the other side is and is not capable of, nor even of what the other side believes.'[26]

The rediscovery of religion: blessing or curse?

The many calls for inter-religious dialogue have made it plain that there is a rediscovery of religion. But is this rediscovery a blessing or a curse? Should people of religion think, 'Finally, the world is seeing what we have been saying all along?' I am not so sure. I doubt that the interest is necessarily prompted by an interest in religion per se. One definite reason for the interest in inter-religious dialogue is the hope that one could nip in the bud the effect of religion in the world. There is fear involved. Getting religious moderates organized in dialogue might keep the fundamentalists at bay, it is hoped, and enable a status quo on the participation of religion in the world, ensuring that it remains an instrument for rites of passage or a tranquilizer in times of distress. It is therefore much more of an attempt to domesticate religion than actually engaging religion in an exchange on what it means to be a human being, what human dignity means and the values to enable people to relate to people, in all, what religion is all about.

The problem becomes even more difficult when realizing that the actual target is Islam. Inter-religious dialogue is sometimes a codeword for dialogue with Muslims, where the dialogue is a method of preventing Islam from enfolding even more in the West and in the world. Islam is above all seen as the threat to world peace. Those trying to understand Islam are seen as wrong, because they

> soft-peddle(s) the dangers of fundamentalist Islam, whose radical elements espouse the world's most virulently anti-American ideology. . . . they hate the entirety of our civilization. . . . The ever-pithy Ayatollah Khomeini put it this way: 'We are not afraid of economic sanctions or military intervention. What we are afraid of is Western universities. . . . [The author warns] . . . about low Western birth-rates and millions of Muslim immigrants to Western Europe and North America. . . . Western European civilisation will start to die at the point when it could have revived with new blood.[27]

While people in general are embarrassed reading words like the above and politely dissociate themselves from islamophobes, some of the arguments nevertheless penetrate the discourse and emerge in many of the underlying reasons in the calls for dialogue.

Fear is not the best opening for dialogue. One's mind is made up and one mainly wants to see how through dialogue one can dissuade the other from being what one thinks he or she is. Lurking behind is of course an attempt to instrumentalize religion through inter-religious dialogue, to condense it to a function, surely useful but controllable. It builds upon an old tradition, which precedes inter-religious dialogue. Power organized religion and reduced it to a set of habits, behaviours, dogmas, forms, which in the truest sense has little to do with spirituality. We have lost something when

> faith is a matter of believing certain creedal propositions. Indeed, it is common to call religious people 'believers', as though assenting to the articles of faith were their chief activity. . . . If the Buddha or Confucius had been asked whether he believed in God he would probably have winced and explained – with great courtesy – that this was not an appropriate question. If anybody had asked

Amos or Ezekiel if he was a 'monotheist', who believed in only one God, he would have been equally perplexed. Monotheism was not the issue.[28]

The peril of religious reductionism

Inter-religious dialogue is lost when religion is delinked from the irrational, the anti-rational, the non-rational, the mysterious, the unknown, the unknowable, the dangerous-to-know or the ineffable. Religion becomes meaningless when it is reduced to dogmas or set into a program with measurable goals and the yearnings, aspirations, and hopes are categorized. In challenging attempts to box in religion as a function, there must be space for the experience of the holy, the sacred; there must be room for humility, gratitude and oblation; for thanksgiving and awe; the sense of the divine; the sense of littleness before mystery; the quality of elatedness and sublimity; the awareness of limits and even powerlessness; the impulse to surrender and to kneel; a sense of the eternal and of fusion with the whole of the universe; even the experiences of heaven and hell.[29]

When reducing religion – and by extension inter-religious dialogue – to a function, we lose a lot more than the other dimensions, we lose a wholeness. In his book *Crazy Mountains* the philosopher David Strong picks up the theme of so-called progress in development, taking as an example the trajectory of heating technologies from the hearth to the radiator:

> [T]he hearth is the correlational coexistent thing that establishes the world of the household [. . .] The device [heater] provides a commodity, one element of the original thing (warmth alone) and disburdens people of all the elements that compose the world and engaging character of the thing.[30]

The hearth represents more than a heater – it is a focus, a marker of home, a symbol of family, it has a mantelpiece where ornaments, trophies, treasures are put. This is the place for the stories to be told. The heater provides heat, maybe better heat, maybe more heat, but has none of these affordances. In focusing only on one aspect of the thing, other aspects are lost, and the qualitative experience is reduced or lessened.

The analogy is here suitable. In many of the calls for inter-religious dialogue we see a certain kind of reductionism at play. Religion is seen as a resource to serve a particular purpose. Religion can be engaged to serve the cause of world peace, the struggle against climate change, the cause of development, etc. While all of this is true, religion is certainly a way of peace, a way of respect for creation, a way of addressing prophetically the scandal of poverty; it cannot be reduced to being an instrument towards a particular goal. When we cease to look upon creation as holy and only look upon it as a resource, there is sense in reflecting on what this does to our relationship with Nature. There is sense in considering the understanding of peace as shalom, that is, much more than the mere absence of war. There is sense in looking upon justice as a principle and not only providing alms for the poor. There is sense in religion as a resource bank for keeping society lawful and moral. There is sense in seeing religion providing creedal propositions as focal points for creating community. But there is a danger if religion is reduced to a tool or instrument for achieving particular goals. If religion is believed to be reducible, to be encompassed, by the above characteristics alone, that they would be sufficient for a complete characterization, then we no longer have a hearth to warm ourselves by. The radiator is not where we come together.

The emphasis on theology and the concern for cooperation are important but will not suffice. Both are needed and more. This dimension is unfolded with the following:

> Mere ethical/social dialogue is useful, and is very much needed. However, dialogue of that kind happens everyday, through purely secular institutions such as the United Nations and its organizations. If religious revelation-based communities are to truly contribute to humanity, their dialogue must be ultimately theologically and spiritually grounded. Many Muslim theologians are not just interested in mere ethical dialogue of 'cultures' or 'civilizations'. We take our Qur'anic/Prophetic revelation solemnly and seriously, as the very foundation of all our living and all our discourses. Islam is a great deal more than a 'culture' or a 'civilization'. It is a prophetical revelatory religion and heart-felt faith that has been the rich font of multiple cultures and civilizations. If dialogue is to be serious, it must be theologically and spiritually deep.[31]

If it is possible, we need to retrieve dimensions in religion that are being lost; lost either through the powers that be in controlling religion or lost because religious organizations want to accommodate so as to make religion and themselves well-dressed and thus more respectable. We need to let the question be heard and not only provide an answer. If mainstream Christianity in the West is in decline, I think one reason is that the churches leave no room for the questions to be heard. There is today a spirituality, which is not satisfied with answers. To go beyond is to question. But we are so sure we have the answer that we fail to ask the question.

Creating space for expansive religious possibilities

The anecdote of the little boy in the Polish town of Lublin is in this context relevant: He comes running out from his Talmud class shouting, 'I have an answer but isn't there anyone who has a good question?' The good question leads to others, and continues. There is no end to it. One question stimulates another question. We need to provide space for the positive dimension in never arriving at the truth as long as we live; there needs to be space for being in uncertainties without any irritable reaching after fact and reason and particularly fact and reason as defined by religious authority. There needs to be space for space. 'Thirty spokes make one wheel. The spaces in between and the spokes both are essential to the function of the wheel.'[32] In this space, there is only silence like the silence of the whirling dervish. In this space of silence there is awe, and I cannot say, whether it is God or the union with God, whether it is meeting or separation, whether it has happened or not happened, whether it is me or you.

There is nothing that I can say! In the silence there is presence.

Notes

[1] Hugo Odeberg, Pharisaism and Christianity, translation from the Swedish *Fariseism och kristendom*, 1943 by AB CWK Gleerup Bokförlag (Lund, Sweden: *Concordia Publishing House, Saint Louis*, 1964), p. 9.

[2] The 'teaching of contempt' was coined by the French-Jewish history professor Jules Isaac, who, during the Nazi invasion of France, began to research the topic of the silence and apathy of Christians toward Nazi persecution of European Jews. In 1947 Isaac published Jesus and Israel, a 600 page analysis of antisemitism and Christianity, which compared the texts of the Gospels with Catholic and Protestant commentaries conveying a distorted picture of Jesus' attitude towards Israel and Israel's attitude towards Jesus, and which he believed were largely responsible for the antisemitic conditioning of European Christians.

[3] Paul van Buren in *Christian Century*, June 17–24, 1981, pp. 665–668.

[4] *Harvard Divinity Bulletin*, November–December 1980.

[5] In October 1975 the WCC General Secretary issued a forceful statement repudiating the UN resolution of that year that equated Zionism with Racism.

[6] *Christian Century*, pp. 665–668.

[7] Romans 11.17.

[8] 'Krister Stendahl', says W. D. Davies, 'is particularly distinguished by a catholicity of mind and spirit, which enables him to look with understanding, sympathy and empathy on all sorts of conditions in what he once unpejoratively called "God's menagerie of religions"'. See 'Christians among Jews and Gentiles: Essays in Honor of Krister Stendahl on His Sixty-Fifth Birthday' in *The Harvard Theological Review*, vol. 79, No. 1/3, (Jan.–Jul., 1986): 44.

[9] I am well aware that there are many who would say that this dialogue is very eclectic when it comes to making theological use of the words of the Bible. But they would say this about any effort to create space for the integrity of the other.

[10] There are of course Bible verses that we can use in support of a more generous attitude to religious plurality: Micah 4.5, 6.8; Psalm 87; Isaiah 19.23–24, etc. But the verses are few and the question is, of course: should we really have to give scriptural reason for openness and generosity?

[11] The story about Abraham sacrificing his son is a case in point.

[12] See, e.g. The International Scholars' Annual Trialogue as reflected in Leonard Swidler, (ed.) *Theoria → Praxis: How Jews, Christians and Muslims Can Move Together from Theory to Practice* (Leuwen: Peeters, 1998).

[13] The relationship with Muslims today is considered to be of utmost priority, whereas the Jewish–Christian dialogue has no longer the same attraction. This is particularly true when it comes to funding; Jewish–Christian dialogue is not seen as an immediate priority. There are therefore many who want to invite Muslims into the Jewish–Christian dialogue, as if the set menu could easily accommodate also the third of the children of Abraham.

[14] Romans 4.20–24.

[15] Genesis 17.7–8.

[16] Genesis 16.12.

[17] Tarek Mitri, 'The Abrahamic Heritage and Interreligious Dialogue: Ambiguities and Promises' in *Current Dialogue*, no. 36, December 2000.

[18] S. 3:68, the Family of Imran.

[19] I am aware that there were also those at the Assembly, who, irrespective of the Gulf War, had made up their minds that there should be no theological conversation on dialogue at the Canberra Assembly.

[20] Prayer composed in 1948 for the new State of Israel.

[21] 'In God's Name' in *The Economist*, 11 January 2007, at http://www.economist.com/specialreports/displaystory.cfm?story_id=10015255.

[22] Even the liberal and a bit disdainful *The Economist* (1 November 2007) repents and says: '"Inter-faith dialogue" may sound a wishy-washy concept; but it is a more realistic idea than presenting a secular peace to competing faiths without the backing of religious leaders.'

[23] Following the latest restructuring in the WCC, there is now a new program called 'Dialogue and Cooperation'.

[24] *Ecumenical Considerations for Dialogue and Relations with People of Other Religions*, WCC 2002, http://www.oikoumene.org/index.php?id=3445. Accessed December 2007.

[25] *Ibid.*

[26] Aref Ali Nayed, http://chiesa.espresso.repubblica.it/articolo/173961?eng=y. Accessed January 2008.

[27] http://www.danielpipes.org/article/882. Accessed December 2007.

[28] Karen Armstrong, *The Great Transformation* (New York: Anchor Book, 2007), p. xviii.

[29] Abraham Maslow, *Religions, Values and Peak-Experiences* (New York: Penguin Compass, 1994).

[30] David Strong, *Crazy Mountains: Learning From Wilderness to Weigh Technology* (Albany: State University of New York Press, 1995), p. 81.

[31] Interview with Aref Ali Nayed, http://www.islamicamagazine.com/Common-Word/CNS-interview.html. Accessed December 2007.

[32] Tao Te Ching, ch.11.

Chapter 5

The Globalization of Localized African Religions: The Case of Kwame Bediako*

James L. Cox

Some 15 years ago, a publication edited by Robert Bates, V. Y. Mudimbe and Jean O'Barr appeared under the title *Africa and the Disciplines*. Its aim, as explained in the subtitle, was to examine 'the contributions of research in Africa to the social sciences and humanities'.[1] The purpose of the book was not to analyse the role African scholars have played in shaping research in the social sciences and humanities, although this aspect was not excluded. The book's primary aim was to 'trace the impact of the research in Africa on the core disciplines'.[2]

Clearly, the volume was approached from the context of the globalizing influences which Western universities exerted on the study of African societies, beginning at the level of undergraduate students and extending to senior researchers. The editors note in their introduction:

> Conscious of the growing significance of international trade, the need for international 'competitiveness', and the continuing dangers posed by misunderstandings and conflicts of interests among nations, academic leaders seek to 'internationalise' the modern university. They encourage students to learn foreign languages, study in universities abroad, and steep themselves in the history and culture of other nations. In addition, they promote faculty exchanges, affiliations with foreign universities, and international programs. The study of Africa can be justified as part of these broader efforts to heighten the awareness of scholars, both students and faculty, of global realities.[3]

Yet, it is equally clear that the globalization envisaged in this book was undertaken from the perspective of Western universities, including those with researchers on their faculties drawn from the African diaspora (like Mudimbe) who in increasing numbers were taking up posts in Western academic institutions. Thus the authors protested against 'those who champion the cause of Africacentricity' and declared an interest instead in advocating 'the study of African culture as a subject equally valid as the study of other cultures, most notably Europe'.[4]

* Professor Bediako died in June 2008, while this volume was still in preparation.

A clear example of the approach adopted in the book is found in the article by Sally Falk Moore, who presented a comprehensive survey of anthropological approaches to the study of African cultures, primarily by examining the history of British and American theoretical schools.[5] Her study pays scant attention to Africans who have contributed to the study of their own cultures. She admits towards the end of her lengthy contribution that post-Cold War Africa may 'present anthropology with new challenges' and that as a result anthropology 'may be poised for yet another phase of theoretical and methodological revision', which may include the contribution of African scholars working in Africa.[6] The history of such contributions reveals very few such scholars. She mentions specifically Jomo Kenyatta, K. A. Busia, J. B. Danquah, F. M. Deng and A. B. Diop but notes that these differ little from Western anthropologists since 'they were all trained in a British or European tradition and wrote very much in the intellectual style of the departments from which they received their degrees.'[7] A major oversight in her list, of course, is Okot p'Bitek, who can be described as a reactionary rebelling against the Western tradition of anthropology in which he was trained, notably under Evans-Pritchard and Godfrey Lienhardt in Oxford.[8]

The volume, *Africa and the Disciplines*, suggests a critical issue that I want to address in this article, which, in my view, the editors have failed to exploit because they deliberately have retained a fully Westernized perspective. My argument is this: Western academic disciplines have 'globalized' quite localized African cultures not solely by applying the methods used in the social sciences and humanities to the study of Africa, but by literally extracting African scholars out of Africa into Western institutions. If such scholars return to Africa, they re-interpret African cultures in terms of their 'globalized' experiences. A scholar's academic credibility thus does not stand or fall simply, as the editors claim, by his or her capacity to generate, analyse and assess arguments regardless of the geographic origin of the scholar.[9] This would hold true only if Western academic disciplines are regarded as somehow privileged and unaffected by context. If African cultures are primarily localized, kinship-based systems, the globalizing effects on such cultures by Africans trained in Western institutions must be significant. The validity of scholarly arguments may not be determined by their origins, geographic or cultural, as Bates, Mudimbe and O'Barr contend, but their appropriation into geographic and cultural contexts by African scholars transforms radically the self-understanding of the 'objects' of study to which the arguments refer.

This process can be seen particularly by African scholars of religion, who, under the influence of Western theological and religious studies methods, have applied globalized religious interpretations to localized African religions. Nowhere can this be seen better than in the writings of Kwame Bediako, who studied in Aberdeen University in the early 1980s under the noted church historian Andrew Walls, and who returned to Ghana to establish a Centre aimed at reaching deeply into the local Ghanaian culture by training theologians and church leaders through a globalized understanding of African indigenous religions. After briefly seeking to establish that African Indigenous Religions indeed are localized, in the remainder of this essay, I intend to illustrate the globalizing process through the writings of Bediako.

The local nature of African religions

Numerous scholars, such as Philipa Baylis, Harold Turner and Andrew Walls, have asserted that African Indigenous Religions direct their attention towards localized deities or spirits, which generally are kinship-based.[10] As a result, the Indigenous Religions of Africa frequently are described as non-missionary in nature. One is born into an extended family, clan or chieftaincy. In Zimbabwe, for example, I have argued that the majority of traditional rituals are performed towards ancestors within extended families by bringing them back to the homestead around one year after their deaths, by regular rituals of respect, by appeals for assistance in times of crisis or through rituals aimed at establishing direct contact with them through possession of selected mediums.[11] Rituals dealing with wider issues such as drought, warfare or pestilence are still aimed at ancestors, although these are generally in the chief's direct lineage. In every case, the immediate ancestors are known by name, and these are presumed to be in communication with those who have died long ago. Frequently, in family rituals, appeals will be made to specific ancestors who are remembered by the living, with an addendum: 'and carry our message to those we no longer remember.'

Jan Platvoet contends that the traditional societies of Africa 'are organised in primary, especially in kinship, relationships' and that 'they live in complex micro worlds'.[12] Hence, relationships are usually 'face to face' 'as they obtain between kin and peers'. The micro-worlds of traditional societies, Platvoet notes, can be compared to the 'macro mental worlds' of modern societies which are marked by 'intensive communication' and 'the cultivation of history'.[13] In traditional African societies, by contrast, most people are 'familiar only with the territory in which they themselves live and part of that of neighbouring communities'. Even when territorial boundaries are extended in traditional societies, they are interpreted in kinship terms since all institutions are 'structured on the model of kinship'.[14]

Platvoet then makes what for the purposes of my argument is the central point: 'Kinship . . . rules religion.'[15] He reaches this conclusion because 'the deceased, for as long as they are ritually approached as ancestors, are treated as the foremost members of the social worlds of these societies.' Even non-ancestral spirits, called by Platvoet 'other meta-empirical beings', are given 'quasi-kinship status'.[16] I have observed this in my own studies of Indigenous Religions in Zimbabwe, where a commonly experienced non-kinship spirit is called the *shavi* (sometimes spelled *shave*) spirit, or alien spirit. This is usually a spirit of one who has died without descendants, or for other reasons has not been able to have been made into an ancestor within a kinship group. The *shavi* spirit roams around and remains potentially dangerous, until it is settled within its new social group. This is usually done by the spirit afflicting a member of a community to which the spirit does not belong, normally by making the person ill, in order that eventually the person will accept the spirit by becoming its medium and thus integrating what is alien into the kinship system.[17] This illustrates the central place of lineage in African Indigenous Religions which, Platvoet explains, are 'co-extensive with their societies', since they regard social life as extending beyond the living to 'unseen beings, foremost with ancestors, kinship being the dominant institution of these societies.'[18]

In her review of the history of anthropological studies in Africa to which I referred earlier, Sally Falk Moore warns us not to reduce African societies entirely to kinship and lineage systems. She refers to the work conducted in the 1950s by C. Daryl Forde in southern Nigeria which 'provided unsettling evidence of the great importance of secret societies and other non-kinship-based associations'.[19] More recently, studies conducted by Richard Werbner on the Mwari shrines in Zimbabwe also point towards an inter-connected network of communication across a wide area of southern Africa that seems to extend beyond kinship.[20] Whereas I acknowledge wide variations of social organization within the whole of sub-Saharan Africa, many of which are not based on kinship, I believe Platvoet is correct by stressing the localized, community-directed nature of indigenous societies in Africa. At the level of immediate, pragmatic, day-to-day concerns, the localized spirits play the most important role – and these, although not always directly related to ancestors, can be interpreted at least in quasi-kinship terms. Even where other manifestations of spirit organization exist, throughout sub-Saharan Africa, ancestors play a pivotal role by providing for the well-being of those within their quite identifiable and localized social groupings.[21]

The globalization of localized African religions: Aberdeen University and Kwame Bediako

Robin Horton has advanced the thesis that as the micro-worlds characteristic of African Indigenous Religions encountered the macro-world of Western colonialism, a shift of ritual attention away from ancestors and local deities towards a supreme God occurred. This explained for Horton why during the colonial period Africans converted in large numbers to the two great missionary and monotheistic world religions, Christianity and Islam.[22] Platvoet observes that Horton 'held that these two monotheistic religions provided ready-made religious models matching the expanded horizons at precisely the time when Africans were in need of some such model and when such change was in the air anyway'.[23] A similar point has been made by Andrew Walls, who argues that it is largely irrelevant today whether or not Africans originally held a belief in a Supreme God, since due to the impact of Christianity and Islam, almost all religious believers in Africa today, even traditionalists, do hold such beliefs.[24] This would suggest, for example, that the Mwari shrines located in southwest Zimbabwe, studied by Werbner, Daneel, Ranger and Nthoi,[25] among others, may today represent a form of globalized African Indigenous Religions (at least on a mini-scale), without contradicting the claim of Herbert Aschwanden that traditionally Mwari may have been a fertility deity closely associated with the quasi-historical myths depicting the migrations of original ancestors.[26] These cases illustrate, at any rate, that, although the process of globalizing the localized religions of Africa is complex and subject to wide variations in interpretation, the central thesis, as put by Platvoet, is correct: 'to wit that the shift from more limited to wider horizons through incorporation into wider contexts of communication caused major changes in the religious scene of Africa.'[27]

This shift, what I am calling the globalization of Africa's localized religions, can be illustrated dramatically through the works of African scholars who studied religions in Western institutions and returned to Africa to re-interpret local situations in global terms. Recently, I have written articles and chapters in books on the development of the study of Indigenous Religions in the Universities of Aberdeen and Edinburgh, both of which had their roots in Africa through the pioneering work of E. G. Parrinder in Ibadan, Nigeria and through the later developments initiated by Andrew Walls and Harold Turner, both of whom had worked together in the University of Sierra Leone and at the University of Nigeria, Nsukka.[28] It is clear throughout these studies that Western academic institutions became centres for the training and development of African scholars and that such training had profound effects on the way in which Africans viewed their own societies.

In the University of Aberdeen, for example, a long list of African PhD students followed the award of the first PhD degree earned in the Department of Religious Studies in 1969 by Godwin Tasie, whose thesis carried the simple title: 'Christianity in the Niger Delta, 1864–1918'. Other theses displayed more philosophical themes, such as the one presented in 1978 by the Cameroon scholar Michael Bame Bame on 'Pastoral Care and Ontic Reality of the Incorporeal Components of Man's Being'. My own colleague at the time, Samuel Prempeh from Ghana, who recently completed a stint as chaplain in Edinburgh University, submitted his doctoral thesis in 1977 exploring the history of the Basel and Bremen mission in what was then the Gold Coast.

In this essay, I am particularly interested in the work of Kwame Bediako, who finished his PhD at Aberdeen in 1983 with a thesis entitled, 'Identity and Integration: An Enquiry into the Nature and Problems of Theological Indigenization in Selected Early Hellenistic and Modern African Writers'. This was subsequently published by Regnum Press in Oxford in 1992 under the title, *Theology and Identity*. This work indicates the direction Bediako was to take in his later career in which he became preoccupied with the indigenizing process of so-called 'foreign' religions, primarily Christianity, into Africa and the effects of this process on African concepts of identity.[29]

Following the completion of his PhD thesis, Bediako became director of the Akrofi-Christaller Memorial Centre for Mission Research and Applied Theology in Akropong-Akuapem, Ghana. Later, he was appointed as special lecturer in African Christianity in the Centre for the Study of Christianity in the Non-Western World in the University of Edinburgh, first under the directorship of Andrew Walls and then David Kerr, a post sponsored under the auspices of the African Christianity Project, which for 7 years received funding from the Pew Charitable Trusts in Philadelphia, Pennsylvania.[30] Bediako, who occupied the post of African Christianity Lecturer from 1992 through 1998, spent one term per year in Edinburgh, which meant that he kept a foot in Europe while maintaining a firm hold in Ghana. During the 1990s, Bediako became closely affiliated with the Oxford Centre for Mission Studies and was a frequent guest lecturer in the United States. During the late 1990s, he forged an academic link with the Department of Contextual Theology in the University of Natal, Pietermaritzburg, South Africa and expanded this link in 2004 into a Postgraduate Diploma in Theological Mission as an introduction to the MTh in African Christianity. He also developed a journal and a publication programme at the Akrofi-Christaller Centre that has made his project an important source for academic literature largely dealing with aspects of Christianity in Africa. Because Bediako remained in Africa, but in large measure due to his extensive ties also in Europe and America, he represented a notable example, with close ties to the Scottish Divinity programmes in Edinburgh and Aberdeen, who globalized African Indigenous Religions in a Christian guise. That this is the case is made evident through what I regard as his most important publication, *Christianity in Africa: The Renewal of a Non-Western Religion*, published jointly in 1995 by Edinburgh University Press and Orbis and which was based on his Alexander Duff lectures presented in the University of Edinburgh between 1989 and 1992.[31]

Bediako and Christianity as Africa's indigenous religion

The most significant re-interpretation of African Indigenous Religions by Bediako has resulted from his claim that Christianity is now a fully non-Western religion, or more specifically, what he calls an African 'primal' religion, but in an entirely transformed way. The 'primal' transcends itself by becoming universal; the universal discovers its roots in the primal. This idea is vividly exemplified by Bediako in chapter four of *Christianity in Africa*, which carries the title, 'Christianity as Africa's Religion'. In one section of the chapter, Bediako refers to the programme of 'Applied Theology' at the Akrofi-Christaller Centre, which

in part relates to 'a still-vital Akan traditional culture'.[32] By studying the Bible in
the vernacular Twi language, Bediako argues, local Christians have been able to
interpret the Christian message in ways that have integrated it into local Akan
culture. He cites an example that occurred during a Bible study group that was
considering the first chapter of Hebrews. The group focused on Hebrews 1.3,
particularly the phrase rendered in the New English Bible as: 'When he had
brought about the purgation of sins'.[33] The Twi word used for 'purgation', Bediako notes, is *dwiraa*, which is associated with the traditional New Year Festival
called *Odwira*. Because *Odwira* marks the end of one year and the start of a new
year, it is, according to Bediako, 'above all a festival of purification, reconciliation and renewal'.[34] Bediako explains that as the study group began to understand the traditional New Year Festival in the light of the biblical passage, they
began to see that '*Odwira* had something to do with Jesus, and that the atoning
work of Jesus could be related to the traditional *Odwira* rituals and its anticipated benefits'.[35]

The application of this text to an indigenous cultural ceremony meant for
Bediako that the tradition was being recreated by the Christian meaning, but at
the same time the Christian Scripture was being illuminated by the original
meaning. In traditional *Odwira*, the ancestors played a central role in the process
of purification and renewal, a place ascribed in the Christian scripture to Jesus.
In this way, the local, kinship-bound system adopted into its context a global
figure, that of Jesus, who could now be regarded as a kind of universal ancestor
for all humanity. The local thereby became the global, but the global was bound
into traditional kinship terminology.

Bediako's main point throughout this is that Christianity is not a 'foreign' or
'alien' religion. This is not because Africans always believed in a Supreme God,
and that they somehow anticipated the Christian message, as has been put
forward by other African theologians like J. S. Mbiti[36] or E. B. Idowu.[37] Rather,
drawing his inspiration from another of his mentors at Aberdeen, Harold Turner,
Bediako describes the 'primal understanding' as disclosing 'a universe conceived
as a unified cosmic system, essentially spiritual, in which the 'physical' acts as a
sacrament for 'spiritual' power.[38] The African worldview clearly is 'this-worldly'
but it is a 'this-worldliness' that, in Bediako's words 'encompasses God and man
in an abiding relationship which is the divine destiny of humankind, and the
purpose and goal of the universe'.[39]

In theological language, Bediako asserts a divine revelatory act in Jesus Christ,
whom he sees as 'the revelation of transcendence'.[40] This describes very clearly
how Christianity historically has understood the meaning of Christ's incarnation.
The African context adds something fundamental to this understanding that
enhances it and one could even say embraces it, making it its own – not foreign or
alien. The revelatory act of Christ in an African understanding, Bediako asserts, 'is
like the rending of the veil, so that the nature of the whole universe as instinct with
the divine presence may be made manifest'.[41] The New Testament language that

affirms, 'God's home is with mankind', becomes transformed by what Bediako calls 'the primal imagination' from a future eschatological event into a 'present existence' testified by typically African forms of Christianity which 'anticipate and *do* experience transcendent happenings like visions, prophecies and healings'.[42]

The task for the African Christian theologian has now become clear. The global religion with its universal revelation must be interpreted in ways that disclose its local characteristics so that the local can adopt the universal and the universal in turn can be moulded – as it is in other contexts – by the local. Bediako concludes: 'I see African academic theology as being challenged to be in close contact with the vernacular apprehension of the Christian faith and with its roots in the continuing realities of the traditional primal world-view.'[43]

The globalizing of a localized religion

What we witness in the case of Kwame Bediako, a graduate from Aberdeen University with its globalizing programme of postgraduate studies during the 1970s and 1980s, exemplifies my argument. Bediako was not just another participant in an academic discipline situated among the humanities, the value of whose contribution depends on the strength of his argument. His 'Africanness' is not irrelevant to the deliberate and calculated role he took in recreating local contexts in Africa. Nor is his Western education irrelevant to his impact on the culture he influenced. Quite clearly, he chose to remain close to the Akan culture by working among indigenous peoples in Ghana, where local, kinship-based religion still thrives. It is equally clear that he sought to globalize the local by elevating vernacular language and thought forms into contexts with universal applicability, something that would never have occurred in traditional thought forms.

The Bediako case can be multiplied in varying degrees beyond Bediako himself, beyond Aberdeen and beyond theology as a discipline. As Bates, Mudimbe and O'Barr have argued, Africa has been the subject of Western academic disciplines in their current forms for at least a century. The disciplines have been influenced by the African context and they have exercised power over African self-perceptions. What Bates, Mudimbe and O'Barr choose not to emphasize is the vast importance for African self-understandings played by African scholars themselves, who have studied in Europe or America, one might say have become globalized in the West, in order to carry the ideologies of globalization into localized contexts. If the case of Bediako is indicative, and more broadly that of the Aberdeen Department of Religious Studies at its height, Western academic institutions have penetrated into the heart of African culture itself by extracting Africans out of local situations and thereby intensifying an ongoing globalization process, a process superbly exemplified by the universalizing of African Indigenous Religions.

Notes

[1] Robert .H. Bates, V. Y. Mudimbe and Jean O'Barr. 'Introduction' in R. H. Bates, V. Y. Mudimbe and J. O'Barr (eds), *Africa and the Disciplines. The Contributions of Research in Africa to the Social Sciences and Humanities* (Chicago and London: University of Chicago Press, 1993), p. xi.

[2] Bates, Mudimbe and O'Barr, p. xi.

[3] Bates, Mudimbe and O'Barr, pp. xii–xiii.

[4] Bates, Mudimbe and O'Barr, p. xi.

[5] Sally Falk Moore, 'Changing Perspectives on a Changing Africa: the Work of Anthropology', in Bates, Mudimbe and O'Barr (eds.), pp. 3–57.

[6] *Ibid.*, p. 33.

[7] *Ibid.*, p. 33.

[8] Okot p'Bitek, *African Religions in European Scholarship* (Chesapeake, VI: ECA Associates, 1990). Previously published as *African Religions in Western Scholarship* (Kampala: East African Literature Bureau, 1971). See also, Henk van Rinsum, *Slaves of Definition* (Maastricht: Shaker Publishing BV, 2001), pp. 89–117.

[9] Robert H. Bates, V.Y. Mudimbe and Jean O'Barr, p. xii.

[10] Phillipa Baylis, *Primal Religions: An Introduction* (Edinburgh: Traditional Cosmology Society, 1989); Harold Turner, *Living Tribal Religions* (London: Ward Lock Educational, 1971); Andrew F. Walls, 'Primal Religious Traditions in Today's World' in F. Whaling (ed.), *Religion in Today's World* (Edinburgh: T. and T. Clark, 1987), 250–78. See also, James L. Cox, 'The Classification "Primal Religions" as a Non-Empirical Christian Theological Construct' in *Studies in World Christianity* 2 (1), 1996, 55–76; James L. Cox, *From Primitive to Indigenous: The Academic Study of Indigenous Religions* (Aldershot, Hampshire and Burlington, Vermont: Ashgate, 2007), pp. 53–74.

[11] James L. Cox, *Rational Ancestors. Scientific Rationality and African Indigenous Religions* (Cardiff: Cardiff Academic Press, 1998), pp. 104–12; James L. Cox, 'Characteristics of African Indigenous Religions in Contemporary Zimbabwe' in G. Harvey (ed.), *Indigenous Religions: A Companion* (London: Cassell, 2000), pp. 230–42; James L. Cox, 'Spirit Mediums in Zimbabwe: Religious Experience in and on behalf of the Community' in *Studies in World Christianity* 6 (2), 2000, 190–207.

[12] J. G. Platvoet, 'African Traditional Religions in the Religious History of Humankind' in *Journal for the Study of Religion* 6 (2), 1993, 36.

[13] *Ibid.*, 38.

[14] *Ibid.*, 38.

[15] *Ibid.*, 38.

[16] *Ibid.*, 38.

[17] Michael Gelfand, *The Genuine Shona* (Gweru, Zimbabwe: Mambo Press, 1973), pp. 60, 64, 129–31.

[18] J. G. Platvoet, 'African Traditional Religions', p. 39.

[19] Sally Falk Moore, p. 13. See, Daryll Forde, 'Double Descent among the Yakö', in A.R. Radcliffe-Brown and D. Forde (eds.), *African Systems of Kinship and Marriage* (London: Oxford University Press, 1987), pp. 285–332.

[20] Richard P. Werbner, 'Continuity and Policy in Southern Africa's High God Cult', in R. P. Werbner (ed.), *Regional Cults* (London, New York and San Francisco: Academic Press, 1977), pp. 179–218.

[21] James L. Cox, 'Ancestors, the Sacred and God: Reflections on the Meaning of the Sacred in Zimbabwean Death Rituals', *Religion* 25 (4), 1995, 339–55.

[22] Robin Horton, 'African Conversion', *Africa* 41 (2), 1971, 85–108.

[23] J. G. Platvoet, 'The Religions of Africa in their Historical Order', in J. Platvoet, J. Cox and J. Olupona (eds.), *The Study of Religions in Africa: Past, Present and Prospects* (Cambridge: Roots and Branches), pp. 56–7.

[24] Andrew F. Walls, 'African Christianity in the History of Religions' in *Studies in World Christianity* 2 (2), 1996, 192–3.

[25] Richard P. Werbner, 'Continuity and Policy'; M. L. Daneel, *The God of the Matopos Hills* (The Hague: Mouton, 1970); T. O. Ranger, *Voices from the Rocks. Nature, Culture and History in the Matopos Hills of Zimbabwe* (Bloomington: Indiana University Press and Oxford: James Currey, 1999); Leslie S. Nthoi, *Contesting Sacred Space: A Pilgrimage Study of the Mwali Cult of Southern Africa* (Trenton, NJ: Africa World Press, 2006).

[26] Herbert Aschwanden, *Karanga Mythology* (Gweru, Zimbabwe: Mambo Press), pp. 205–7.

[27] J. G. Platvoet, 'The Religions of Africa in Their Historical Order', p. 57. See also, M.F.C. Bourdillon, *Where Are the Ancestors?* (Harare: University of Zimbabwe Publications, 1997), pp. 7–17.

[28] James L. Cox, 'From Africa to Africa: The Significance of Approaches to the Study of African Religions at Aberdeen and Edinburgh Universities from 1970 to 1998' in F. Ludwig and A. Adogame (eds.), *European Traditions in the Study of Religion in Africa* (Wiesbaden: Harrassowitz Verlag, 2004), pp. 255–64; James L. Cox, *A Guide to the Phenomenology of Religion. Key Figures, Formative Influences and Subsequent Debates* (London and New York: Continuum, 2006), pp. 141–70; James L. Cox, *From Primitive to Indigenous*, pp. 16–29.

[29] Kwame Bediako, Theology and Identity. The Impact of Culture upon Christian thought in the Second Century and Modern Africa (Oxford: Regnum Books, 2000).

[30] James L. Cox, 'Setting the Context: The African Christianity Project and the Emergence of a Self-Reflexive Institutional Identity' in J. L. Cox and Gerrie ter Haar (eds.), *Uniquely African? African Christian Identity from Cultural and Historical Perspectives* (Trenton, NJ: Africa World Press, 2003), pp. 1–7.

[31] Kwame Bediako, *Christianity in Africa. The Renewal of a Non-Western Religion* (Edinburgh: Edinburgh University Press and Maryknoll, NY: Orbis, 1995).

[32] *Ibid.*, Christianity in Africa, p. 70.

[33] *Ibid.*

[34] *Ibid.*, 71.

[35] *Ibid.*

[36] John S. Mbiti, *African Religions and Philosophy* (London: Heinemann, 1969), pp. 29–74.

[37] E. Bolaji Idowu, *African Traditional Religion: A Definition* (London: SCM Press, 1973), pp.140–65.

[38] Kwame Bediako, *Christianity in Africa*, p. 101.

[39] *Ibid.*

[40] *Ibid.*, p. 102.

[41] *Ibid.*

[42] *Ibid.*, p. 103.

[43] *Ibid.*, p. 86.

Part Two

The African Context

Chapter 6

The Ngoni Struggle for Land and Identity in Colonial Malawi[1]

T. Jack Thompson

The Ngoni of northern Malawi are not nearly as famous as their 'cousins' the Zulu in South Africa. Yet, at least in terms of nineteenth-century European historiography of Africa, they have much in common. Both were regarded as fierce, war-like, often cruel and brutal, and at the same time brave and resourceful. Ethnographically they come from a similar Nguni stock, and, indeed, the Ngoni were quite often described as 'Zulus' in nineteenth-century accounts. In actual fact, they had fought on opposite sides in the early nineteenth-century disturbances in south-eastern Africa, generally known as the *Mfecane*. As a result of being on the losing side, the Ngoni under their leader Zwangendaba had begun a 35-year migration around 1820, which brought them eventually to settle in the Mzimba district of what is now northern Malawi.

Once settled in Malawi, the group of Ngoni, now led by M'mbelwa, began a period of adjustment to a number of different external factors. First was the very fact of 'settlement' itself. After 35 years of migration, raiding and the assimilation of subject peoples, they had to come to terms with a more settled agricultural way of life. Yet because this was a gradual and resisted process, there also followed a period of often difficult and sometimes violent relationship with surrounding peoples. To use a modern term, the Ngoni were often regarded as 'the neighbours from hell', and certainly that is how they were portrayed by many early European writers. Second, soon after the Ngoni settled in northern Malawi, the area saw a new incoming group: the Scottish missionaries – small in number but large in influence – with whom they had to come to terms. Third, although other European presence in the area was very limited, the Ngoni, on one very trying occasion in 1899, had to react to the violent incursion of one particular European adventurer, William Robert Ziehl. Finally, the Ngoni had to deal with the increasingly invasive intentions of the British colonial authorities culminating in 1904, in the absorption of the Ngoni state into British Central Africa – an entity formally established 13 years earlier in 1891.

This essay will look briefly at each of these interactions. In doing so, it will challenge the traditional stereotype of the Ngoni as 'bloodthirsty savages', and argue that Ngoni understandings of land-culture and identity emerged from a thoughtful re-assessment of core Ngoni values brought about by the enforced interaction with new and external forces.

Ngoni origins

M'mbelwa's Ngoni (sometimes known as the northern Ngoni) had arrived in what is now the Mzimba district of Malawi in around 1855, having migrated from the area of Lake St Lucia in KwaZulu-Natal, beginning around 1820.[2] Most nineteenth-century European commentators identified them as Zulu, though this is really an anachronism, since, at the time of the beginning of their migration, the Zulu were merely one of many clans of the Nguni peoples of south-eastern Africa. It would be more accurate to describe the Ngoni as belonging to the Ndwandwe branch of the Nguni peoples, and as speaking a language somewhere between Zulu and Xhosa, though nearer to the former.

In a short essay such as this there is no space to look in any detail at the origins of their migration–not least because some strands of recent South African historiography query the whole idea of the *Mfecane* as being a major cause of mass migrations such as that of the Ngoni. Suffice it to say here that a group comprising not more than a few hundred Ngoni, led by Zwangendaba Jere, left KwaZulu-Natal around 1820, and began a slow, gradual movement northwards, during which they assimilated many people along the way, and eventually moved as far north as southern Tanzania – where Zwangendaba died around 1847. The group then splintered, and the major section, now led by M'mbelwa Jere, moved south into Malawi, where they settled around 1855.

The Ngoni were predominantly pastoralists, and during the long migration had become accustomed to a pattern of life centred on raiding other groups – both to obtain food, and to capture and incorporate extra personnel into their social structure. It was this, as much as anything else, which led to the impression given by European commentators, that they were a powerful and fearsome people. It is possible to interpret the facts in a different way, however. The fact that they migrated for 30 years and travelled around 1,500 miles from their point of departure can be seen as much as a sign of weakness as of strength. Had they been stronger than they were, they might have settled much earlier than they did. Some Ngoni traditions speak of them searching for a particular type of long-horned cattle, which they greatly valued, and/or an ideal land in which to settle. The reality is more likely to be that this small and increasingly heterogeneous grouping continued to migrate simply because they had not the strength or numbers to overcome local groups any earlier.

Certainly this first period of Ngoni history is characterized by an understanding of the land that is not closely tied to a particular place. Most nineteenth-century writers on the Ngoni (and indeed many in the twentieth century) have spoken of their territory as *Ngoniland*. This terminology closely equates land with territory. For the Ngoni, however, the term *uNgoni* (or *ubuNgoni*)[3] while indicating the area where the Ngoni lived and ruled, may almost be better translated *Ngoni-ness*, or 'the essence of being Ngoni'. Thus land is understood, not so much within the narrow confines of territory, but more widely in terms of culture and identity. It is likely that such an understanding was strengthened by the long migration, and by the fact, for example, that the Ngoni had no physical access to the graves of their ancestors.

The settlement in Malawi

Around 1855 M'mbelwa (following the death of his father Zwangendaba around 8 years earlier in Tanzania) finally came to settle in northern Malawi. Even now, however, it is a slight misnomer to speak of him finally settling, for while the Ngoni have remained in much the same area ever since, the paramount chief has moved his headquarters on several occasions for pastoral or political reasons. The settlement in Malawi came after 35 years of migration. Of course, this migration had not been continuous, but had been a series of short settlements, interspersed with periods of travelling. One major characteristic marked this period. This was the pattern of raiding surrounding peoples for cattle and food-stuffs and the associated capturing of what the Ngoni called *abafo* (domestic slaves). Once they had finally settled in Malawi this pattern of behaviour did not disappear overnight. It continued for many years and was largely responsible for the very negative reputation that the Ngoni enjoyed both with surrounding peoples, and with passing Europeans, including David Livingstone. Like several other early European travellers, however, Livingstone got his ideas about the Ngoni (or the Mazitu, as he called them) not by direct contact, but largely by second hand accounts provided by their enemies. This is not to say, of course, that the Ngoni were blameless in the matter. Undoubtedly they continued with an intermittent policy of raiding for many years. Increasingly, however, surrounding groups became more adept at dealing with such raids, and even began to make counter-raids. One result of this pattern was that the boundaries of *uNgoni* remained very indefinite for many years, with patches of frontier disputed and shifting. Such a situation meant also that it was in such borderlands that it was most difficult for the paramount and other Ngoni chiefs to maintain control. Given also the fact that many of the young men involved in such raiding were not *abaZansi* (i.e. from the core Ngoni clans who had left southern Africa), they sat rather loosely to the core values of Ngoni culture. In addition, the Ngoni pattern of chieftaincy – with a paramount and four or five strong chiefs under him – meant that there was a good deal of political manoeuvring for control, not least as we moved into the next period of missionary influence.

Early missionary interaction

The Scottish missionaries of the Livingstonia mission of the Free Church of Scotland had first entered Malawi in 1875, but several years before they had moved into the area of the country controlled by the Ngoni. They made first contact with the northern Ngoni in 1878, when they had established a temporary station at Kaning'ina on the outskirts of present-day Mzuzu, on the borderlands of Ngoni control. During this period the major missionary influence on the Ngoni was the Xhosa evangelist William Koyi from Lovedale in South Africa, who was able to communicate with the Ngoni, as isiXhosa and siNgoni were closely related languages. At this point (and indeed for many years to come) the Ngoni had little interest in converting to Christianity. Rather, they saw the missionaries as potential allies – both political and spiritual – in their disputes with the Tonga of the lakeshore, where the major mission station of Bandawe was situated. I have written extensively about this relationship elsewhere; here I want to highlight just two examples of early Ngoni interaction with the missionaries, and how it impacted on the question of identity.

In June 1879 Koyi and the Scottish artisan Miller went up from Kaning'ina to M'mbelwa's village of Echigodhlweni to be formally welcomed by the Ngoni. Part of this welcome involved the gift of 11 cattle to the mission.[4] Gifts of individual cattle to important guests were reasonably common in Ngoni society. For example, both M'mbelwa and Mtwalo gave a cow to the mission in 1878, and Mzukuzuku gave one in March 1879.[5] It would seem however, that the gift of cattle in June 1879 had a far greater symbolic significance than has generally been recognized. Several factors point to this conclusion.

First, in spite of internal disagreements among the Ngoni at this time, it is clear from the speeches made during the welcome that the chiefs regarded the occasion as of considerable importance, and were making a real effort to present a united front.[6] Second, the gift of eleven cattle, rather than one or two, is a clear indication of the seriousness with which the Ngoni regarded the occasion. Third, the Ngoni at first insisted on keeping the cattle in *uNgoni*, and in July Miller had to go up from Kaning'ina to build a kraal for them, most probably at M'mbelwa's village.[7] Fourth, the physical transfer of the cattle to the mission took place only after the mission had settled permanently at Njuyu in 1882;[8] and fifth, continued Ngoni references to the gift as late as 1887 make it clear that they regarded the transfer as an event of considerable significance. These Ngoni references suggest that they regarded the gift as a pledge of friendship – not in an ordinary sense, but in a mystical and binding way. In many respects the gift bore strong resemblances to the transfer of the *lobola* cattle on the arrangement of an Ngoni marriage, and the Ngoni certainly spoke of the relationship of M'mbelwa and the mission in these terms. Furthermore, the Ngoni feared that, unless the mission clearly acknowledged acceptance of the gift and its consequences (in their view) of a mission–Ngoni alliance,[9] then other tribes would be encouraged to attack them. Once the cattle had been accepted, however, their safety became a mission responsibility, and as late as 1887, M'mbelwa warned the Lovedale evangelist George Williams that 'your safety and the safety of all the missionaries depended upon the keeping of the cattle that was given to Dr. Laws.'[10]

Though William Koyi himself was not clear about the precise significance of the gift, he did recognize that it was of considerable symbolic importance and urged Laws to be cautious in respect of it.[11] In retrospect it would seem that the gift was a symbolic gesture of considerable significance, perhaps representing a mystical marriage between the Ngoni and the mission, and that Koyi's sensitive handling of the situation at this very early stage may have helped to ensure Ngoni acceptance of the missionary presence at a time when some elements in the Ngoni leadership would have preferred confrontation. Just a few months ago, and following a lecture I gave in his presence, the present Ngoni paramount M'mbelwa IV, when I mentioned the transfer of the 11 cattle, confirmed in public that my interpretation of these events was correct, and that the Ngoni regard the transfer of cattle as a symbolic marriage between the Scottish mission and the Ngoni people. In terms of our present concerns, the significance of the events is that the Ngoni saw the alliance as part of their continuing struggle to establish their land and identity, and regarded the support of the missionaries as an important element in their continuing disputes with the Tonga.

A second example of this early interaction can be seen in the way that the Ngoni used the missionaries as religious practitioners to fulfil their own religious needs. In a letter to Robert Laws, the leader of the mission, in 1882, William Koyi mentioned a request from M'mbelwa that he should come to his village and pray for the success of the crops for the coming year. Koyi goes on to describe the service that he led there on the last Sunday of December 1882. He reports that one and a half thousand people turned up at the service to pray for a successful planting season, and while we may have to take his statistics with a pinch of salt, clearly something quite significant was taking place. Obviously it was not a mass conversion to Christianity – the first Ngoni baptisms were still more than 7 years in the future. The real significance of the event may lie in its timing. Before leaving South Africa, the Ngoni had regularly followed the traditional ritual of the *incwala*. I have described this ritual in more detail elsewhere. Suffice it to say here that it was a traditional first-fruits ritual among several Nguni groups in southern Africa, and was concerned both with agricultural fertility, and with the annual renewal of the spiritual power of the king. In the southern African context from which the Ngoni had migrated in the 1820s, the ritual took place at the end of December – the precise time that M'mbelwa asked Koyi to come and pray for the crops. As a result of several factors – the long migration, the changing composition of the Ngoni group itself, as it assimilated new non-Zansi elements, the changes in the timing of the agricultural year as the Ngoni moved more than 1,500 miles to the north – the *incwala* had died out amongst the Ngoni by the time that Koyi settled at Njuyu. Nevertheless, it seems reasonable to assume that, particularly among the Zansi-Ngoni themselves a clear memory of, and perhaps even a feeling of need for, the *incwala* (or at least something which fulfilled a similar function) remained. If this were the case, what the Ngoni were actually doing in asking Koyi to pray for the crops, was (as I have indicated above) using him as a religious practitioner to fulfil their own traditional religious needs, rather than, in any real sense, agreeing to adopt the new religious allegiance being offered by the missionaries. At this period, as various external influences made regular raiding more difficult, the Ngoni were struggling to adapt to a new way of life. Their early interactions with the Livingstonia missionaries (not least with the Xhosa William Koyi, who understood their dilemma better than any Scottish missionary could) indicate clearly that they were attempting to consolidate their grip on the land (in both physical and metaphysical senses) by attempting to cement an alliance with the newcomers. While the Scottish missionaries were only partly aware of what was going on, the Ngoni tactic succeeded, at least to the extent that the missionaries did not abandon the Ngoni and throw in their lot entirely with the Tonga.

The Ziehl case

By 1891 the British had declared most of the area of what is now Malawi a Protectorate (at first known as British Central Africa). The Ngoni area had, however, been specifically excluded from this takeover, partly, at least, because of perceived Ngoni opposition to the possibility of losing what had by then become a strong a fairly cohesive political entity, and partly because of the British fear of having to deal with any subsequent reaction with very limited forces at their disposal. In the section after this we trace briefly the process by which the Ngoni were finally brought under colonial control. Here, it is sufficient to say that as the nineteenth century drew to a close, *uNgoni* remained the only part of Malawi not under colonial control; but that this in turn left it particularly vulnerable to incursions from a small number of ruthless European entrepreneurs. One such was William Robert Ziehl, who entered *uNgoni* in January 1899, hoping to buy cattle cheaply following a recent outbreak of rinderpest disease, which had wiped out large numbers of cattle both in Malawi and countries to the south.

During several weeks in *uNgoni* Ziehl and his followers were accused not only of forcing people to sell cattle to them, but also of stealing cattle, whipping villagers with a *chikoti*, raping women and killing at least two people. At one point he came into conflict with several mission teachers (the most prominent of whom was Daniel Nhlane). By this time Christianity was beginning to make steady progress among the Ngoni, and though the vast majority remained loyal to Ngoni traditions at this point, the general influence of the Scottish mission was considerable. The ambiguous reality of the situation was highlighted when Nhlane informed Ziehl that he should leave the area immediately because 'this is Mission country. It does not belong to the Administration.' For Christian teachers in particular identity was increasingly becoming more hybrid. They clearly regarded themselves as Ngoni, but Ngoni who were taking on a new identity. This is shown by the fact that in the same conversation in which he informed Ziehl that the area belonged to the Mission, Nhlane also spoke of 'his own country'. For most Ngoni still the area was *uNgoni*: The place where Ngoni-ness prevailed. But even for such traditionalists, the ability to control their own territory was reaching its end.

Ziehl fled the area, and the Ngoni wanted to pursue him with an army. Amazingly, the Scottish missionary Donald Fraser agreed to lead out the army (in order to try to keep it under control). At the last moment the government Collector from the lakeshore area, C. A. Cardew, arrived. His involvement highlighted the ambiguous position of a continued Ngoni independence, for while they were technically independent the 'glory days' of their old raiding period were clearly gone. Eventually, Ziehl was arrested and brought back to the mission station of Ekwendeni where he was put on trial by the British authorities. Technically *uNgoni* was still an independent territory, but the legal justification for the trial was probably that Ziehl was a British citizen. Ziehl was charged with nine offences – the most serious of which were that he had levied war against the Ngoni, and illegally armed the Africans travelling with him.

The trial aroused a huge amount of interest among the Ngoni, several of whom gave evidence. It was also attended by the paramount chief, Chimtunga. Ziehl was found guilty on eight of the nine charges against him, and sentenced to 6 months imprisonment, or a fine of £50. He also had to pay compensation to those he had wronged, including the derisory sum of £1.50 to the families of each of the two men who had been killed by his followers.

One might have thought that this verdict would have angered the Ngoni; but the opposite seems to have been the case. Many years later paramount chief M'mbelwa (the son of chief Chimtunga) in explaining to the Bledisloe Commission why his father had agreed to consider coming under British rule, explained:

> This is one of the reasons why my father willingly placed himself under the imperial government rule, because the Deputy Commissioner, Mr. Pearce, had displayed justice and showed great protection by fining the European and making him pay all damages made to people.[12]

So by the beginning of the twentieth century a very complex situation had developed among the Ngoni with regard to their self-perception of their own land and identity. There remained a strong pride in the old Ngoni military tradition, though by the turn of the century raiding as a regular activity had all but died out. Politically Chimtunga was regarded as a somewhat weak chief, and had never been given the title M'mbelwa, which would have sealed his acceptance as paramount. While the number of Ngoni converts to Christianity still numbered hundreds rather than thousands, the influence of the mission was considerable. In May 1899, within a couple of weeks of Ziehl's trial, a great open-air religious convention took place at Ekwendeni. Missionary accounts estimated the attendance at six thousand six hundred – ten times the number of those actual baptized as Christians. This indicates that a new Ngoni identity was beginning to emerge which included Christian as well as traditional elements. With regard to the land several years of bad harvests (and in 1902 a plague of locusts) forced some sections of the Ngoni to migrate to new areas on the southern edges of their previous territory. Once again, Ngoni ideas of the land were not tied firmly to particular territory, but to the authority of particular chiefs.

The coming of colonial government

By the end of the Ziehl affair, it seemed certain to most outside observers that it was only a matter of time until the Ngoni came under British colonial control. That they had remained independent for a decade after the rest of the area had been colonized was in itself very surprising, yet even now the colonial authorities seemed reluctant to force the issue – confident that the Ngoni themselves would soon request the move. Yet the Ngoni were not keen on being taken over by the government. It would seem that they regarded their alliance with the mission as an alternative to colonial absorption and reckoned that they could retain more independence under mission than government control. There was also a sense in which the mission gave more respect to the Ngoni chiefs than the colonial government might do. One weakness with the Ngoni position was that most of the Scottish missionaries themselves felt that the time for Ngoni independence was coming to an end.

By 1903 several small-scale incidents had arisen which once again raised the question of who had ultimate jurisdiction within Ngoni territory, or when disputes arose between the Ngoni and neighbouring groups. The most serious of these incidents arose in 1904 and involved a small but direct clash between the Ngoni and the colonial authorities themselves. Early in 1904 a group of colonial policemen entered *uNgoni*, began collecting hut tax and burning the huts of those who refused to pay. They were intercepted by the Scottish missionary Donald Fraser, who sent them back to the lakeshore, with a letter of complaint to the Collector there. Here again we see the mission and the Ngoni acting as allies apparently against the colonial authorities; an alliance which the Ngoni were happy to support, but with which the Scottish missionaries felt increasingly unhappy.

Though in this particular case the fault seems to have lain almost entirely with the local colonial authorities, the Governor-General, Sir Alfred Sharpe took exception to the strong pro-Ngoni line taken by Fraser, and decided that the time had come to annex *uNgoni*. The *indaba*, at which negotiations leading to annexation took place, met at Ekwendeni on 2 September 1904. Sharpe pointed out that one of the reasons why annexation was necessary was that the Ngoni had spread out well beyond their original boundaries, and gave them the choice of returning to their original boundaries or accepting British annexation. Here, again the question of land was central to the issue. There was no practical possibility of the Ngoni moving back to boundaries which they had occupied 13 years previously. In any case, for the Ngoni, boundaries were a not a matter of lines on a map, but of areas of political control.

Even so, their eventual acceptance of British rule was not a matter of surrender, but of negotiating the most advantageous terms they could get. These included that as far as possible the local police force to be set up should be made up of the Ngoni themselves, that hut tax should not be levied until January 1906, that the slate should be wiped clean of any remaining disputes involving the Ngoni, and that six Ngoni chiefs would receive annual subsidies from the colonial government.

While it is true that the Ngoni would probably have preferred to remain independent of British control, the conditions that they managed to negotiate protected their understanding of land and identity in several important ways. First, their chiefs were confirmed in their authority. Second, they were able to remain on the land they actually controlled, rather on the more limited territory which the British had originally assigned them when taking over the rest of the country in 1891. Third, the policing of the area was to be carried out mainly by Ngoni policemen, rather than those of other groups the Ngoni may have regarded as inferior. The Ngoni would have liked much more, of course. They felt that they had been promised a status of semi-independence similar to that of King Khama in Botswana. Nevertheless the settlement reached in many ways gave them a superior status to that enjoyed by many neighbouring peoples.

Clearly one of the reasons why the British had been slow and cautious in approaching the annexation of *uNgoni* had been the fear of violence and uprising. The Ngoni themselves were proud of their military prowess, even though it had almost certainly declined considerably since their settlement in Malawi. Yet it is interesting to note that one leading Ngoni Christian writer, Yesaya Chibambo, in recording the events of September 1904 in his book *Makani gha waNgoni* (later translated as *My Ngoni of Nyasaland*) wrote:

Para Boma likanjira mu *uNgoni* pa 1904 kuti donto limoza la ndopa likatirikapo cara; ndipo nkongono ya wayeni yirive kutayapo wonga wake kutereska fuko litu; nga ndi umo kuli kucitikira mu vyaru vinyake. Bwana Mkubwa Sir Alfred Sharpe, wakiza yeka na muwoli wake kwambura msirikari wa nkondo, ndipo pa September 2, iyo na waNgoni wakazomerezgana kuti Boma liwenge mu *uNgoni*.[13]

When the government entered Ngoniland in 1904 not a drop of blood was shed, as was done in some other parts of the land. The Governor, Sir Alfred Sharpe, came alone with his wife and with no armed force, and on 2nd September he and the Ngoni agreed that the Government be established in Ngoniland.[14]

Conclusion

From their inception as a small fleeing group of refugees in KwaZulu around 1820, to their annexation by the British colonial authorities in Malawi more than 80 years later, M'mbelwa's Ngoni had struggled both to maintain a distinctive identity, and to establish their own concept of *ubuNgoni* (as both territory and culture). Rather than attempting to summarize the events described above, let me finish with a very brief account of an incident which took place in 2004 – exactly a century after the annexation of *uNgoni* by the British. The scene was in the heart of *uNgoni*, at the village of Njuyu, where the Scottish missionaries had set up their first permanent station among the Ngoni in 1882. There, celebrations were taking place to commemorate the origins of that work, and I had been invited to deliver a celebratory lecture as a part of the wider commemorations. Just a few days before the event, which was to be attended by several thousand people, I was asked if I would take part in a short play to commemorate the first meeting of the Ngoni paramount M'mbelwa with the Scottish missionary Robert Laws. The request came from senior Ngoni leaders themselves, and the present paramount *nkosi yamakosi* M'mbelwa IV was to play his own great-grandfather M'mbelwa I. I was to play Robert Laws. The paramount chief and his entourage were in full traditional dress, complete with spears and shields. Parts of the play (including my traditional greeting to the paramount chief) were in the *siNgoni* language. The occasion, while in some respects light-hearted, in others summed up very well the Ngoni struggle for identity. The short play, lasting less than 10 minutes was performed in the open air for an audience including the then President of Malawi Bakili Muluzi, and later went out on news programmes on Malawi television. Here symbolically was how the Ngoni would still like to see themselves: The head of state as a spectator, the white man doing obeisance at the feet of the paramount chief. Yet while in most respects this is a mere dream of a long lost reality, in another way it is not so far from the truth. Ngoni culture has survived many struggles, the head of state was present at a remote village in the midst of *uNgoni*, the European historian had flown thousands of miles to celebrate the occasion. Among the celebrations that followed were traditional Ngoni dances and praise songs to early Ngoni figures such Mawelera Tembo, the first Ngoni convert to Christianity.

While politically, and certainly militarily, Ngoni power had largely ended even before the British annexation of 1904, in other ways the Ngoni have managed over the last century to maintain their own culture and identity. True, the *siNgoni* language is on the verge of extinction, though efforts are presently under way to revive it. Yet for all that, it is possible to argue that at the beginning of the twenty-first century, and more than a hundred years after an independent Ngoni state came to end, it is still possible to speak authentically of the concept of *ubuNgoni*.

Notes

1 An earlier version of this paper was presented at the 19th Congress of the International Association for the History of Religions in Tokyo, in March 2005. It is published here for the first time.

2 See T. Jack Thompson, *Christianity in Northern Malawi* (Leiden and New York: E. J. Brill, 1995), chapter 1, 'Ngoni Origins'. For an indigenous Ngoni account of their origins see, Yesaya Chibambo, 'Makani gha waNgoni' in *Midauko* (Malawi: Livingstonia Synod, 1965).

3 In this essay I shall use the term *uNgoni* to indicate the territory of the Ngoni people, and *ubuNgoni* to indicate the culture concept of 'Ngoniness': what it means to be Ngoni.

4 Kaning'ina Journal, 12 June 1879, Ms. 7910, National Library of Scotland (NLS).

5 W. P. Livingstone, *Laws of Livingstonia*, 156; Bandawe Journal, 1 April 1879, Ms. 7910, NLS.

6 Kaning'ina Journal, 12 June 1879, Ms. 7910, NLS.

7 *Ibid.*, 5 July 1879.

8 Koyi to Laws, 26 August 1882, Shepperson Collection, NLS.

9 Kaning'ina Journal, 24 June 1879, Ms. 7910, NLS.

10 Williams to Laws, 21 September 1887, Ms. 7890, NLS.

11 Koyi to Laws, 13 September 1882, Shepperson Collection, NLS.

12 Chief M'mbelwa's evidence to the Bledisloe Commission, quoted in Bridglal Pachai, 'Ngoni Politics and Diplomacy in Malawi, 1849-1904' in B. Pachai (ed.), *The Early History of Malawi* (London: Longmans, 1972), p. 206.

13 'Makani gha waNgoni', p. 85.

14 Y. M. Chibambo, *My Ngoni of Nyasaland* (London: United Society for Christian Literature), n.d., [1940], p. 59; Charles Stuart's translation.

Chapter 7

Familiar Ground: Origins and Trajectories of African Biblical Scholarship

Misheck Nyirenda

The premise of typology

L. S. Thornton noted so long ago that, 'It is doubtful whether we can hope to understand the contents of any mind whose presuppositions we have not yet learned to recognize.'[1] This observation captures the starting point for Africans, particularly those within a prominent trajectory in African biblical scholarship. The familiarity that Africans generally find with respect to several features in the Hebrew Bible and, for others, the Gospels,[2] has led to much research. In this essay, we aim to introduce this phenomenon and its ramifications for African encounters with the Bible.

In African biblical scholarship, this trajectory encompasses, in keeping with similar currents in postcolonial discourse, disparate approaches where the consistent feature is the 'who' that is undertaking the scholarship. *African* biblical scholars want to own the critical encounter between themselves and the Bible.

Sugirtharajah defines Postcolonialism as space for the masses in postcolonial societies to be themselves, 'an attempt to go 'home' . . . a call to self-awareness, aimed at creating an awakening among people to their indigenous literary, cultural and religious heritage'.[3] The fact he is writing with the Indian context in mind explains the allusions to an indigenous 'literary heritage' and the view that colonizers set out to impose their values and ways of life in the 'colony' against the will of the colonized.

In South Africa, there is evidence that white settlers initially opposed missionary efforts to 'civilise' 'natives'. Their reasons ranged from belief that Africans were biologically incapable of such civilization to fear that they would be empowered to be critical of and to rebel against the status quo. There is also evidence in Old Calabar that the 'natives' had their own agendas for pursuing the white man's education, often related to equipping their children for trade. For example, the chiefs of Bonny told missionaries that they did not want religious teaching for their children as they already had that. They wanted them to learn 'how to [measure] palm-oil and other mercantile business as soon as possible.'[4] These examples suggest that, in Africa, the 'colonisation of the

African mind' as Ngugi Wa Thiong'o calls it[5] was a rather complex affair with different agendas and rationale on both sides.

Some in Modern biblical scholarship have also entertained the notion that we can only understand biblical traditions through a specific conceptual filter. James Barr's largely successful criticism of the Biblical Theology Movement[6] demonstrates the tensions and dangers associated with: (1) making presuppositions *prima facie* evidence for understanding biblical texts and (2) examining the texts inductively in order to come up with cues for understanding the material. Both approaches presuppose method(s). The first explicitly declares the epistemological framework for its methods regardless of the merits or demerits of such a framework in relation to the texts. In the Biblical Theology Movement, a reconstructed 'Hebrew mind-set' was the presumed epistemic filter for understanding biblical theology. The second approach attempts critical and inductive analysis of the texts without paying too much attention, if at all, to its own epistemic criteria and presuppositions. Within Modernity, it has operated under the assumption of a methodological 'objectivity' predicated on a presumed minimization or even lack of epistemic bias. Some within this approach believe that all data contains self-evident criteria that is inductively accessible and ought to be the basis for analysing it.[7]

Without endorsing the caricature that all biblical scholarship prior to the Enlightenment failed to appreciate the historically conditioned nature of the biblical material,[8] it is clear that, 'the Bible's time-conditioned quality became a major hermeneutical problem in the wake of the Enlightenment and the rise of the historical critical method.'[9] However, it is now apparent that historical–critical scholarship is weak at the very point of facing its own subjectivities, its own historical conditioning. Under '*The Sitz im Leben of the Exegete*', Erhard Gerstenberger notes that

> [i]n the European hermeneutical discussion there is hardly ever any reference to the exegete's real predisposition, that is, to the interpreter's affiliation with certain social, economic, ethnic, sexual, political, or cultural groups. This is very strange indeed, because one no less than Rudolf Bultmann long ago called attention to the prime importance of 'preconceived ideas' in all interpretive proceedings.[10]

Barton agrees that the 'conventions' governing specific material ought to be paramount in the understanding of it. He also argues that without some assumption of methodological affinities between such conventions and a scholar's own culture, the very task of analysis cannot proceed.[11] He makes his point in the context of literary criticism without offering a critique of such an assumption. Childs points to this oversight in the historical–critical method when he notes that, 'One of the disastrous legacies of the Enlightenment was the new confidence of standing outside the stream of time and with clear rationality being able to distinguish truth from error, light from darkness.'[12] We find here an allusion, then, to an oversight in historical–critical scholarship to factor in the subjectivities of its method(s).

From the perspective of postcolonial scholars, this oversight is inexcusable. Andrew Walls notes that Africans are now engaged in re-interpreting Christianity through their social–cultural realities and *Sitz im Leben*.[13] Including their subjectivities in appropriating the Scriptures and constructing theologies is gaining momentum.

The Africa referenced here is sub-Saharan Africa in keeping with the new identities arising from the 'nations' created by the powerful and disruptive phenomena of colonialism and imperialism and created by 'the partition of the continent among European nations, signified by the Berlin Congo-Conference 1884/5'.[14] According to Richard Werbner, colonialism re-defined ethnic, cultural and political-social reality in Africa. By imposing new national identities based on arbitrarily created borders, it drastically altered the identities, values and associations of the societies involved to the effect that the average African is still in the process of re-negotiating his or her terms of self-reference in an attempt to accommodate the new realities.[15]

Colonialism and imperialism came to Africa in the context of another disruptive phenomenon, the Modern Missionary Movement with can be functionally dated from 1792–1992 although Roman Catholic missions to Africa predate the eighteenth century.[16] 1792 represents the era of formation of several missionary societies within the church that became instruments for foreign missions in Europe. The year 1992 is representative of the end of the inviolability of 'scientism'.[17] Perhaps even more than colonialism and imperialism, the Modern Missionary Movement is responsible in Africa for negative portrayals of African cultures, particularly religious beliefs and practices because of its twin agendas, the 'civilizing mandate' and conversion to Christianity. Colonists and imperialists were fundamentally concerned with control and exploitation, not transformation of the African. We noted how white settlers in South Africa initially opposed missionary activities aimed at civilizing Africans.

By contrast, negative portrayals of African realities in the Modern Missionary Movement generally undermined African societies, cultures and religious beliefs and practices. Ironically, the Bible was responsible for empowering Africans to rebel against European interpretations of the Bible and colonialism itself. Translation of the Bible into vernacular languages was a key activity for missionaries in their efforts to *convert* Africans to Christianity in keeping with the Protestant Principle to 'supply every man with the Holy Scriptures in his own mother-tongue'.[18] According to Lamin Sanneh, ability to access the Scriptures in vernacular languages unleashed a process of direct appropriation of the Bible by Africans that missionaries were not able to control. By this act, missionaries compromised their role as mediators of the message of the Bible to the African. This led to local criticism of missionary theories and practices and, on the political front, to the rise of nationalistic sentiments.[19] Notably, most (if not all) the leaders of African independent churches and political independence movements were graduates of missionary schools.

However, there were exceptions. For example, John Philip stood for the autonomy of Africans (against colonization) and racial equality in South Africa during the first half of the nineteenth century.[20] However, Ukpong's unsympathetic portrayal of missionary attitudes towards things African and how these inspired African biblical scholarship is generally accurate:

> The beginning of modern biblical studies in Africa . . . was in response to the widespread condemnation of African religion and culture in the Christian missionaries of the 19th and 20th centuries. African religion and culture were condemned as demonic and immoral and therefore to be exterminated before Christianity could take root in Africa.[21]

From the outset, Africans found the Scriptures, particularly the Old Testament, to be epistemologically and culturally familiar. Kwesi Dickson credits this with the 'African predilection for the Old Testament',[22] 'the Old Testament atmosphere that makes the African context a kindred atmosphere'.[23] Mercy Amba Oduyoye and Musimbi Kanyoro assert that, 'the Bible was written in a culture similar to our African culture.'[24] This familiarity was largely unacknowledged and even discouraged by missionaries given the popular view that African cultures and religious beliefs and practices were primitive and evil. In addition, Christian doctrine and practice tended to elevate the New Testament at the expense of the Old Testament. For example, some early missionaries in South Africa cautioned that Africans should have restricted access to the Old Testament lest they uncritically adopt practices in it as Christianity.[25] Consequently, converting to Christianity generally entailed renouncing one's African cultural roots, including exchanging your 'pagan' name for a 'Christian' (European or biblical) one.

Ngugi Wa Thiongo's life illustrates the disruptive nature of imperialism, colonialism and the Modern Missionary Movement for an African. He was born in 1938, a Gikuyu, Kenya's largest ethnic group. His father, a peasant farmer, was forced to become a squatter after the British imperial Act of 1915. Ngugi attended the mission run school in Limuru and eventually alliance High School in Kikuyu. During these years, he became a devout Christian. However, at school, he also learnt Gikuyu values and history and underwent the Gikuyu rite of passage ceremony. In 1963, he obtained a BA in English at Makerere University College in Kampala (Uganda) and worked as a journalist. In 1964, he left for England to pursue graduate studies at Leeds University. In 1964, while at school in England, he published his first novel, *Weep Not, Child*. He worked as a lecturer at several universities – the University College in Nairobi (1967–1969), Makerere University in Kampala (1969–1970) and Northwestern University in Evanston, the United States of America (1970–1971). He had resigned his faculty position at Nairobi University College as a protest against government interference in the university after criticizing the decision made by the British government in the 1950s making instruction in English mandatory. He rejoined this faculty in 1973 to chair the Literature Department. Later, he rejected Christianity, and, in 1976, changed his original name from James Ngugi, which he saw as a sign of colonialism, to Ngugi wa Thiong'o in honour of his Gikuyu heritage. In December 1977, he was imprisoned for a year without trial by the Kenyan Government on the orders of the then vice president, Daniel Arap Moi for writings that essentially attacked what he called 'neo-colonial elites' because they were corrupt and continued to champion Euro-centric values at the expense of indigenous ones. While in prison, he abandoned using English as the primary language of his work in favour of Gikuyu, his mother tongue. In 1982, he left Kenya to live in self-imposed exile abroad. He has since held several faculty positions elsewhere.[26]

Failure to acknowledge, harness and exploit this familiarity in missionary-originated churches led to breakaway movements, predominantly involving indigenous and charismatic converts. Perceived disparities between the teachings and practices of missionaries and those in the Bible, which often bore close resemblance to daily African realities, contributed to the rise of these movements and African independent churches:

> In the Bible, [Africans] discovered a Jesus who healed the sick, made the lame walk, and restored sight to the blind – a reality that held great attraction for them and that they sought to appropriate but which the Christian church to which they belonged consigned to the past history of Jesus. They discovered a Jesus who drove out demons from people and confronted the power of Satan, another reality they sought to actualize in their communities but which the church chose to ignore.[27]

A history of typology in African biblical scholarship

African nationalism and developments in the African academy aimed at the re-evaluation of African societies, cultures and religious beliefs and practices emerged from the same consciousness, during what Adogame calls the 'cultural-nationalist period of the 1950s and 1960s'.[28] African biblical scholarship may be understood as research that embraces and builds on these re-evaluations.

Comparative religions

Williams is often cited as the forerunner to such research. In *Hebrewisms of West Africa*,[29] he sought to show correlation between biblical Hebrew and *Ashanti*

(Ghana) based on phonetic similarities. He also sought similarities between the worship of deities (apart from *Yahweh*) in the Old Testament and *Ashanti* worship of 'God' and divinities. From these comparisons, he postulated either Jewish ancestry for the *Ashanti* or very early contact with Jews.[30]

Subsequent scholarship, the framework of Comparative Religion, focused on religious themes and practices as opposed to extrinsic resemblances. It faulted Williams' methodology and undermined his conclusions.[31] Initially Westerners sympathetic to the African cause and subsequently Africans sought to defend, redeem and legitimize African cultures and religious beliefs and practices. They explored continuities and discontinuities between the religious culture of Africa and the Bible, particularly the Old Testament, and generally sought to 'illustrate similarities in patterns of thought and feelings, and to show how certain basic notions have been expressed by people in different places and times.'[32]

Developments in Europe shaped this research. Tendencies in European rationality towards 'articulation,' 'systematisation' and 'generalisation of beliefs and other cultural concepts'[33] were introduced in Africa through missionaries and the new educated indigenous elite educated in systems patterned after European universities or in Europe. For example, E. G. Parrinder justified his synchronistic comparative approach to African Traditional Religion(s) because they lacked texts and therefore could not yield histories.[34]

Scholars extrapolated 'key' categories from data from specific ethnic groups into 'a common Africanness' and used these categories to analyse African cultures and societies, and African Traditional Religions. Parrinder revised E. W. Smith's categories ('Supreme Being', 'a sense of dynamic power', and 'localised kinship focus on ancestral spirits')[35] to 'Supreme Being,' 'Chief divinities' (generally non-human), 'the cult of ancestors', and 'powers associated with charms and amulets'.[36] Portrayals of African social–cultural and religious realities in sources like Mbiti's *African Religions and Philosophy* (1969),[37] or Kagame's writings from this period on Bantu philosophy[38] reflect such research.

Later research is generally more critical of synchronic views of African societies, cultures and religious traditions although it makes concessions to demonstrable synchronic bases for understanding African realities. For example, Platvoet acknowledges the unusually high incidence of language similarities among the Bantu-speaking parts of Africa. He attributes these to the so-called glottochronological depth, the difference in time between two related languages, or families, to a hypothetical parent language, from which linguists assume they both developed. This is supposedly a theoretical device for explaining both the differential development and the similarities between two modern languages or groups of languages. Thus, the Bantu have a 'glottochronological depth' of 2000 years while that for West and Sudanic Africa is 5000 years (leading to the greater number of languages and diversity there).[39] Historical considerations also suggest a common past for the Bantu. For example, histories of migrations for Bantu ethnic groups in southern Africa trace their origins to the Luba Lunda empires of the upper Congo basin.[40]

In Europe, liberal theology began to produce missionaries who progressively broke ranks with their more radical predecessors in their views of African societies, cultures and, in particular, African traditional religions.

> These dropped the *vera/falsa religio* dichotomy of traditional Christian orthodoxy, and postulated on various theological grounds that non-Christian religions were also proper religions, permitted, or even ordained by God, and with at least some function in the divine economy, and some salvific efficacy.[41]

This led to portrayals of African traditional religions in theological categories in order to identify continuities and discontinuities with Christianity. For example, Kiernan attributes the presence of the concept of 'Supreme Being' in Southern Bantu religions (with the exception of *Nomkhubulwana*, the Zulu goddess of spring) to 'conceptual conquest' by Christian missionaries.[42] Close examination reveals that African societies, as also the highly dynamic and adaptable African traditional religions, continually changed:

> Instead of being encumbered by rigidifying canonical scriptures in which some system of religious beliefs, deemed to have its source in a unique, complete, exclusive and immutable 'revelation', was codified, as are the so-called world religions, they consisted of complex combinations of several, loosely articulated, adaptable systems of belief, for example, in a creator God; in several types of gods and/or spirits of nature; and/or in ancestors and deceased of several sorts; in a constantly renewable collection of charms and 'medicines'; in witches and/or sorcerers; in oracular devices, mantic procedures and spirit possession; in other beings, such as dwarfs, which are non-verifiable by empirical means etc.; and in cults: not only towards God, and gods, spirits, ancestors and 'medicines' of several sorts, but also related to several institutions, or sets of social relations.[43]

Studies from this period include Mbiti's *New Testament Eschatology*,[44] Bolaji Idowu's *God in Nigerian Belief*[45] and Kwesi Dickson's several publications, including 'The Old Testament and African Theology' in the *Ghana Bulletin of Theology* (1973). 'Theology' in these studies betrays the fact that they generally sought to explore the evident familiarity of the Bible to Africans, particularly the Old Testament, within an apologetic agenda.

Such studies extend to 1980s and 1990s and include the work of African scholars trained in biblical studies. Most colonies attained political and ecclesiastical independence (exceptions include the then North-West Africa, Southern Rhodesia and South Africa) during the 1960s. This decade also witnessed the 'rapid growth of theological seminaries and university departments of religion throughout the continent, and . . . a sudden wave of publications on Africa and the OT.'[46] However, African biblical scholars with higher degrees during this period were foreign-trained, typically in Europe and the United States of America.[47] Ukpong's *Sacrifice, African and Biblical: A Comparative Study of Ibibio and Levitical Sacrifices* (1987)[48] is typical of their scholarly output.

At this stage, distinguishing between studies under the Comparative Religions framework and African biblical studies is academic. The former were judged to be weak because they were merely apologetic and polemical. Their value was merely heuristic, to consolidate the view that African culture and religion(s) are *praeparatio evangelica*. They raised the profile of African culture and religion and 'helped to articulate the values of African culture and religion for the appropriation of Christianity'.[49]

African biblical scholarship

Studies under the Comparative Religions framework 'remain foundational to all biblical studies that link the biblical text to the African context'.[50] Ukpong regards the 1970s–1990s to be 'the most dynamic and rewarding periods of biblical studies in Africa.' During this time, the reactive approach gradually gives way to the proactive approach.

> The African context is used as a resource in the hermeneutic encounter with the Bible, and the religious studies framework characteristic of the former phase gives way to a more theological framework. Two main approaches, which can be identified as inculturation and liberation crystallize.[51]

'Inculturation', unlike 'enculturation', is a term generated in the context of theology in reference to the process of relating the Gospel to culture. 'Enculturation', generated from the social sciences, is

> the process of learning about a new cultural tradition through, for example, the process of socialization into that culture. It is process by which a person, as a kind of *tabula rasa*, is introduced to and gradually learns and grows into a particular culture.[52]

The difficulty, even impossibility of any person overcoming their 'enculturation' is at the heart of the debate concerning the possibility of scholars to be 'critical' in the sense of surmounting their 'enculturation' in order to analyse material as 'objective' researchers.

Sanneh situates 'inculturation' within 'enculturation':

> The inculturation of Christianity is not a one-way process through which the Christian faith and way of life are superimposed on a culture; rather, through

inculturation, Christian teachings and practices are integrated into the given culture, and the local culture and practices in turn are integrated in the Christian message. In other words, there must be a mutual and critical dialogue and integration.[53]

The Comparative Religions approach did not lead to inculturation: 'Christianity in Africa was still looked upon as a foreign religion expressed in foreign symbols and idiom.'[54] African biblical studies seek to remedy this anomaly predominantly through two models: *Africa-in-the-Bible* and the *Evaluative* studies.

Africa-in-the-Bible studies:

Investigate the presence of Africa and African people in the Bible and the significance of such presence. The overall purpose is to articulate Africa's influence on the history of ancient Israel and Africa's contribution to the history of salvation, as well as correct negative interpretations of some biblical texts on Africa. . . . They belong to the same category of studies as those which, in the field of philosophy, have been able to show the contribution of Ancient African nations to world culture.[55]

They often take one of two directions. They attempt to correct negative images about Africa and African peoples embedded in certain traditional readings of some biblical texts such as the so-called curse of Ham.

Ham's descendants were Cush (Ethiopians), Mizraim (Egypt), Phut and Canaan.[56] Ham saw the nakedness of his drunken father and, instead of covering him, informs his two brothers. The two took a garment, walked backwards and covered him without seeing his nakedness. When Noah woke up and realized what had happened, he cursed Canaan, Ham's descendant, to be a 'servant of servants', to his brethren.[57]

A fifth century AD *midrash* on this narrative places Noah's curse directly on Ham as: 'Your seed will be ugly and dark-skinned.'[58] The sixth century AD Babylonian Talmud states: 'The descendants of Ham are cursed by being black and are sinful with degenerate progeny.'[59] Such interpretations led to the idea that Africans were black *because of* the curse of Ham. Whites in South Africa used such interpretations as support for their subjugation of blacks. *Africa-in-the-Bible* studies seek to show that such interpretations have no basis in the text. For example, see David Tuesday Adamo's work.[60]

They also seek to make explicit the presence of Africa and contributions of Africans in the Bible thereby targeting perceptions of de-emphasis and exclusion regarding Africa in Western scholarship. A keen subject of debate is whether Egypt belongs to the ancient Near East or Africa. *Africa-in-the-Bible* studies are not concerned with the search for theological meaning for contemporary Africans.

Their 'value' lies in creating awareness of the importance of Africans in the biblical story.[61]

Evaluative studies focus on the encounter between African religion and culture, and the Bible, and evaluate the theological consequences of that encounter:

> They go beyond similarities and dissimilarities between African religion and [culture] and the Bible to interpreting the biblical text on the basis of these similarities and differences. The aim is to facilitate the communication of the biblical message within the African milieu, and to evolve a new understanding of Christianity that would be African and biblical. Generally, the historical-critical method is used for the analysis of the biblical text, and anthropological or sociological approaches are used in analysing the African situation.[62]

Up to five approaches may be isolated within this model.

1. Evaluating elements of African culture(s), religion(s), beliefs, concepts or practices in the light of the biblical witness in order to arrive at an understanding of both and bring out their value for Christian witness.[63] Examples include Kalilombe's[64] and McFall's[65] works.
2. Critique from a biblical text or theme of a particular issue in African society and finding the lessons that may be drawn from the text for a particular context.

This differs from (1) above in that there 'the contextual realities studied are assumed to be values or at least contain values whereas [here] they are presented as liabilities to be challenged by the biblical message.'[66]

Examples of such scholarship include Igenoza's critique of the practice of medicine and healing in African Christianity,[67] Manus's use of Paul (attitudes towards ethnicity) to critique ethnic discrimination in Nigeria,[68] and Abe's treatment of the relevance of the Old Testament concept of 'covenant' for Nigerian society.[69]

3. Interpreting biblical themes or texts against the background of African culture, religion and life experience. The goal is to facilitate a new understanding of the biblical texts that is informed by the African situation and would be both African and Christian. This approach, more than the others, takes seriously the premise of the 'enculturation' of every interpreter of the Bible. As such, it logically leads (or should lead) to a critique of the nature and practice of the historical method. Examples include Wambudta's[70] and Abijole's[71] works.
4. Erecting bridges for communicating the biblical message. The major concerns here are homiletical (communication) rather than exegetical and the goal is to make use of concepts from either the Bible or African culture and

Christianity in aid of comprehension. For example, John Pobee has identified 'kinship' and the anthropological concept of 'grand ancestor' (a familiar concept to Africans) in his Akan (Ghana) context as key concepts for communicating Christ's humanity in Christology.[72] Conversely, John Mbiti has identified New Testament images of Christ as 'miracle worker' and 'risen Lord' as those that Africans can easily identify with 'because they show Jesus as the conqueror of evil spirits, disease and death'.[73] Diane Stinton's *Jesus of Africa* includes several other such themes.[74]

5. The study of biblical texts to discover biblical models or foundations for aspects of contemporary church life and practice in Africa. For example, Buetubela has studied the relationship between the churches in Jerusalem and Antioch, with mission churches and has shown how it was marked by autonomy as opposed to dependence. Using this model, he argues for the development of autonomy for young churches in Africa.[75]

Joseph Osei-Bonsu[76] and Ukpong[77] have argued for an African 'inculturation' of Christianity because they see biblical antecedents for it. As noted above, Lamin Sanneh sees this process as integral to the 'translatability' of Christianity everywhere and argues that it is well under way in Africa.

Evaluative studies are the most common approach to biblical studies in Africa today. Through them, African culture(s) and religions have advanced from being *praeparatio evangelica* to becoming '*indispensable resources in the interpretation of the gospel message* and the development of African Christianity'.[78]

A third model, *Liberation*, deserves mention. Influenced by socialist ideology and driven by a need for theology to engage with secular issues, it finds expression in biblical interpretation as *liberation hermeneutics, black theology* and *feminist hermeneutics. Liberation* scholars have criticized *Evaluative* approaches for not paying attention to social, economical and political issues in Africa today.[79]

> *Liberation hermeneutics* uses the Bible as a resource in the struggle against oppression of any kind based on the assumption that the Bible does not sanction oppression and that God sides with the oppressed. In African contexts (except South Africa), political and economic oppression are often in mind and Exodus is often the key text. Examples include the works of Jean-Marc Ela[80] and Canaan Banana.[81]
>
> *Black theology* is race-focused and typically the preserve of black South Africans. Black consciousness[82] is its point of departure and the Bible is used as a resource from two perspectives: (1) as a liberating book quite opposed to Apartheid and on the side of the oppressed[83] and (2) as a book written by elites to serve their interests and to be read critically as a resource for liberation.[84] The latter reflects the fact that the Apartheid regime used the Bible to subjugate blacks. However, it employs *Marxist* and *liberal-Western* presuppositions and methods, not African ones.

Feminist hermeneutics focuses on the oppression of women and uses the Bible as a resource for the struggle against the subordination of women in contemporary society and church life. Since the Bible has also been used to support this subordination, a feminist critique of the Bible and conventional modes of interpretation is part of feminist hermeneutics. At least five approaches are evident.

1. Challenging conventional hermeneutics by which Scripture and the history of Christianity are interpreted in androcentric terms, including the assumption that God is male to the exclusion of female attributes and the corollary rendering of God using the masculine pronoun. A key proponent is Mercy Oduyoye.[85]
2. Critique or interpretation of biblical texts that are perceived to oppress women or portray them as inferior to men through 'a close reading' of such texts 'in their literary and cultural contexts.'[86]
3. Focus on texts that show the positive role of women in the history of salvation or in the life of the church. Examples include the works of Anne Nasimiyu-Wasike,[87] Joyce Tzabedze[88] and Mbuy-Beya.[89]
4. Inquiry into biblical theological themes that can function as guide in interpreting both negative and positive texts. For example, Oduyoye uses the 'theology of creation' to affirm the basic equality of man and woman as created in the image of God.[90]
5. Interpreting biblical texts from the perspective of African women's experience. For example, Nasimiyu-Wasike has interpreted stories of polygamy in the Old Testament from an African woman's experience and argued that the Old Testament itself contains a critique of this institution, contrary to the common assumption that it extols it.[91]

Proponents of feminist hermeneutics use a vast array of tools, including historical and literary criticism, and other disciplines like sociology and anthropology.[92]

Further developments

Further developments build on the above. For example, in his quest to make 'ordinary readers' (i.e. non-biblical scholars) important partners in the academic study of the Bible, Gerald West's[93] 'contextual method' intentionally brings 'ordinary readers' and their concrete situations into the equation with a commitment to transformation.[94]

His methodology involves interaction between academic and ordinary readers. 'Ordinary readers' bring their culture and historical life experiences to the task or interpretation to complement conventional critical tools of biblical exegesis. In this way, academic biblical scholarship is directly relevant to the community of believers.

His design to incorporate relevance to the task of reading the Bible is commendable. However, from an inculturation perspective, the 'complimentary' role of 'ordinary' readings to 'academic' ones needs further clarification. West does not address the critical matter of the epistemological conventions at play in the 'conventional critical tools' of 'academic' readings, those of 'ordinary' readers and those in the texts and the epistemological relationships among them in the interpretation process.

Justin Ukpong's 'inculturation hermeneutics' builds on the third approach under *Evaluative studies*. He both urges critical awareness of one's context and that of the biblical text under examination and wants to address both 'relevance' and 'inculturation' by making the African the 'subject' of interpretation. His goal is the 'actualisation of the theological meaning of the text in today's context so as to forge integration between faith and life, and engender commitment to personal transformation.' The 'root paradigm of African culture' that informs his interpretive framework includes the following: (1) reality as holistic (not matter vs. spirit, sacred vs. profane, visible vs. invisible); (2) divine origin of the universe; (3) interconnectedness between God, humanity and the cosmos and (4) individuality within community (as opposed to apart from it).[95]

Scholars in the field of African Religious Studies have criticized the inclusion of (2) and (3) in a 'root paradigm of African culture' because they supposedly reflect the influence of Christian doctrines rather than African beliefs in themselves.[96] The contention is that African beliefs scarcely address the questions of the 'origin of the universe' or the 'interconnectedness between God, humanity and the cosmos.' However, in that these are finer points arising from 'reality as holistic' (1) and 'individuality within community' (4), such differences do not detract from the spirituality and holistic nature of the African 'culture' or worldview.

This, then, is the theatre where Africans are pitting their concerns and enculturation against the Bible and histories of its interpretation elsewhere. In the words of Ukpong, 'African questions are now being put to the Bible and African resources are being used in the answering of them.'[97]

Notes

[1] G. W. H. Lampe, 'The Reasonableness of Typology' in *Essays in Typology*, ed. G. W. H. Lampe and K. J. Woollcombe (London: SCM, 1957), p. 18.

[2] Mugambi sees African cultural predilection for biblical traditions as extending to the synoptic Gospels. J. N. K. Mugambi, 'Foundations for an African Approach to Biblical Hermeneutics' in *Interpreting the New Testament in Africa*, ed. M.N. Getui, Tinyiko Maluleke, and Justin Ukpong (Nairobi: Acton Publishers, 2001), p. 16.

[3] R. S. Sugirtharajah, *The Bible in the Third World: Precolonial, Colonial and Postcolonial Encounters* (Cambridge: Cambridge University Press, 2001), p. 177.

[4] S. A. Crowther, 'Brief Statements exhibiting the characters, habits and ideas of the Natives of the Bight' 1874; C.M.S. CA3/04. Cited in J. F. A. Ajayi, *Christian Missions in Nigeria 1841–1891* (London: Green and Co. Ltd., 1965), p. 133.

[5] Ngugi Wa Thiong'o, Decolonising the Mind: The Politics of Language in African Literature (London: James Currey Ltd., 1986).

[6] E.g. in James Barr, *The Semantics of Biblical Language* (Oxford: Oxford University Press, 1961).

[7] E.g. R. Descartes, *Discourse on Method, Optics, Geometry, and Meteorology*, trans. Paul J. Olscamp (New York: The Bobbs-Merril Co., Inc., 1965), pp. 4–5. Smith claims that there are 'self-evident criteria' or 'empirical transcendentals' within the object interpreted. J. K. A. Smith, *The Fall of Interpretation: Philosophical Foundations for a Creational Hermeneutic* (Downers Grove, Illinois: InterVarsity Press, 2000), p. 169.

[8] For example, historicity was a key principle in the biblical exegesis of Renaissance humanists such as Erasmus and Calvin. Gerald Bray, *Biblical Interpretation: Past and Present* (Downer's Grove, Illinois: InterVarsity Press, 1996), pp. 221–222.

[9] B. S. Childs, *Old Testament Theology in a Canonical Context* (London: SCM Press Ltd, 1985), p. 14.

[10] E. S. Gerstenberger, 'Canon Criticism and the Meaning of "Sitz Im Leben"' in *Canon, Theology, and Old Testament Interpretation*, ed. G. M. Tucker, D. L. Petersen, and R. R. Wilson (Philadelphia: Fortress Press, 1988), p. 27. However, Bultmann 'limited preconception to intellectual, emotional and religious dispositions'.

[11] John Barton, *Reading the Old Testament: Method in Biblical Study*, New ed. (London: Darton, Longman and Todd, 1996), pp. 26–28.

[12] Childs, 14. Cf. p. 12.

[13] See the lecture by Professor Andrew Walls, 'The Appropriation of Christianity in Africa: Three Historic Modes' (Edinburgh: University of Edinburgh, 2007).

[14] Frieder Ludwig and Afe Adogame, 'Introduction: Historiography and European Perceptions of African Religious History' in *European Traditions in the Study of Religion in Africa*, ed. Frieder Ludwig and Afe Adogame (Wiesbaden: Harrossowitz Verlag, 2004), p. 7. Andrew Ross dates the so-called scramble for Africa within the decade 1885–1895. A. C. Ross, *David Livingstone: Mission and Empire* (London, England: Hambledon and London, 2002), p. 241.

[15] Richard Werbner, 'Multiple Identities, Plural Arenas' in *Postcolonial Identities in Africa*, ed. Richard Werbner and Terence Ranger (London and New Jersey: Zed Books Ltd., 1996), p. 8.

[16] W. A. Smalley, Translation as Mission: Bible Translation in the Modern Missionary Movement. The Modern Missionary Era, 1792–1992: An Appraisal (Macon, Georgia: Mercer University Press, 1991), pp. xi–x.

[17] '1: Methods and attitudes typical of or attributed to the natural scientist 2: an exaggerated trust in the efficacy of the methods of natural science applied in all areas of investigation (as in philosophy, the social sciences, and the humanities).' *Merriam-Webster's Collegiate Dictionary*, 10 ed. (Springfield, Massachusetts: William-Webster Incorporated, 1996), p. 1046.

[18] Have Ye Never Read?: A Popular Report of the British and Foreign Bible Society 1910-1913 (London: The Bible House, 1913), p. 145.

[19] Lamin Sanneh, *Translating the Message: The Missionary Impact on Culture* (Maryknoll, NY: Orbis Books, 1989), pp. 1, 62, 172–173, 193; '"They Stooped to Conquer": Vernacular Translation and the Social-Cultural Factor' in *Research in African Literatures* 23, no. 1 (1992): 106.

[20] See A. C. Ross, 'John Philip 1775–1851: Standing for Autonomy and Racial Equality' in *Mission Legacies: Biographical Studies of Leaders of the Modern Missionary Movement*, ed. G. H. Anderson (Maryknoll, NY: Orbis Books, 1994).

21 J. S. Ukpong, 'Developments in Biblical Interpretation in Africa: Historical and Hermeneutical Directions' in *The Bible in Africa: Transactions, Trajectories and Trends*, ed. Gerald O. West and Musa W. Dube (Leiden, Boston, MA and Köln: Brill, 2000), p. 12.

22 K. A. Dickson, *Theology in Africa* (Maryknoll, NY and London: Orbis Books and Darton, Longman and Todd Ltd., 1984), p. 145.

23 K.A. Dickson, 'The Old Testament and African Theology' in *The Ghana Bulletin of Theology* 4, no. 4 (1973): 141–184.

24 M. A. Oduyoye and M. R. A. Kanyoro, *The Will to Arise: Women, Tradition, and the Church in Africa* (Maryknoll, NY: Orbis Books, 1995), p. 4.

25 G. E. Philips, *The Old Testament in the World Church* (Guildford: Lutterworth, 1942), pp. 6–10.; B. G. M. Sundkler, *Bantu Prophets in South Africa* (Oxford: Oxford University Press, 1961), p. 277.

26 *Ngugi Wa Thiong'o (1938–) – Formerly Known as James Ngugi*, available from http://www.kirjasto.sci.fi/ngugiw.htm. Accessed 7 February 2007).

27 J. S. Ukpong, 'Rereading the Bible with African Eyes: Inculturation and Hermeneutics' in *Journal of Theology for Southern Africa*, no. 91 (1995): 3.

28 Ludwig and Adogame, pp. 14–15, 18.

29 Cf. J. J. Williams, *Hebrewisms of West Africa: From the Nile to Niger with the Jews* (London: 1930; reprint, New York: Biblo and Tanner, 1967).

30 *Ibid.*, p. 7.

31 Ukpong, 'Developments in Biblical Interpretation' p. 6.

32 *Ibid.*, p. 5.

33 Jan G. Platvoet, 'From Object to Subject: A History of the Study of the Religions of Africa' in *The Study of Religions in Africa: Past, Present and Prospects*, ed. Jan Platvoet, James Cox, and Jacob Olupona (Cambridge: Roots and Branches, 1996), p. 113.

34 *Ibid.*, p. 115.

35 E. W. Smith, African Beliefs and Christian Faith: An Introduction to Theology for African Students, Evangelists and Pastors (London: The United Society for Christian Literature, 1936), p. 29; and African Ideas of God: A Symposium (London: Edinburgh House Press, 1950), p. 34.

36 James L. Cox, A Guide to the Phenomenology of Religion: Key Figures, Formative Influences and Subsequent Debates (London and New York: T & T Clark International, 2006), p. 148.

37 J. S. Mbiti, *African Religions and Philosophy* (London: Heinemann, 1969).

38 E.g. A. Kagame, *La Philosophie Bantu Comparee* (Paris: 1976).

39 Jan G. Platvoet, 'The Religions of Africa in Their Historical Order' in *The Study of Religions in Africa: Past, Present and Prospects*, ed. Jan Platvoet, James Cox and Jacob Olupona (Cambridge: Roots and Branches, 1996), pp. 53–55.

40 Brian M. Fagan, ed., *A Short History of Zambia from the Earliest Times until A.D. 1900* (London, England: Oxford University Press, 1966), p. 103.

41 Platvoet, 'From Object to Subject', pp. 111–112.

42 Platvoet, 'Religions of Africa', p. 55, note 39.

43 *Ibid.*, p. 55.

44 J. S. Mbiti, *New Testament Eschatology in an African Background: A Study of the Encounter Between New Testament Theology and African Traditional Concepts* (London: London University Press, 1971).

[45] E. B. Idowu, *God in Nigerian Belief* (Lagos: Federal Ministry of Information, 1963).

[46] Knut Holter, *Yahweh in Africa*, Bible and Theology in Africa, vol. 1 (New York: Peter Lang, 2001), pp. 10, 45.

[47] *Ibid.*, p. 12.

[48] J. S. Ukpong, Sacrifice, African and Biblical: A Comparative Study of Ibibio and Levitical Sacrifices (Rome: Urbaniana University Press, 1987).

[49] Ukpong, 'Developments in Biblical Interpretation', p. 6.

[50] *Ibid.*

[51] *Ibid.*, p. 7.

[52] Joseph Osei-Bonsu, 'The Inculturation of Christianity in Africa', ed. Johannes Buetler, Werner Kahl and Thomas Schmeller, *New Testament Studies in Contextual Exegesis* (Frankfurt: Peter Lang, 2005), p. 19.

[53] *Ibid.*, p. 21. Cf. Sanneh, *Translating the Message*.

[54] Ukpong, 'Developments in Biblical Interpretation' p. 7.

[55] *Ibid.* Cf. C. Williams, The Destruction of Black Civilization: Great Issues of a Race from 4500 B.C. to A.D. 2000 (Chicago: Third World Press, 1976).

[56] Gen. 10.1–14, esp. v.6, and 1 Chronicles 1.8–16, esp. v.8.

[57] Gen. 9.18–27.

[58] Gene Rice, 'The Curse That Never Was (Genesis 18–27)' in *Journal of Religious Thought* 29 (1972): 17, 25. Cited in Ukpong, 'Developments in Biblical Interpretation', p. 8.

[59] Ephraim Isaac, 'Genesis, Judaism and the Sons of Ham' in *Slavery and Abolition* 1, no. 1 (1980): 4–5.

[60] E.g. David T. Adamo, 'The Table of Nations Reconsidered in African Perspective (Genesis 10)' in *Journal of African Religion and Philosophy* 2 (1993): 138–143. Cf. M. Prior, *The Bible and Colonialism* (Sheffield: Sheffield Academic Press, 1997). For similar work from an African-American perspective, see C. H. Felder, ed., *Stony the Road We Trod: African American Biblical Interpretation* (Philadelphia, PA: Fortress Press, 1991).

[61] Ukpong, 'Developments in Biblical Interpretation', pp. 8–9.

[62] *Ibid.*, 9.

[63] *Ibid.*

[64] P. Kalilombe, 'The Salvific Value of African Religions: A Contextual Bible Reading for Africa' in Christianisme Et Idente' Africanine: Point De Vue Exegetique – Actes Du Ier Congress Des Biblistes Africaines, Kinshasa, 26–30 Decembre 1978, ed. A. Angang (Kinshasa: Facultes Catholiques de Theologie, 1980), pp. 205–220.

[65] E. A. McFall, *Approaching the Nuer through the Old Testament* (Pasadena: William Carey Library, 1970).

[66] Ukpong, 'Developments in Biblical Interpretation', p. 10.

[67] A. D. Igenoza, 'Medicine and Healing in African Christianity: A Biblical Critique' in *Africa Ecclesial Review* 30 (1988): 12–25.

[68] C. Manus, 'Galatians 3:28 - a Study of Paul's Attitude towards Ethnicity: Its Relevance for Contemporary Nigeria' in *Ife Journal of Religion* 2 (1982). 18–26.

[69] G. O. Abe, '*Berith*: Its Impact on Israel and Its Relevance to the Nigerian Society' in *Africa Journal of Biblical Studies* 1 (1986): 66–73.

[70] D. N. Wambudta, 'Savannah Theology: A Reconstruction of the Biblical Concept of Salvation in the African Context' in *Bulletin of African Theology* 3, no. 6 (1981): 137–153.

[71] B. Abijole, 'St. Paul's Concept of Principalities and Powers in African Context' in *Africa Theological Journal* 17, no. 2 (1988): 118–129.

[72] J. S. Pobee, *Towards an African Theology* (Nashville: Abingdon Press, 1979), pp. 88–94.

[73] J. S. Mbiti, 'Some African Concepts of Christology' in *Christ and the Younger Churches*, ed. George F. Vicedom (London: SPCK, 1972), p. 54.

[74] D. B. Stinton, 'Jesus of Africa: Voices of Contemporary African Christology from Selected Textual and Oral Sources' (PhD, The University of Edinburgh, 2001).

[75] Ukpong, 'Developments in Biblical Interpretation', p. 11.

[76] Osei-Bonsu; J. Osei-Bonsu, 'The Contextualization of Christianity: Some New Testament Antecedents' in *Irish Biblical Studies* 12, no. 3 (1990): 129–148.

[77] J. S. Ukpong, 'Inculturation and Evangelization: Biblical Foundations for Inculturation' in *Vidyajyoti* 58, no. 5 (1994): 298–307.

[78] Ukpong, 'Developments in Biblical Interpretation', p. 11.

[79] *Ibid.*

[80] Jean-Marc Ela, 'Christianity and Liberation in Africa' in *Paths of African Theology*, ed. R. Gibellini (Maryknoll, NY: Orbis Books, 1994), pp. 146–147.

[81] Canaan Banana, *The Gospel According to Ghetto* (Gwero: Mambo Press, 1981).; Canaan Banana, *Theology of Promise* (Harare: College Press, 1982).

[82] 'Black' here includes all those discriminated against under Apartheid.

[83] E.g. Desmond Tutu, 'The Theology of Liberation in Africa' in *African Theology En Route*, ed. Kofi Appiah-Kubi and Sergio Torres (Maryknoll, NY: Orbis Books, 1979), p. 166.

[84] E.g. I. J. Mosala, *Biblical Hermeneutics and Black Theology in South Africa* (Grand Rapids, MI: Wm. B. Eerdmans Publishing House, 1989), pp. 13–42. Mosala uses a historical–materialist analysis to 'expose the interests of the elites'. Ukpong, 'Developments in Biblical Interpretation', p. 13.

[85] E.g. M. A. Oduyoye, 'Violence against Women: A Challenge to Christian Theology' in *Journal of Inculturation Theology* 1, no. 1 (1994): 47. Cf. Oduyoye and Kanyoro, *Will to Arise*.

[86] For example, Teresa Okure argues that 'the creation of Eve from Adam's rib, far from denoting a situation of inferiority . . . denotes their identity in nature, their destined marital status and their equality.' T. Okure, 'Biblical Perspectives on Women: Eve, the Mother of All the Living (Gen 3:20)' in *Voices from the Third World* 8, no. 3 (1985): 82–92.

[87] A. Nasimiyu-Wasike, 'Christology and an African Woman's Experience' in *Faces of Jesus in Africa*, ed. Robert Schreiter (Maryknoll, NY: Orbis Books, 1991), pp. 73–80.

[88] J.S Tzabedze, 'Women in the Church (1 Timothy 2.8–15, Ephesians 5.22)' in *New Eyes for Reading: Biblical and Theological Reflections by Women from the Third World*, ed. J. Pobee and Barbel von Wartenberg-Potter (Geneva: WCC, 1986), pp. 76–79.

[89] M. B. Mbuy-Beya, 'Doing Theology as African Women' in *Voices from the Third World* 13, no. 1 (1990).

[90] Oduyoye, 'Violence against Women' pp. 48–51.

[91] A. Nasimiyu-Wasike, 'Polygamy: A Feminist Critique' in *The Will to Arise*, ed. M.A. Oduyoye and Musimbi R.A. Kanyoro (Maryknoll: Orbis Books, 1992), pp. 108–116.

[92] Ukpong, 'Developments in Biblical Interpretation', p. 15.

[93] See G. O. West, *Biblical Hermeneutics of Liberation: Modes of Reading the Bible in the South African Context*, second ed. (Maryknoll, NY: Orbis Books, 1995); G. O. West, *Contextual Bible Study* (Pietermaritzburg: Cluster Publications, 1993).

[94] Ukpong, 'Developments in Biblical Interpretation', pp. 15–16.

[95] J. S. Ukpong, 'Towards a Renewed Approach to Inculturation Theology' in *Journal of Inculturation Theology* 1 (1994): 3–15.

[96] E.g. Okot p'Bitek, *African Religions in Western Scholarship* (Nairobi: East African Publishing Bureau, 1971), p. 105.

[97] Ukpong, 'Developments in Biblical Interpretation', p. 18.

Chapter 8

Prophetic Ministry Amid Conflict in Africa

Diane Stinton

I watched with fascination as he sipped his coffee from a large brown earthenware mug. Carefully but deftly, the claw hand on his prosthetic arm tightened around the mug and in a relaxed manner, he brought it to his lips. A certain gentleness, perhaps even shyness, exuded his one good eye as he examined our group of forty or so international scholars in mission studies. He then called us together, that quiet Sunday afternoon, 23 January 2000, at a Dutch Reformed Church in Pretoria, South Africa, and in a steady voice with deep passion, began to tell us his story.[1]

Born in New Zealand, Father Michael Lapsley trained for the priesthood in Australia and joined the Anglican Society of the Sacred Mission (SSM). In 1973 his religious community transferred him to South Africa, where he studied at the University of Natal in Durban and subsequently became the National Chaplain of Anglican Students. By his own confession, he expected to find three groups of people in South Africa: the oppressed, the oppressors and a third group of 'humanity'. However, he found that no such third group existed, and he felt caught in the duality of either being one of the oppressors or the oppressed. At the time he was a convinced pacifist, which he notes is untypical of Anglicans. Yet he explains that the turning point came in 1976 with the Soweto Uprising and the killing of schoolchildren that 'changed me very radically.'[2] He began speaking out against the torture and killing of schoolchildren, and as a result, he was expelled from South Africa that same year.

Fr Lapsley then went to Lesotho, where he continued in ministry as a priest and also joined the African National Congress (ANC) of South Africa. In 1979–1980 the first indications came that he was likely on a South African government hit list. At the end of 1982 the South African Defence Force attacked Lesotho and shot dead 42 people. Although Fr Lapsley happened to be away at the time, the Church authorities believed he was a key target in the attack and therefore forced him to leave Lesotho.

From there he went to Zimbabwe, where he lived from 1983 to 1992 and served as a Chaplain of the ANC, engaging in educational, pastoral and theological work. In 1988 the Zimbabwe authorities confirmed that he was on a South African Government Hit List, and therefore placed him under 24 hour armed police guard. Reflecting on his situation, he explains:

I came to the conclusion that the only way that I could be a threat to the apartheid system was because of my theology, because I believed that apartheid was a choice and an option for death carried out in the name of the Gospel of Life, and my work was the work of mobilising the Religious Community in South Africa and internationally, to oppose apartheid as an issue of faith.[3]

After 2 years of living as a hostage within his own home, he began to relax only after the news that Nelson Mandela was to be freed from prison on 2 February 1990. Following assurances from Magnus Malan that there would be no further attacks on frontline states, Fr Lapsley's guards were removed.

Then on 28 April 1990, on the eve of the first talks between F. W. de Klerk's government in South Africa and the ANC, Fr Lapsley opened a package in the post which contained two religious magazines. Opening one of the magazines detonated a bomb which blew the ceiling off three rooms in the house and left a large hole in the floor. Miraculously, Fr Lapsley survived the blast. He recalls:

One of the extraordinary things was that I, and the doctors don't know why, I didn't become unconscious. I didn't go into shock. . . . I can still remember what happened, the actual explosion is still with me. I remember pain on a scale that I didn't think a human being could ever experience. I remember going into darkness, being thrown backwards by the force of the bomb. . . . It blew off my hands. I lost an eye, my ear drums were shattered. I think perhaps the most extraordinary thing of all was that I felt the presence of God with me. I felt also that Mary who had watched her son being crucified also understood what it was that I was going through.[4]

Many months of recovery followed, first in Harare and later in Australia, where he underwent extensive reconstructive surgery. During this prolonged process his struggle became, in his words, 'to get well, . . . to live my life as fully, as joyfully, as completely as possible, and that would be my victory'. He concludes:

I also realized that if I was filled with hatred, bitterness, self pity, desire for revenge, that they would have failed to kill the body but they would have killed the soul, and I would be a permanent victim. And today I would say that I see myself not simply as a survivor, but I am a victor over the evil and hatred and death that apartheid represented, a sign of the triumph of good.[5]

Fr Lapsley's experience of making the transition from victim, to survivor, and eventually to victor, was fuelled by his passion for participating in creating a different kind of world, particularly in South Africa. When he returned to Zimbabwe, now jobless, the Bishop who was supposed to employ him said, 'Ah well, you are disabled now, what can you do?' Lapsley replied, 'I think I can be more of a priest with no hands than I ever was with two hands.'[6] Certainly his ministry since then has borne out the truth of these words. After repatriating to South Africa in 1992, he became one of the first two employees of the Trauma Centre for Victims of Violence and Torture in Capetown. He continued in this post until 1998, when he helped launch the Institute for Healing of Memories. Over the years, he has developed a model for assisting faith communities in the process of healing from the psychological, emotional and spiritual wounds of violence. In addition, he has travelled extensively around the globe in his mission of reconciliation and healing, for example, to Rwanda, Eritrea, Zimbabwe, Uganda, Palestine, Sri Lanka, Northern Ireland, Germany, Australia, Fiji, and more recently to New York, to meet with those who lost loved ones in the terrorist attack on September 11, 2001.[7] Hence the fitting tribute from Archbishop Desmond Tutu, at the close of Fr Lapsley's testimony before the Truth and Reconciliation Commission:

> I in a way give thanks to God for what happened to Michael. It is a very difficult thing to say, but he knows that I am saying it . . . as one who loves him very dearly, because the Michael after the Bomb Outrage has been an incredible person. He has been an icon . . . a living example of the kind of thing that we are trying to help be incarnated, be enfleshed in our country.[8]

If a picture paints a thousand words, then a single portrait of prophetic ministry in the context of conflict speaks volumes. In Fr Michael Lapsley we find a powerful example of such prophetic ministry in the context of conflict in South Africa and beyond. Yet what exactly do we mean by prophetic ministry, and how is it exercised in relation to conflict, reconciliation, and healing today? What are some of the key insights offered by those currently involved in such ministry? And what resources are there for Christians today who are called to engage in peacemaking and reconciliation?

This essay provides a brief introduction to prophetic ministry in biblical tradition and then examines it in relation to conflict and reconciliation today. In addition to biblical and theological analysis, my methodological approach interweaves aspects of Fr Lapsley's narrative – not as a case study to be critiqued, nor as a hero to be idolized. Rather, following Desmond Tutu's observation above, Fr Lapsley serves as a true icon in the original Greek sense of *eikōn* as image – one who does indeed incarnate or enflesh the kind of ministry under consideration here – or in the religious definition of an icon as a portrait that opens up a window on spiritual reality. While he is simply one of a multitude of Christians across Africa who lend powerful witness to Christ midst situations of conflict, an in-depth look at his story serves to illuminate aspects of prophetic ministry.

Prophetic ministry in biblical tradition

While the literature on biblical prophecy is vast, a few summary comments will suffice for the purpose of this essay. First, contrary to common misconception, biblical prophecy was not primarily a matter of foretelling or predicting future events, as in soothsaying. While at times the prophets did make announcements concerning the future, the future dimension was inextricably linked to the present situation of the hearers, for example warning of impending judgement for present sin.[9] From the period of Israel's monarchy onwards, the classical prophets associated with the Old Testament prophetic literature increasingly used word – first spoken, then written oracles – as the predominant means for proclamation. Thus their primary function was to *forth*-tell, or 'to *speak* for God to their own contemporaries'.[10] Central themes included prophecies of judgement, which generally explain the reason for the judgement and exhort the audience to repent so as to avert the impending doom, and prophecies of salvation. Colin Brown sums up the all-encompassing concept of salvation as follows:

> Salvation becomes a reality in the renewal of the relationship between Israel and God, in the eschatological king (the messiah), in the new ordering of the cult, the renewal of the state and political liberation of the nation. Majestic representation of salvation is often followed by an explanation of the ground on which it is based: not the faithfulness or holiness of the people, in its zeal for God and the covenant, but the faithfulness, holiness, zeal and unconditional love of God alone.[11]

If the OT prophets were essentially spokespersons for God, then the clear corollary is that their message was not their own, but God's. Gordon Fee and Douglas Stuart note that 'the prophets were, on their own, neither radical social reformers nor innovative religious thinkers.'[12] Rather, they functioned to enforce the covenant that God had previously established with Israel, by announcing the blessings and curses that would ensue depending on Israel's faithfulness. Whoever violated the covenant, be they royalty (e.g., 2 Sam. 12.1–14; 24.11–17; Hos. 1.4), clergy (Hos. 4.4–11; Amos 7.17, Mal. 2.1–9), or any other individual or group, the prophets called them to account according to the covenant stipulations and pronounced God's word into the situation.

Likewise the New Testament materials on prophecy are complex, yet a strong line of continuity exists between the two testaments in terms of prophets proclaiming divinely inspired messages. Again, while prophets might know the past (Jn 4.19) or predict the future (cf. Acts 11.28), essentially they are not soothsayers or magicians but proclaimers of God's word. One main difference from OT prophecy, however, is that while there was a special group of prophets set apart for the ministry of prophecy in the NT, every member of the Christian community is now called to prophesy (Acts 2.4, 16–21; 4.31), or at least has the potential to do so. Paul in particular makes use of the verb *prophēteúō*, 'to prophesy' (11 of 28 occurrences), with the following range of meanings:

a. 'to proclaim a divinely imparted message' (1 Cor. 11:4-5); b. 'to foretell' (Mk. 7:6; Lk. 1:67), c. 'to bring to light something that is hidden' (Mk. 14:65),

d. 'to teach, admonish, comfort' (1 Cor. 14:3, 31), e. 'to glorify God ecstatically' (Acts 10:46-47), f. 'to have a prophetic gift' (Acts 21:9), and possibly g. 'to act as a prophet' (Mt. 7:22).[13]

In sum, the NT prophet spoke God's word to the people under inspiration of the Holy Spirit, and all prophesy was to be tested or 'discerned' by the Spirit-filled community. Just as the OT prophets were not religious innovators but reinforced the covenant law delivered by Moses, so the NT prophets were not sources of new doctrine in the Church but rather expounded the truth revealed by Christ and delivered by the apostles. As Gordon Fee concludes, '"Prophecy" was a widely expressed and widely experienced phenomenon, which had as its goal the building up of the people of God so as to come to maturity in Christ (Eph. 4.11–16).'

Finally, according to the biblical prophets of both the Old and New Covenants, that goal of spiritual maturity encompasses both orthodoxy, or right belief, and orthopraxy, or right action. A true prophet was one who not only *spoke* God's word with authenticity, but also one who *lived* out God's word with faithfulness and integrity, and usually at great personal cost – for example, Jeremiah and Hosea in the Old Testament, and John the Baptist and John the Apostle, the presumed writer in exile of the Apocalypse, in the New Testament. Conversely, a false prophet (*psuedoprophētēs*) was one who distorted God's word, who compromised it through personal disobedience, or who manipulated it to seek personal gain. Throughout the Scriptures, very harsh judgement was pronounced upon such false prophets, for example the Jewish magician in Acts 13.8 whom Paul denounced, and the prophetess Jezebel in Revelation 2.20 who is thoroughly castigated for misleading God's people. Prophetic ministry, then, essentially means proclaiming God's word, both orally and in action, to the contemporary context so as to call people back to covenant faithfulness to God, to humanity, and to the cosmos. It entails pronouncing God's judgement and declaring his salvation, so that God's people might grow in orthodoxy and orthopraxy – or in right relationship with God and with one other.

Prophetic ministry in relation to conflict today

If ever there was a 'kairos' moment for prophetic ministry in relation to conflict, that historical moment is now. Tragically, the twentieth century is considered to be the most violent of all centuries known to humanity, with estimates exceeding one hundred million who have died in wars and civil conflict.[14] Hostilities continue unabated in the twenty-first century with the unprecedented rise in international terrorism, the deepening geo-political polarizations across the planet, and the humanitarian disasters in places like Darfur. Just as conflicts rage on the global scene – for example, in the Middle East, in Afghanistan and Iraq – so they flare across the continent of Africa. According to a 2004 report from Human Rights Watch:

Over the last 10 years at least eighteen countries in Africa have been consumed by war, usually internal. At present there are several active conflicts in Africa – . . . Cote d'Ivoire, the Darfur region of Sudan, Northern Uganda, Burundi, and the Democratic Republic of Congo.[15]

In sum, and indicative of the ongoing conflicts globally, a recent report by the same organization highlights human rights abuses in Pakistan, Kenya, China and Somalia. It then condenses the current situation worldwide as follows:

In its *World Report 2008*, Human Rights Watch surveys the human rights situation in more than 75 countries. Human Rights Watch identified many human rights challenges in need of attention, including atrocities in Chad, Colombia, the Democratic Republic of Congo, Ethiopia's Ogaden region, Iraq, Somalia, Sri Lanka, and Sudan's Darfur region, as well as closed societies or severe repression in Burma, China, Cuba, Eritrea, Libya, Iran, North Korea, Saudi Arabia and Vietnam. Abuses in the 'war on terror' featured in France, Pakistan, the United Kingdom, and the United States, among others.[16]

Not only does conflict fill the news on the international and national scene, but a glance at any local newspaper reveals the extent of conflict within Kenyan society today: interpersonal discord, domestic disputes, organizational conflicts, church wrangles, ethnic clashes, rows over revising the Constitution, and the recent eruption of violence following the disputed parliamentary and presidential elections of 27 December 2007, resulting in hundreds of deaths and over three hundred thousand internally displaced persons (IDPs). Without a doubt, the experience of conflict is intrinsic to human existence, yet the need for conflict management and conflict resolution is perhaps more critical than ever before. Therefore, it is both timely and essential to consider what it means to exercise prophetic ministry in relation to conflict.

One of the leading theologians in this area is Robert Schreiter. On the basis of his work for justice and peace in various conflict zones around the world, Schreiter has become a leading proponent of reconciliation as a new paradigm for Christian mission. He acknowledges that there is no single understanding of reconciliation among human societies but that every culture has concepts of who needs to be involved in reconciliation, how it should be accomplished, what constitutes justice in the new situation and what marks the end of the reconciliation process.[17] Moreover, there is no single Christian understanding of reconciliation, as the concept has developed various nuances depending on the context and circumstances. Furthermore, no two situations in need of reconciliation are the same. Schreiter therefore contends that the best approach is to merely outline elements that must be considered in any process of reconciliation.

For Schreiter, these fundamental elements are summarized in the subtitle of his 1998 publication, *The Ministry of Reconciliation: Spirituality and Strategies.*

This volume follows his 1992 publication, *Reconciliation: Mission and Ministry in a Changing Social Order,* in which he reached the conclusion that 'reconciliation is more a spirituality than a strategy'. While certainly acknowledging specific tasks and measurable outcomes in a process of reconciliation, he insists that it cannot be reduced to a technical rationality of problem-solving strategies. Rather,

> [w]hat undergirds a successful process of reconciliation is a spirituality, a view of the world that recognizes and responds to God's reconciling action in that world. That is why reconciliation is largely discovered rather than achieved. We experience God's justifying and reconciling activity in our own lives and in our own communities, and it is from that experience that we are able to go forth in a ministry of reconciliation. Thus, reconciliation becomes a way of life, not just a set of discrete tasks to be performed and completed.[18]

Reflecting further on reconciliation as spirituality, Schreiter outlines two necessary faces of reconciliation: social and spiritual. Social reconciliation is concerned with providing structures and processes for a fractured society to be reconstructed as truthful and just. It entails dealing with the past, punishing wrongdoers and providing reparation as far as possible to the victims. Spiritual reconciliation is concerned with 'rebuilding shattered lives so that social reconciliation becomes a reality.'[19] Schreiter emphasizes that the state can appoint commissions to examine past evils, but it cannot legislate the healing of memories; it can punish wrongdoers, but it cannot guarantee forgiveness; it can attempt to set the conditions for making reconciliation possible, but it cannot itself affect the process. For this reason, secular non-governmental organizations (NGOs) often seek assistance from their religious counterparts in addressing the necessary spiritual dimension in conflict resolution. Yet even where indigenous cultures and Christian communities offer means of reconciliation, given the scale of need for it in the world today, Schreiter laments that it remains 'an elusive spiritual practice'. He therefore examines the spiritual dimensions of reconciliation from a Christian perspective.

The concept of reconciliation, he notes, is found throughout the Bible, with OT stories like the reunion of Isaac and Esau (Gen. 33) and of Joseph and his brothers (Gen. 45), as well as NT parables like the lost sheep and the prodigal son (Lk. 15). However the term 'reconciliation' is used only 13 times in the NT, and exclusively in the Pauline corpus. The Greek term *katallassein* means to make peace after a time of war, and following J. Comblin, Schreiter suggests that the concept functions on three levels in Paul's thought: (1) Christologically, with God reconciling the world through Christ (Rom. 5.11); (2) ecclesiologically, with Christ reconciling Jew and Greek (Eph. 2.12–16) and (3) cosmically, with Christ reconciling everything in heaven and earth to himself. Finally, and crucially for the purpose of this essay, Christ's work of reconciliation is now entrusted to the Church in its ministry to the world (2 Cor. 5.11–21).[20]

From these biblical foundations, plus theological reflection upon years of ministry experience within conflict-ridden zones, Schreiter offers a framework of five central points on the Christian ministry of reconciliation. This framework warrants analysis in light of the insights and experiences of other theologians and activists engaged in reconciliation.

Schreiter's first point spells out his most fundamental premise, that '*reconciliation is the work of God, who initiates and completes in us reconciliation through Christ.*'[21] Certainly people participate in the process, but ultimately, reconciliation is not a human achievement, but the work of God's grace within us. This assertion is not simply a spiritual platitude, but a theological reality that is borne out by the experience of the Apostle Paul. Examining 2 Corinthians 5.17–21, Miroslav Volf highlights Paul's distinctive use of the term reconciliation, indicating that it is never God who is reconciled, or who reconciles himself, to humanity. On the contrary, it is only human beings who need to be reconciled to God, and this is accomplished not through their own repentance or good works, but only by the grace of God. Volf follows Seyoon Kim in tracing the origin of Paul's unique understanding of reconciliation to his own encounter with Jesus on the road to Damascus. There Saul, the persecutor of Jesus and his followers, underwent the most dramatic experience of God's reconciling action. Through this encounter, Saul discovered that his sins were forgiven, he was transformed into a new creature, received into the very human community he had sought to destroy, and called to a radically new vocation of reconciliation and community-building.[22]

Volf draws out two significant features of a theology of reconciliation from this passage. First, while grace without justice is inconceivable, 'justice is subordinate to grace'. Saul, as the enemy of God persecuting the Church, did not encounter a wrathful God in pursuit of strict justice, as the 'victim', but instead a loving God who offered to reconcile Saul to himself. Yet this was no cheap grace, or cheap reconciliation that overlooked the injustice that had taken place. On the contrary, the divine voice specifically named the injustice of 'persecution', and confronted the oppressor with the direct question 'why?': 'Saul, Saul, why do you persecute me?' (Acts 9.4). As Volf points out, 'Jesus Christ himself named the injustice and made the accusation in the very act of offering forgiveness and reconciliation.'[23] So although justice is indispensable to reconciliation, reconciliation is not simply the automatic consequence of justice established.

Second, while the doctrine of reconciliation has all too often been interpreted spiritually, in terms of reconciliation of the soul with God (particularly by pietists and socially conservative evangelicals), Volf insists that 'reconciliation between human beings is intrinsic to their reconciliation with God'.[24] The account in Acts makes clear that Saul was ravaging the Church, and even on the road to Damascus he was breathing murderous threats against the disciples. Yet the voice from heaven identifies itself explicitly as the voice of Jesus Christ: 'I am Jesus, whom you are persecuting' (Acts 9.4–5). Hence Volf concludes, 'So from the start and at its heart, the enmity toward God is enmity toward human beings, and the enmity toward human beings is enmity toward God. Consequently, from the start, reconciliation does not simply have a vertical but also a horizontal dimension.'[25] Thus the grace that the Apostle Paul received both from God and from the Christian community that welcomed him into their midst becomes the very core of his message of reconciliation with God and the core of his ministry of reconciliation between Jews and Gentiles.

Are these insights merely a matter of abstract theology, or are they actually enfleshed in people's lives today? In developing his first point about reconciliation being the work of God, Schreiter stresses that God initiates this work of reconciliation in the lives of the victims. While one would expect that reconciliation would begin with repentance on the part of the wrongdoers, experience shows that this is rarely the case. Instead, Schreiter observes:

> God begins with the victim, restoring to the victim the humanity which the wrongdoer has tried to wrest away or to destroy. This restoration of humanity might be considered the very heart of reconciliation. The experience of reconciliation is the experience of grace – the restoration of one's damaged humanity in a life-giving relationship with God.[26]

Certainly Fr Michael Lapsley's transition from victim, to survivor, to victor, bears witness to this transformation by God's grace. By his own account, there were times when he questioned whether it would have been better had he died. Yet he explains his recovery as follows:

> When I was bombed I became a focus of evil, because there is something very personal about a letter bomb which was supposed to kill me. However in the response of people all over the world I became a focus of all that is beautiful in the human community, our ability to be tender, loving and compassionate. I think that is what enabled me to take that situation and make it redemptive, to bring the life out of the death, the good out of the evil.[27]

As he regained a sense of his own humanity and dignity through God's grace, and through the overwhelming love and support from people around the world, Fr Lapsley became committed to extending that grace to others who have suffered violence and injustice.

Despite such moving stories of triumph, however, there is no detracting from the complexities involved in reconciliation. For example, Schreiter continues by asserting that 'it is through the victim that the wrongdoer is called to repentance and forgiveness.'[28] Therefore Schreiter views repentance and forgiveness not as preconditions but as consequences of reconciliation. Undoubtedly, South Africa's Truth and Reconciliation Commission brought these truths to light through the testimony of various victims of apartheid.[29] Yet undeniably, issues of repentance and forgiveness remain among the thorniest matters in the ministry of reconciliation, especially in situations like South Africa where despite the offer of amnesty, the perpetrators of crimes against humanity remain anonymous. Accordingly, forgiveness is very difficult when there is no one to forgive. Fr Lapsley is therefore critical of the 'cheap, glib, easy' discussions of forgiveness often presented by adherents of most orthodox religions.[30] His own view warrants citing, despite the length, for the light it sheds on the complex issue of forgiveness:

> While I may be clear that I'm not full of hatred and bitterness, and that I don't want to spend my life focusing on what I cannot now do, forgiveness is not yet even on the table for me. In my case, I lost my hands due to a letter-bomb. I know that this letter-bomb was sent by the proponents of apartheid, but no individual has ever claimed responsibility. No-one has said 'I did it.' Without someone acknowledging responsibility, I cannot even consider whether forgiveness is something I can or cannot grant.
>
> Of course, this could change at anytime. Perhaps when I get home this evening someone will ring my doorbell and when I meet them at the door they will say 'I'm the one who sent you the letter-bomb and I have come to seek your forgiveness. Will you forgive me?' If this occurred, I think my first response would be to ask some questions of my own, the first being, 'do you still make letter-bombs?' And if the person concerned said 'no, no, actually I work at the local hospital,' then perhaps I'd respond by saying, 'Yes, of course I forgive you. I would prefer that you spend the next 15 years working at that hospital rather than locked up in prison, because I believe in restorative justice rather than retributive justice.' Perhaps over tea I might also say 'While of course I've forgiven you, you can't give me back my hands. They've gone forever and I will need to employ somebody to assist me for the rest of my life. Of course, you will now help pay for that person.' And, you see, this would be a part of reparation and restitution. These are the sorts of reciprocal acts that become possible as part of a journey of forgiveness. And these are the sorts of stories that are shared at the Healing of Memories Workshops. They are not easy, glib or cheap stories. Journeys of forgiveness are costly, painful and difficult. At the same time they are graceful. Journeys of forgiveness require a generosity of spirit and this, to me, is representative of grace.[31]

So despite the many complexities entailed, Fr Lapsley's concluding comments confirm Schreiter's fundamental point concerning reconciliation, that it is indeed the work of God, at God's initiative, and though human action is required, it is ultimately a gift of grace. Hence the element of surprise, like the profound shock of St Paul on the road to Damascus, when either the perpetrator or the victim discovers reconciliation with God and with others, even one's former enemies.

The second main point that Schreiter puts forward, already mentioned above, is that '*reconciliation is more a spirituality than a strategy.*'[32] Definitely there are strategies or particular procedures that enhance the process of conflict resolution, such as the use of rituals and peacemaking practices and the formulation of laws and policies regarding amnesty. However, reconciliation in its theological sense calls for 'a way of living that creates the space for new possibilities'.[33] It is precisely here that the ministry of reconciliation intersects, or overlaps, with the prophetic ministry addressed in this essay. As Walter Brueggemann puts it, 'The task of prophetic ministry is to nurture, nourish, and evoke a consciousness and perception [which is an] alternative to the consciousness and perception of the dominant culture around us.'[34] Thus in contexts of conflict, violence or injustice, prophetic ministry or the ministry of reconciliation conjures up new ways of thinking, imagining, acting and being.

Schreiter proposes various spiritual practices in this quest for healing, for justice, and for new possibilities. One is to cultivate truth-telling as a means of overcoming the lies propagated through situations of injustice.[35] Another is to create 'communities of memory', or safe places in which those who have suffered conflict, violence or injustice can expose and explore their experience of pain as a major step towards healing. Additionally, 'communities of hope' can be created to encourage those who have suffered to imagine and to celebrate new possibilities for the future. Finally, Schreiter notes that often those victims who discover reconciliation themselves then receive a call or vocation in helping to heal others – both victims and wrongdoers – through practices of truth-telling, pursuing justice and peacemaking.[36]

This profile of prophetic ministry seems to fit Fr Lapsley so closely, one wonders if Schreiter had him in mind when he wrote it. Certainly these three spiritual practices are foundational to the Institute for the Healing of Memories. As the Director, Fr Lapsley places this ministry in the wider context of South Africa as a country that chose not to 'forgive and forget', nor to reproduce Nuremburg trials for prosecuting those responsible for the grave injustices of apartheid. Instead, South Africa devised its own Truth and Reconciliation Commission in an attempt to 'remember and heal' as a nation. Drawing parallels with other nations such as the United States of America, Canada, Australia and New Zealand, Fr Lapsley states:

> This is a time in the world of confronting the genocidal effects of colonialism and racism. This confrontation is happening during our generation, our time on earth. I think it calls us to be part of acknowledging the truth of what happened, and to find ways to heal the memories and to create something different for future generations.[37]

Thus the heart of the Institute's ministry is healing memories through storytelling. Their approach differs from therapy in that everyone has a story to tell of their experience in South Africa, or other contexts of their ministry. They therefore seek to provide a safe place to tell these stories, and to witness one another's stories, in ways that transcend the barriers that have previously divided them from one another. The healing workshops then seek to analyse those memories that are constructive, those that are destructive and those that might be redemptive. In other words, they seek those qualities and experiences from the past, such as courage and commitment, so as to invite participants to link these aspects of the past with the present and to carry them forward in envisioning new possibilities for the future.[38] Additionally, the Institute seeks to educate people and to address issues of conflict, violence, racism and injustice, with due attention to matters of reparation and restitution. Hence the Institute serves as a prime example of the spiritual practices Schreiter advocates in terms of truthtelling, communities of memory and communities of hope. Moreover, Fr Lapsley himself exemplifies those whose own experience of deep suffering and reconciliation form the foundation for a new vocation of helping to heal others who have likewise suffered.

Schreiter's third main point is that '*the experience of reconciliation makes of both victim and wrongdoer a new creation* (2 Cor 5.17).'[39] This is an important point, for strategies of reconciliation that operate without this spirituality often view reconciliation as a restoration of the previous condition, and justice as restitution. Yet all too often in situations of conflict, it is simply impossible to restore the earlier situation, and how can restitution be made for the dead? Instead, reconciliation involves God restoring the humanity that had been wrested through the conflict, and then refashioning a new humanity that now includes the experience of reconciliation. In other words, the painful memories of injustice are neither denied nor obliterated; these necessarily remain part of the person's identity, yet they are transformed in the process of healing to become life-giving channels of healing to others. In the resurrection appearance of Jesus to Thomas, the glorified body of Christ still bears the scars from his torture, yet they minister in profound, life-changing ways to Thomas (Jn 20). In the radical transformation of Saul, the persecutor of Jesus, to the Apostle Paul, he neither denies nor downplays his murderous past. Instead, he never ceases to marvel at how God's grace reached out to him, 'the worst' of sinners (1 Tim. 1.15–16). This new-found humanity, or re-creation in Christ, remains foundational to his apologetic for the Gospel and to his ministry of reconciliation. In regaining his dignity and a renewed sense of identity following the letter-bomb blast, Fr Lapsley admittedly becomes much more of a priest with no hands than he ever was with hands, and his ministry of healing grows exponentially in breadth and depth. So whether on the part of the perpetrator or the victim, the very experience of reconciliation can indeed create a new humanity.

According to Schreiter's fourth main point, '*The process of reconciliation that creates the new humanity is to be found in the story of the passion, death and resurrection of Jesus Christ.*'[40] This observation may seem so fundamental to Christian theology that it hardly needs mentioning. Yet the Paschal Mystery which forms the very heart of the Gospel must be recounted, and celebrated in the Eucharist, as a continual reminder of how God subverted power that was used to perpetrate violence and injustice. Likewise it is the grand narrative that invites our individual and communal stories of suffering to be subsumed and transformed into accounts of healing and resurrection into new life. Once again, abstract theology becomes concretized in the witness of Fr Lapsley, who speaks of his own experience as 'a journey that has included suffering, crucifixion, a kind of death and resurrection'.[41] Archbishop Desmond Tutu lends further affirmation in his concluding statement following Lapsley's testimony before the TRC:

> I give thanks to God for you, Michael, and I also give thanks for the experience through which you went, because you can talk about crucifixion and resurrection because it is real, it is in your body. You should see when he celebrates the Eucharist, I have sometimes stood next to him and I got a little worried whether he was not going to overturn the Chalice or something, and there is an incredible kind of hush in almost every service that I have been with you, because people somehow feel that they are in touch with goodness, in an awful situation somehow they are aware that they are in touch with light in darkness, that they are in touch with life in death, and somehow they know goodness is going to triumph over evil.[42]

Finally, it also goes without saying that '*the process of reconciliation will be fulfilled only with the complete consummation of the world by God in Christ.*'[43] Both the enormity and the complexity of the ministry of reconciliation in today's world evoke deep humility and the acknowledgement yet again that ultimately reconciliation is God's work. Certainly it involves human agency and strategies, yet it cannot be programmed from the outset nor presumed in its outcome. Thus Schreiter concludes that since 'it is the work of God, it is more spirituality than strategy, it is a new creation, it is encompassed in the mystery of the cross – it ultimately can only be grasped cosmically and perhaps eschatologically.'[44]

Conclusion

Given the magnitude, the gravity, and the complexity of conflict in Africa, the Apostle Paul's charge in 2 Corinthians 5.17–18 sounds a clarion call across the continent: 'Therefore, if anyone is in Christ, he is a new creation; the old has gone, the new has come! All this is from God, who reconciled us to himself through Christ and gave us the ministry of reconciliation' (NIV). The foregoing discussion has underlined that this ministry of reconciliation is not simply abstract theology. On the contrary, as Schreiter sums up, 'It is about coming to terms with a very concrete past and working towards a different future within the constraints – political, economic, social, cultural, and religious – of the context.'[45] As ambassadors for Christ, believers are called to prophetic ministry, speaking God's word and living it out in the contemporary context. Whatever the situation of conflict and injustice, be it personal, domestic, organizational, ethnic, religious, national or international, our mandate is to call people back to covenant faithfulness to God, to humanity and to the cosmos.

Without a doubt, the scope of this calling is both daunting and costly. Yet like the biblical prophets before us, the message we proclaim is not our own but of God who is reconciling all things unto himself. Likewise the resources are not our own, but rather we participate with God in his work of reconciliation. Consequently it entails both spirituality – seeking to foster Gospel transformation in ourselves and in others – and strategies. As the yeast permeates the dough, this ministry of reconciliation must penetrate every avenue of human existence and draw upon every strategy possible in the particular context of reconciliation – whether it is constitutional review and political and judicial reform, whether it is establishing justice in economic relations locally, nationally and internationally, or whether it is addressing the myriad of social ills which create suffering and conflict. The panoply of biblical prophets offers wisdom and inspiration for speaking God's peace into virtually every human situation.

Finally, the Christian Church has particular resources for accomplishing this ministry of reconciliation. First and foremost it has the message of reconciliation in Christ and the Spirit of Christ to effect it. It also has the power of ritual, such as the sacrament of reconciliation, plus the opportunity to creatively inculturate indigenous rites of reconciliation into its worship and praxis. In addition, the Church has strategic opportunities for education, integral community development and for participating in the public space, particularly here in Africa. Ultimately, the Church is perhaps best placed, among human organs of society, to create communities of reconciliation and communities of hope, thereby demonstrating genuine reconciliation to the wider society. Would that she – would that we – live up to this calling. Against all the natural cynicism and despair that may arise, may we recall that a single candle can light up a dark room. A single prophet can transform the life of a nation. And a single person, like Fr Michael Lapsley, can illuminate reconciliation in Christ to a country, to a continent, to a troubled globe. In such prophetic ministry do we discover the truth of the Kenyan proverb, 'Peace is like a treasure that shall never part from you.'[46]

Notes

[1] Participant Observation, Truth and Reconciliation Exposure Group Workshop, 10th International Conference of the International Association of Mission Studies, January 21–28, 2000, Hammanskraal, South Africa.

[2] 'Transcript of the evidence given by Fr Michael Lapsley, S. S. M., together with Michael Worsnip to the Commission for Truth and Reconciliation at the hearings of the Human Rights Violations Committee at Kimberley on Monday 10 June 1996', p. 2, http://www.healingofmemories.co.za/articles/TCR%20transcript%20of%20evidence%20to%20the%20HR%20Violation%20Commiteee,%20June%2096.htm. Accessed December 2007.

[3] *Ibid.*

[4] *Ibid.*

5   *Ibid.*

6   *Ibid.*

7   http://www.anglicord.org.au/faces/sa_lapsley.html. See also the annual reports and articles at http://www.healingofmemories.co.za. Accessed September 2007.

8   'Transcript of the evidence given by Fr. Michael Lapsley', p. 10.

9   *The New International Dictionary of New Testament Theology* (Grand Rapids, MI: Zondervan Publishing House, 1986), s.v. 'Prophet', by Colin Brown, p.79.

10 Gordon D. Fee and Douglas Stuart, *How to Read the Bible for All Its Worth: A Guide to Understanding the Bible* (Grand Rapids, MI: Zondervan Publishing House, 1982), 150; emphasis in original.

11 Brown, p. 79.

12 Fee and Stuart, p. 153.

13 *Theological Dictionary of the New Testament*, Ed. Gerhard Kittel and Gerhard Friedrich, translated and abridged in one volume by Geoffrey W. Bromiley (Grand Rapids, MI: William B. Eerdmans, 1985), s.v. 'Prophet,' by Gerhard Friedrich, p. 960.

14 Robert J. Schreiter, *The Ministry of Reconciliation: Spirituality and Strategies* (Maryknoll, NY: Orbis Books, 1998), p. 3.

15 Corinne Dufka, 'Combating War Crimes in Africa' in *Human Rights Watch*, English, http://hrw.org/english/docs/2004/06/28/africa8974.htm, June 28, 2004.

16 '2008 Report: Democracy Charade Undermines Rights: Human Rights Watch Highlights Abuses in Pakistan, Kenya, China, Somalia' in *Human Rights Watch*, English, http://hrw.org/englishwr2k8/docs/2008/01/31/usint17940.htm, 31 January 2008.

17 Schreiter, *The Ministry of Reconciliation*, p. 13.

18 Robert J. Schreiter, *Reconciliation: Mission and Ministry in a Changing Social Order* (Maryknoll, NY: Orbis Books, 1992), p. 60.

19 Schreiter, *The Ministry of Reconciliation*, p. 4.

20 *Dictionary of Mission: Theology, History, Perspectives* (Maryknoll, NY: Orbis Books, 1997), s.v. Schreiter, *Reconciliation* , pp. 379–380.

21 Schreiter, *The Ministry of Reconciliation*, 14; emphasis original in all five points.

22 Miroslav Volf, 'The Social Meaning of Reconciliation,' pp. 4–5, http://www.globalconnections.co.uk/pdfs/reconciliation.pdf. Accessed December 2007.

23 *Ibid.*, p. 5.

24 *Ibid.*

25 *Ibid.*

26 Schreiter, *The Ministry of Reconciliation*, p. 15.

27 'Transcript of the evidence given by Fr Michael Lapsley,' pp. 3–4.

28 Schreiter, *The Ministry of Reconciliation*, p. 15.

29 See the testimonies to this effect in Antjie Krog, *Country of My Skull* (Johannesburg: Random House, 1998), and Piet Meiring, *Chronicle of the Truth Commission* (Vanderbijlpark, SA: Carpe Diem Books, 1999).

30 Simon Bowen, 'To Heal and Remember, or to Bury and Forget?' A personal summary of Fr. Michael's Presentation at The Forgiveness Conference, 18th October 1999, http://www.findhorn.org/events/conferences/archives/forgive/frmichael.html. Accessed September 2007.

31 'Interview: Healing Memories with Michael Lapsley,' pp. 3-4, http://www.gracecathedral.org/enrichment/interviews/int_20030507.shtml. Accessed December 2007.

32 Schreiter, *The Ministry of Reconciliation*, p. 16.

33 Schreiter, *Reconciliation*, p. 380.

34 W. Brueggemann, *The Prophetic Imagination* (Philadelphia, PA: Fortress Press, 1982), p. 12; quoted in Raymond S. Mosha, 'The Prophetic Role of the Church in Tanzania Today' in *The Prophetic Role of the Church in Tanzania Today*, ed. Laurenti Magesa (Eldoret, Kenya: AMECEA Gaba Publications, 1991), p. 14.

35 See Schreiter's discussion of 'Violence as a Narrative of the Lie' in *Reconciliation*, pp. 34-36.

36 Schreiter, *The Ministry of Reconciliation*, p. 16.

37 'Interview: Healing Memories with Michael Lapsley,' p. 1.

38 *Ibid.*, pp. 1–2.

39 Schreiter, *The Ministry of Reconciliation*, p. 17.

40 *Ibid.*, p. 18.

41 'Feature Interview: Michael Lapsley,' http://www.abc.net.au/sundaynights/stories/s1237649.htm.

42 'Transcript of the evidence given by Fr. Michael Lapsley', p. 10.

43 Schreiter, *The Ministry of Reconciliation*, p. 19.

44 Schreiter, *Reconciliation*, p. 381.

45 Schreiter, *The Ministry of Reconciliation*, p. 105.

46 Annetta Miller, compiler, 'African Wisdom on War and Peace: A Calendar' (Nairobi: Paulines Publications Africa, 2004), 1 January.

Part Three

The Latin American Context

Chapter 9

Mission in Reverse: The Case of Latin America

Miguel A. Palomino

This essay is about the practice of mission by the Latin American Church in today's world. It springs out of the climate of missionary activity, not the climate of academic discovery, though it has sociological, theological and missiological research components. Ever since the centre of Christianity moved from the United States of America and other Western countries to the 'Global South', there are now more Christians residing in those areas than in the West. Because of this, we can no longer assert that the Church in the West is the 'sending' Church and that the rest of the world is the mission field. In the early days of missions, churches sent people and financial resources expecting their mission-aries to administer the resources and 'do missions'. Today, because we live in a world that is much more connected, many American churches have direct rela-tionships with national pastors, and national churches are also involved in part-nerships with other churches to do projects outside the United States of America. As a result, some question the value of the old missionary pattern with the preeminence of the 'sending Church'. This paradigm ought to change if we do not want the Church to become artificially polarized by one approach alone. We can minimize the limitations of both by maximizing the strengths of both so the Church can be methodologically progressive. The future of world missions in the twenty-first century will be even brighter if the participation of both forces are viewed with these bifocal lenses.

From a 'mission field' to a 'mission force'

As noted above, the centre of Christianity has shifted. The Church overseas continues to grow and mature to the point that many non-Western countries are sending missionaries. COMIBAM (Congreso Misionero Ibcroamericano) is an organization that exists to transform Latin America from 'a mission field to a mission force'. At the organization's recent meeting in Grenada, Spain, it was estimated that there are between 10,000 and 15,000 missionaries from Latin America serving around the world, mainly in Muslim countries.[1] Similar patterns are developing in Africa and Asia.

In 1987, at the first COMIBAM gathering, it was estimated that there were about 1,600 cross-cultural Latin American missionaries. By 1997, this figure had grown to a little more than 4,000. Today, after some 20 years of Latin American involvement in the world missionary force, there are 400 mission agencies sending out 9,000 Latino missionaries. Some leaders believe the actual number is probably closer to 12,000, as many have gone out on their own, outside of a traditional missionary-sending structure.[2]

The vision cast in 1987 was for Latin America to be transformed from a 'mission field' to a 'mission force'. And now 20 years later, this vision is coming into full bloom as experienced Latin American missionaries are able to share their victories, as well as the challenges they have met. According to field research presented at the congress, many of those missionaries have suffered due to the lack of preparation and adequate support and the inherent difficulties that are part of the work. Dr Levi DeCarvalho, who led the research, emphasized that

> in spite of the fact that most of those interviewed expressed the lack of minimum resources to accomplish their ministries, all of them remain firm in their calling. If there is something praiseworthy in our Iberoamerican missionaries it is their sacrificial spirit to do the work that the Lord has entrusted in their hands.[3]

Latin America: a role player in world missions

In many parts of the world Latinos are better accepted and are having success at breaking through barriers that are becoming harder for missionaries from North America and Europe to transcend. In Latin America, as well as several other places around the world, the role of many missionaries from 'the North' is transitioning into that of mobilizing and equipping the national churches and believers to 'take the baton' and step into the trenches of frontline missionary service and proclamation.

What a Korean mission leader said during the COMIBAM may illustrate what the congress meant to those who were not Latin Americans. When asked 'What would you take back from this conference?', his answer was, 'Koreans are not the only ones doing missions.' The Latin mission has its own distinct identity. There are many things we can learn from them, regardless of how long we have been in missions. Latino churches are blessing the world by the design and power of the Holy Spirit. With more than 85 million evangelicals in this region, they have a major role to play in world missions today.

Contextualization of mission

Missions history is the history of how the Church has responded to her missionary nature, how she has fulfilled her role in the world and how she perceives her past and interprets the present in light of the eschatological future that reveals itself in the second coming of Jesus Christ, and the restoration of all things including cultures and ethnic groups. Mission is the dynamics of the *Missio Dei* (mission from God) and the *Missio Ecclesiae* (the missionary practice of the community of faith), crossing socio-cultural, ideological, technological and ecological barriers to reach peoples from different backgrounds and situations.

In the case of Latin America, although many goals have been achieved as the COMIBAM III reported, mission is still a work in progress. The big challenge the Latin American Church faces today is finding the way to show its own missionary ethos from a context of poverty, exclusion, injustice and other social ills that afflict the region. Contemporary missiology, reflecting on past and present experiences, raises the question of how to develop new missionary practices for the twenty-first century, taking very seriously the diverse dynamics between the Word and culture. Latino mission leaders are trying to answer this question, which no doubt will affect the way we perceive issues like social ethics, approaches for doing missions and evangelism, and even how we should conduct our inter-ecclesiastic relationships in the years to come.

I do not intend to deal with these issues here. I will limit the discussion to distinguish two developing missionary models that portray the issues mentioned above.

The migratory model

The first model is the migratory model characterized by the spontaneous missionary participation of the whole community and not only of a few professional missionaries. This natural missionary drive has led Christian immigrants to share their faith and make disciples wherever they go, resembling what the first Christians did in Acts 8.4. Missions is certainly not just a matter for professional workers but for every believer in Jesus Christ who takes seriously the Great Commission.

As a consequence of tougher US immigration policies after the terrorist attacks of September 11, 2001, Latin American immigrants now typically face a bewildering array of needs and problems – as does the host country. These policies are meant to manage or restrict the flow of people entering the United States of America. As Mario Vargas Llosa has pointed out, however,

> anti-immigrant policies are destined to fail because they will never stop immigrants. These policies will only have the perverse effect of undermining the democratic institutions of the nations that apply them to give xenophobia, racism and authoritarianism an appearance of legitimacy. Immigrants do not take jobs away from locals. On the contrary, they create them, and bring progress, rather than

deterioration. . . . [Immigration] is a shot of life, energy, and culture, which should be considered a blessing by receiving countries.[4]

An important dimension of this 'blessing' of immigration relates to mission, for immigrants represent a clear challenge and opportunity for spiritual and church growth. We will consider this idea after first reviewing the phenomenon of migration.

The migratory phenomenon

It is said that 195 million people around the world – more than 3 per cent of the world population – have left their place of origin in search of better life somewhere else. According to the United Nations Population Fund (UNFPA), about 25 million people from Latin America and the Caribbean had emigrated by the year 2005. This constitutes 4 per cent of the total population of the region,[5] which represents 13 per cent of the worldwide migratory wave. In some parts of the Caribbean one out of five people have left their country to go to the United States of America, a favourite destination for Latinos who now number about 18 million in this nation.

The promise of a better future motivates new settlers to endure the difficult situations they encounter daily. From 1990 to 2002, more than 3,000 people – mainly Mexican citizens – died or disappeared on the border between Mexico and the United States of America.[6] 'Unauthorised' immigration has not diminished; it only forces immigrants to look for other border-crossing points, making their journey even more dangerous than before.

Arrests and deaths are not the only risks immigrants have to endure. According to the US Department of State, every year 100,000 Latinos and Caribbeans are subjected to trafficking. Women and children are the main victims and are forced to work in the sex industry in distant places such as Spain and Japan. The fact that sexual tourism has increased in the region has made trafficking flourish in certain countries.[7] In 2002 Guatemalan police found more than 2,000 under-aged girls from other Central American countries working in local brothels. Interpol reports that every year 35,000 women who leave Colombia will likely become victims of trafficking.[8]

Because of the similarity of language, historical connections, and culture, Spain and Portugal are now becoming the most popular gateways for Latino immigrants. These countries have granted special status to Latin Americans for years because of their strong ties with the region.[9] Jorge Moragas, secretary of international relations of the Partido Popular in Spain, has stated, 'We need laborers. For that reason we favor Latin American immigration. Latin Americans who experience social instability and economic depression in their societies play an important role in the Spanish labor market.'[10] With one of the fastest-growing economies in Europe, Spain certainly needs foreign workers for its strong tourism and construction sectors, and immigrants are in demand because they tend to be highly reliable, punctual, stable, hard-working and flexible.

In Switzerland, Italy and Britain, Latinos also represent the fastest-growing immigrant community. Hundreds of illegal immigrants ride the rails from Spain to the French Alps and then slip into Switzerland, Italy and other nations. Because of their low birthrate, these countries have been able to support a progressively aging population, thanks to the immigrants. A similar shift is occurring in England, where Latinos take jobs that Britons and the children of earlier immigrants reject.

All these sacrifices and efforts by Latino immigrants are paying off in terms of the economies for Latin America. Remittances – that is, migrant earnings sent back to countries of origin – are the main reason for poverty reduction in the region. Although exact numbers are hard to pin down, the sums are enormous. The World Bank estimates that in 2005 formally transferred remittances rang in at about US$232 billion – of which Latin America received US$45 billion.[11] The actual amount of remittances is considered to be substantially higher, since this figure does not take into account funds transferred through informal channels. So great is the impact on developing world economies that the World Bank theorizes that a 10 per cent increase in remittances as a proportion of a country's GDP could result in a 1.2 per cent reduction in the share of people living in extreme poverty.[12] According to the Economic Commission for Latin America and the Caribbean (ECLAC), remittances from abroad in 2002 helped to boost 2.5 million people living in Latin American and the Caribbean above the poverty line.[13]

However, immigration not only means low-wage labour and economic improvement for Third-World nations, but also a clash of cultures. Observers say that Western values on the continent are at stake. Most European immigrants are Muslim, and most are not assimilating well, while others openly and actively reject liberal values such as secular education or the rights of women and homosexuals. In this case, some say that the United States of America is fortunate that most of its immigrants are from Latin American cultures that accept Western values as their own.[14] While 'Americans worry about the threat of occasional terrorist acts that do not directly endanger basic institutions, Europeans worry that immigrants could turn back the clock on centuries of costly social gains'.[15] EU members looked to the Middle East to import guest workers and bolster their diminishing populations. Unfortunately, many of these immigrants, both legal and illegal, bring with them a strong theocratic, totalitarian background that keeps them from accepting notions of a liberal society based on freedom of choice. Since Latino immigrants, whatever their status, possess a strong work ethic, a respect for Western laws and an appreciation of the heritage of Western Europe, coupled with a foundation in Catholicism, it would appear unproblematic for governments to receive them. In this sense, some Europeans argue that drawing labourers from a new source – Latin America – may help stem the flow of illegal arrivals from Muslim lands.[16]

Immigration and mission

Missiologist Ray Bakke affirms that the migratory phenomenon is one of the biggest challenges for the Church and mission today. He says that when God communicated with the human race, He did it through his Son who was born in Asia but went to Africa as a refugee where he spent the first years of his life. The fact that half of the world's children are born in Asia, and half of the refugees anywhere in the world are Africans, means that Jesus somehow can appeal to them. Also, like today's refugees, Jesus knew about poverty because he was born in a borrowed manger, was buried in a borrowed tomb and never owned a house. Certainly, the pain, needs, frustrations and humiliation that many immigrants and refugees experience now, would not be strange to Jesus if he were here today.[17] Immigrants serve as a reminder of the incarnational nature of the Church in times when changes are required in order to accomplish God's mission. In this sense, the South-to-North migratory movement might be instrumental in the completion of this task thanks to the huge mobilization of believers.

Immigrants, especially those who come from nations where churches are experiencing a spiritual awakening, are shocked when they see half-empty churches on Sundays or church buildings converted into theatres, coffee shops and fitness clubs. Evangelical immigrants cannot understand how these churches that used to send missionaries to Latin America are now in such a poor spiritual condition. Immigrants normally prefer to attend masses and services conducted in their own language. The ethnic church thus is key for the spiritual and moral support of the immigrant, and the priest or minister becomes an authority figure who helps reaffirm the immigrant's identity and culture. Although churches are not social clubs, sociologically speaking, they are seen as havens,[18] communities that become the immigrants' extended families.

For believers in Jesus Christ, the idea of being pilgrims in the world holds strong symbolic meaning that enables them to better adjust to their new place than is possible for immigrants with no religious connection. Viewing the church as the people or house of God undoubtedly offers the believer the possibility of finding in local congregations the family warmth needed in times of difficulties and loneliness.

In the early 1990s a former missionary to Peru, Estuardo McIntosh, was one of the first missiologists in Latin America to draw attention to the potential missionary force that immigrants represent today:

> According to official statistics, 200,000 Peruvians leave the country every year. We know there is a 5 percent of evangelical population in Peru. If we took the hypothesis that evangelicals are also fleeing, then we have around

10,000 'missionaries' per year leaving from Peru. Obviously, this pattern surpasses any other 'formal' pattern of mission.[19]

Who are these evangelical immigrants? A good number of them are part of the new breed of revitalized and fast-growing independent Pentecostal/charismatic Churches that are so common now in Latin America. They emerged in the midst of the deep cultural and social changes that the region has experienced in the past three decades. Now they are reshaping the religious landscape of the whole continent, as well as the way to do missions. These immigrants, and many others like them, have a double purpose in mind: work hard to give their families a better life and plant new churches wherever they go. Three factors here should be considered:

Organization. This movement of evangelical immigrants challenges the idea that a sophisticated organization and timetable are fundamental to accomplishing the task. For them, flexibility and spontaneity are equally appreciated, and sometimes even more important, since these elements may help with moving in accordance with God's leading, regardless of existing programmes and schedules.

Leadership. Generally speaking, the concept of leadership emphasizes the leader as patron or a father figure, in contrast to the Western notion that understands leadership as a function or a job, based on rules and regulations. The Latino leader usually has a strong personality and is expected to be always moving forward and showing results. A weak or indecisive leader would likely have little following. In contrast to the norm in Latin America, Westerners have a democratic and egalitarian view of leadership, with a small 'power-distance' between leader and the sheep.

Spiritual world. Evangelical immigrants come with a natural sensitivity to the spiritual world that is not as common for Westerners. This characteristic has proved to be useful when dealing with the supernatural in the field. When things go wrong, it is necessary to discern whether the problem is due to bad organization or to demonic attacks. In many occasions the latter turns out to be the cause.

The cooperative model

The second model is in some way related to the migratory model, for it seeks to unite human resources of churches in poor countries to the financial resources of churches in rich countries in order to do missions anywhere in the world. This model suggests team work rather than individualistic work, whose final goal is to make disciples for Christ and not only to win converts for the church. 'Despite the fact that the African and Latin American churches are poor and face dramatic challenges by the social and economic crisis of their regions, they are sending missionaries out to other parts of the world,' states Escobar.[20] This is true thanks to partnerships and other types of agreements with denominations and missionary agencies that understand that missions have now gone global. It is not a secret that career missionaries are now scarce both in the United States of America and Europe,[21] so cooperation between North and South may help fulfil the completion of the task.

Consider the Comunidad Cristiana de Londres (CCL), a Latino church founded by Edmundo Ravelo in the early 1980s, and one of the first to begin working with immigrants. In those years just a few Latinos lived in London. Today, however, Ravelo meets them in the streets, buses and subway every day. This increase in the Latino population led him to revise his outreach strategy, with remarkable results. After many years of struggling with a congregation of around 80 members, the Church has grown in the past 8 years to more than 3,000 members.

During the first years, the CCL sought legal covering from missionary agencies and local churches to freely operate in the country. Kensington Temple, a solid, well-known, and established church in London, assimilated this Latino fellowship into its organization as one of the many satellite churches working with them in the city. The agreement, which ended in 2005, basically consisted in legal representation for renting premises where the CCL worshipped, and opportunities for Ravelo to meet with other church leaders.[22] This helped the CCL to mature and cast a vision that would reflect its own ethos in doing Church and mission. The CCL then launched an aggressive evangelistic outreach among the Latino community, having as a priority the formation of similar congregations in other European nations. Two aspects are significant in this approach. First, the worship service was transformed to be regarded as a spiritual fiesta. Second, the cell group work was restructured to reproduce many features of the extended family.

Culto

For evangelicals, the *culto* (worship service) is an important part of both the church's life and missionary work.[23] Believers meet together to celebrate God, and then go out to share the Gospel with others. In the case of the CCL, the *culto* emphasizes the emotional and supernatural, targeting primarily the immigrant.

In this schema, the *unción de poder*, or 'anointing of [God's] power', takes place in the celebration. Empowered by the Holy Spirit, the worship leader expels the territorial demons that control towns, cities and the nation, reclaims authority over the principalities, and declares the sanctuary holy. During the time of ministry the pastor feels free to preach and then to perform healings and work wonders. Here he prays for those who are unemployed, have no place to live, want to bring their families or need to adjust their legal status. This is a moment when people feel cared about and supported by hundreds who understand them because they are also going through the same situation. Participants naturally tell others what happened to them and find it easy to bring relatives and friends along with them the next Sunday.

The *culto* as a fiesta brings up two issues to be considered. The first is the validity of the emotional in worship. The current tendency to structure very emotional services can be a reaction to the time when churches would only pay attention to intellectual sermons, and perceived any sign of emotionalism with suspicion. As a result the *culto* became ritualistic, lacking motivation for believers to express their feelings to God. In trying to rescue the fact that humans are not only intellectual but emotional and physical beings too, the renewed *culto* is creating a theological perspective whereby the whole person is a worshiping being. As Chilean sociologist Cristián Parker argues, individuals are to be seen as mind and heart in one unity, and spirit and body holistically.[24] Regrettably, Western rationalism 'made us believe for a long time that we were nothing else but reason, nothing else but thinking beings', where symbolism and religion had no place in life. The challenge then is to re-assess the different worship styles now widely present in effective and emotional *cultos*, for they are legitimate forms of spirituality, bringing with them a new worldview that helps to understand worship from new perspectives.

The second to be considered is the validity of practices involving supernatural phenomena as part of the worship service. Changes that have occurred in the *culto* are forcing traditional evangelical church leaders and believers alike to rethink their spirituality. But solid theological foundations need then to be defined and taught to sustain whatever is practised in the *culto*. Topics such as falling backwards when a person is prayed for or the legitimacy of signs and wonders demand an elaboration of a theology of liturgy.

Cell groups

Along with the *culto* the CCL places a high priority on the work with small groups, which complements whatever is said and done in the Sunday service. Believers meet at homes on weekdays to discuss the Sunday sermon, share their worries and emotional burdens, and pray about them. Each cell leader oversees the group's activities and functions as the cell pastor, since the nature of the small group, limited to a maximum of twelve people, allows him or her to build a close relationship with the people as if it were an extended family. These relationships enable the immigrant to adjust himself or herself in the foreign country with more confidence, knowing that now he or she can lean on others.

Sociologists of religion tell us that the extended family is important in the process of assimilation to the new culture. Writing about Pentecostals in Chile back in the 1960s, Christian Lalive d'Epinay observed that for the migrants who came from the provinces to the capital city, the small Pentecostal fellowships would resemble the *hacienda* they left back home.[25] These fellowships gave them security and shelter in the big city, providing them a place of transition while they adjusted to the new city. In the case of the CCL, the cell groups accomplish a similar role but with a richer dynamic because the leader can relate much better to the situation of the group, since he or she is also an immigrant. This combined effort, uniting the *culto* and the cell group, has certainly strengthened this community, to the point that its members feel good about themselves, support each other and are always looking after the newcomers. As a result, the CCL now has a daily radio programme (the only Spanish broadcast in the London area) and holds seminars for local English churches that want to develop similar programs.[26]

As Samuel Escobar has noted, this type of evangelical movement may further the completion of the unfinished missionary task in other parts of the world.[27] Latino evangelical immigrants are already doing missions among their peers, and also among their host Europeans in what could be called missions in reverse. It remains to be seen, however, whether European churches will endorse what they are doing.

Implications for missions

In missions, as in any other human activity, there always will be the temptation to ignore what others are doing and engage in a lonely journey in the belief that 'our way' is better than anybody else's way. Yet the question that remains is, 'What can be done to facilitate a "two-way mission" partnership?'

Networking

It's been said that 'networking' is one lettre away from 'not working' – 'networking' being the excuse that 'very important church leaders' use to justify long meetings and fancy lunches. However, networking holds some key truths for mission that we cannot afford to miss.

We are people born into community (the family) and brought into community (the Church) by a God of community (the Trinity). In practical terms, community conveys the idea of relationships – connecting with others, learning from others, sharing with others, rejoicing with others, struggling with others.[28]

The Western Church can provide and receive tremendous benefit by sharing her 200 years of missionary experience with those coming from Latin America. By networking with them, the Church in the United States of America and Europe will learn from the Latinos how to deal with issues of poverty, violence, spiritual warfare and other areas in which they might lack expertise. 'Networking' then is a two-way street rather than a paternalistic mindset, and this can certainly bring net gains to both parties engaged in missions.

Consulting

Recently, some church leaders have begun talking about the need for effective consultants for churches that are charting new territory. Richard Houston, a former missionary to Colombia, says:

> Consulting represents a new role for mission agencies . . . and one that is becoming increasingly important. Some missiologists have identified this type of enabling ministry as one of the most significant contributions that America mission agencies can make toward the future of world missions.[29]

The whole idea behind consulting is that an outside observer sometimes can accurately diagnose a situation, and help the church or missionary to not lose sight of their main goals by providing them with the right tools to accomplish their task. The method used in consulting may vary, but it usually involves suggesting training programs available in the city, or introducing the candidate to missionary boards and agencies, or facilitating resources like books, materials and information. But regardless of the method, partnership is crucial for the success of any consultant – working side by side to enable the missionary to develop his or her own missionary skills and plans.

Former missionaries may find consulting an attractive and feasible ministry today. It does not fit the traditional image of a missionary, but it can be highly useful for the younger generation of mission workers who would appreciate the experience and wisdom of their predecessors. In the end, we are neither interested in re-inventing the wheel nor in doing things 'our way', but in learning from those who were on the field before us and now may say with the apostle Paul, 'I have fought the good fight, I have finished the race, I have kept the faith' (2 Tim. 4.7).

New missionary winds are blowing in the United States of America and Europe and evangelical Latinos seem to be part of it because the Latin American Church is maturing at a surprisingly rapid rate, fostering a vigorous indigenous missionary movement that is at work in places that once were regarded as missionary-sending countries.

Conclusion

It is hard to forecast the impact of these two models on missions. More Spanish-speaking and Portuguese-speaking churches will emerge, churches of neo-Pentecostal style that will target other immigrants and will also help local congregations become spiritually revitalized – something that is already happening in the United States of America and Europe. Collectively, the enormous movement of immigrants now occurring will have a profound effect on these continents to transform the Church and mission. May the huge church growth in Latin America spill over to the rest of the world.

Notes

[1] Taken from Reporte Preliminar del III Congreso Misionero Iberoamericano.

[2] Ted Limptic has reported that there may be up to 3,000 Latin missionaries not accounted for.

[3] See Strengths and Weaknesses of the Iberoamerican Missionary. Research report to COMIBAM, p. 2.

[4] Mario Vargas Llosa, 'Los Inmigrantes' in *Caretas*, No. 1470, Lima, 19 June 1997. This article won him the Mariano de Cavia Prize, awarded by the Madrilenian daily news *ABC* in October 1996. For the electronic version, see http://www. caretas.com.pe/1470/mvll/mvll.htm. Accessed January 2007.

[5] Claudia Florentin, 'Día del migrante: rutas de dolor y esperanza'in *Agencia Latinoamericana y Caribeña de Comunicación*', 18 December 2006.

[6] There were 472 deaths recorded alone in 2005. See Illegal Immigration Border-Crossing Deaths Have Doubled Since 1995; Border Patrol's Efforts to Prevent Deaths Have Not Been Fully Evaluated. August 2006, p. 4. Online at http://www. gao.gov/new.items/d06770.pdf. Accessed January 2007.

[7] Dawn Herzog Jewell. 'Child Sex Tour. The average victim is 14, and Americans make up 25 percent of the customers' in *Christianity Today*, January 2007. See the article online at http://www.christianitytoday.com/39887. Accessed January 2007.

[8] Florentin, 2006, p.5.

[9] The escalating black market in Spanish birth certificates and passports also attracts many Latinos who want to move freely within the EU.

[10] 'Europa, el nuevo destino de los latinos,' *La Semana del Sur* (Tulsa, Okla. / Houston, Tex.), year 3, no. 149, 19–25 November 2003. It is worth mentioning that many ordinary Spanish citizens do not necessarily agree with this policy that welcomes Latinos. Racist comments and discriminating attitudes against Latin Americans are documented and well known.

[11] The World Bank, *Global Economic Prospects 2006: Economic Implications of Remittances and Migration*. Washington, DC: The International Bank for Reconstruction and Development and the World Bank, 2006, pp. 85, 88.

[12] R. H. Adams, Jr, and J. Page, 'The Impact of International Migration and Remittances on Poverty.' Paper prepared for DFID/World Bank Conference on Migrant Remittances, London, 9–10 October 2003. Washington, DC: Poverty Reduction Group, the World Bank. Based on an analysis of data of 72 countries.

[13] ECLAC (Economic Commission for Latin America and the Caribbean), 'The Number of Poor People in Latin America has Fallen by 13 Million Since 2003', November 2005, p. 3. Also at www.eclac.cl/prensa/noticias/notas/0/23580/ NOTAS43ING.pdf. Accessed 19 May 2006.

[14] For an account of Latino immigration in the United States, see Robert Suro, Strangers Among Us: Latino Lives in a Changing America (New York: Vintage Books, 1999).

[15] Andrew Reding, 'Can Europe Keep Its Western Values with Unassimilated Immigrants?' in *NCM*, 22 May 2002. Available at http://news.ncmonline.com/news/view_article.html?article_id=387. Accessed January 2007.

[16] Joel Millman, 'Europe Dances to Latino Moves,' *Wall Street Journal* (Madrid), 20 September 2003.

[17] Ray Bakke, 'World Mission Has Come to America.' *IUA*, International Urban Associates. Chicago, IL: n/d.

[18] Christian Lalive d'Epinay, Haven of the Masses: A Study of the Pentecostal Movement in Chile (London: Lutterworth 1969).

[19] Estuardo McIntosh, 7 Ensayos de la realidad misiológica en América Latina. Lima: PUCEMAA, 1990, p. 29.

[20] Samuel Escobar, *Tiempo de Misión: América Latina y la misión cristiana hoy.* Ediciones Clara/Semilla (1º edición), Colombia, 1999, p. 57.

[21] Robertson McQuilkin, president emeritus of Columbia International University, says that 'While the number of long-term missionaries from North America has stayed basically static, the number of American laity involved in short-term projects grew from 22,000 in 1979 to more than a million today.' See his article in 'Lost Missions, Whatever happened to the idea of rescuing people from hell?' *Christianity Today*, vol.50, No 7, July, 2006, p. 40.

[22] Personal conversation with Ravelo in his church office in London. July 2005.

[23] 'Worship service' does not carry the whole meaning of the Spanish and Portuguese word *culto*. It is more than the regular Sunday service, for *culto* conveys the idea of any meeting where prayer and Bible reading are performed both formally and informally. These gatherings may take place at church, in homes, or at any other location that people might find suitable.

[24] Christián Parker, 'La sociología de la religión y la modernidad: Por una revisión crítica de las categorías durkhenianas desde América Latina'in *Sociedad y Religión*, No. 13, 1995, pp. 35, 36.

[25] Swiss sociologist Christian Lalive d'Epinay observed that Pentecostal Churches in Chile served this purpose for the rural immigrants who came to the capital city. In a sense, the same phenomenon might be taking place in Europe with the ethnic churches. See the reference above.

[26] Not only is this church reaching out to the growing Latino community arriving in England, but it has also led Kensington Temple to adopt the same strategy for church growth. See 'The G-12 Vision Explained,' *Revival Times* (Kensington Temple magazine) 3/2. February 2001.

[27] Samuel Escobar, 'Conflict of Interpretations of Popular Protestantism' in *New Face of the Church in Latin America* , Guillermo Cook, ed. (Maryknoll, N.Y.: Orbis Books, 1994), p. 112.

[28] 'Learning from each other,' in *Idea*, Nov–Dec 1997, p. 5.

[29] Richard Houston, 'Navigating Uncharted Waters' in *Encounter Magazine*, vol. 6, No. 1, Spring 1999, p. 4.

Part Four

The Eastern European Context

Chapter 10

The Evolution of Nationalism Within the Bulgarian Orthodox Church

James L. Hopkins

The Bulgarian Orthodox Church has served Bulgarian nationalism for a thousand years in conditions of infinite diversity. . . . It is not the gospel that the patriarch and bishops in Sofia hold high for the Bulgarian people . . . It is the national cause in its church wrappings that they propagate today.[1]

The inspiration behind the writing of this chapter is a positive one. Twenty-first century Europe has changed dramatically in light of the integration of many countries from the former Communist Bloc, a great number of which are predominantly Eastern Orthodox. Another reason, however, is negative, for the history of Eastern Christianity has for most Western Europeans remained a closed book. As such they know nothing about Orthodox tradition or the dynamic interrelationship which developed between church and nation. This is a relationship which historically has not taken kindly to interference from alien cultural, political or religious influences. Greek, Polish, Bulgarian, Romanian and Cypriot churches have now become part of a considerable Orthodox community within Europe which will have the right to make significant contribution to defining the future development of Europe. Many questions have therefore been asked regarding the acceptance of these countries into the European Union, specifically relating to their affect on the Western economy. However, Michael Kuttin, Austrian Minister of Finance, asked a fundamentally important question during deliberations on Europe's eastward expansion, 'Can Orthodox Christianity be a part of Europe?'[2]

It has been impossible to contemplate this question for almost seventeen hundred years, as there remained substantial political and spiritual division between East and West. Kuttin's question reflects the ancient history of Europe, recognizing a 'fault-line' that has split Europe going back in time to the division of the Roman Empire into Eastern and Western halves by Emperor Diocletian (246–316). This reveals the challenge which lies before us as East and West reunite. The 'clash of civilizations' of which Samuel Huntingdon wrote has now not only transpired, primarily at a political and economic level, but also as a cultural and ultimately spiritual confrontation.[3] The outcome of this confrontation will be revealed over time. It is my desire in this chapter to investigate the immediate consequences of Europe's eastward expansion upon one small branch of Christendom, the Bulgarian Orthodox Church (BOC).

Spas Raikin's comment regarding the relationship between the BOC and nationalism serves to portray the passion for which the Bulgarian church holds the nation. The co-existence of church and nation reaches into the very nature of every Bulgarian. Orthodox Christianity, national identity, culture and politics have become deeply intertwined in the life of the nation. Indeed, Bulgaria's socio-political environment has been forged by the dominant themes of religion and nation, so much so that it may be argued that Bulgaria's acceptance into a Greater Europe is the antithesis of Bulgarian Orthodox national identity. The Bulgarian government's Euro-centric journey has challenged the Orthodox Church, either to welcome European expansion and accept the accompanying incorporation of Western cultural and spiritual trends or else to construct a barricade around its traditional ethnocentric mentality. In this essay we will investigate the themes of church and national identity analysing the development of the relationship between church and nation in Bulgaria and conclude with an examination of contemporary developments in the church since Bulgaria's acceptance into the European Union in January 2007.

An investigation of national identity in Bulgaria requires that special attention be given to that ancient relationship between church and nation, particularly as the old alliance between religion and politics has recently reappeared with potentially disquieting consequences. Historically the Church in Bulgaria has been used as an inspiration for nationalism and as a political instrument in conflict situations.[4] With the advent of Bulgaria's European integration, is history simply repeating itself or, has the BOC taken a radically new nationalistic direction?

Ecclesiastical nationalism

In a 1992 article Peter Kuzmić argued that nationalism had been one of the major challenges facing the traditional Balkan churches during the process of replacing communist ideology: 'The major problem for the Christian Church and its mission may be the temptation to return to a quasi-Constantinian model of Church-State co-operation. In this process . . . there is an intense and valid rediscovery of national-religious identity.'[5] The weakness of Kuzmić's theory is its situational generality, for in the Bulgarian context that 'quasi-Constantinian model' has never been terminated by the Bulgarian Church. That intimate relationship between church, state and nation is a service which Bulgaria's Orthodox ecclesiastical hierarchy has performed throughout the centuries with enthusiasm and without reservation:

The Holy Orthodox Church is the traditional confession of the Bulgarian people. The Bulgarian Orthodox Church is linked with the history and the development of our nation. It is a Church of the people, a democratic church.

For more than 1100 years now our church has been educating and cultivating unflinchingly and with zeal the believing fellow countrymen of the mother country and outside it in loyalty to Holy Orthodoxy, which is the history of the nation over the centuries. The Bulgarian Orthodox Church has made an exceptional contribution in keeping alive national self-consciousness, and in creating a rich spiritual culture within our borders . . . it has helped during the years of slavery to preserve the mother tongue, the morality and the religious and moral traditions of the Bulgarian people. It is with good reason that our Orthodox Church is called a Church of the people.

Our Church has lived and will continue to live with the successes and hardships of the mother country . . . With good conscience the church will in every way contribute towards achieving national unity . . . and will teach the people to labour diligently where their duty requires it.[6]

Such public utterances are evidence that, for the BOC, religion and nationhood are identical realities, dependent upon one another, the nation providing the body and the church the soul to Bulgaria.[7] One of the recurrent themes in Bulgarian Orthodox publications is the parallel continuity between church and nation, linking that progression historically to the Patriarchates of the First and Second Bulgarian Empires. This doctrine is not new, the close identity of church, state and nation has been advanced by every Bulgarian historian from Paisii Hilendarski (1722–1798) to the present day and by every leader of the BOC past and present.[8] The Church's strength, it appears, has been founded more in Bulgaria's particularity and unity with political and national history, than in the ecumenism and mission of universal orthodoxy.

Historical foundations of Bulgarian nationalism

The difficulty in attempting to define nation and nationalism is to find any agreement within the diverse formulae encompassing the subject. Nevertheless, it is necessary to comprehend the historical foundation behind these theories as this will enable us to analyse and interpret them in relation to our subject matter. Within the context of this essay the term 'nationalism' will be used to convey devotion to a cultural-linguistic collectivity which has manifested itself in its respect toward the history, culture, traditions and religion of a particular nation and seeks to promote a specific culture and way of life identified as that of the nation.[9]

Balkan nationalism was initially affected by the German nationalist movement, particularly the eighteenth century work of philosopher Johann Gottfried von

Herder (1744–1803). At the height of the German nationalist period Herder emphasized the importance of respecting, preserving and advancing national groupings. He argued that nations were not defined by imperial dynastic power structures but were differentiated by linguistic and historical–cultural factors.[10] This theory coincided with the situation in South-eastern Europe where religion had been the dominant cultural differentiation in people's lives for centuries. By the nineteenth-century Bulgarian nationalism had developed into what has been termed 'Christoslavism', the theory that all Slavs are Christian by nature and therefore are racially Christian.[11] This theory continues to be implicit in the contemporary religio-cultural debate over the issue 'to be Bulgarian is to be Eastern Orthodox.'

Eugene Lemberg rejects the theory that common qualities such as religion, language and culture are what make a nation. He prefers to talk of nationalism as a 'system of notions, values and norms . . . an ideology,' which demarcate a group from its environment.[12] In Bulgaria's social environment during the nineteenth century that defining 'system' was religion. Indeed, sociologists have pointed out that the intimate relationship between nationalist and religious movements in the nineteenth century both had inspirational and revivalist characteristics.[13] Opposing the unifying cultural and ideological theories of nation, and thus contradicting the ecclesiastical Bulgarian definition of nationalism, Eric Hobsbawn suggests that the political and modern nature of nationality were born purely of nineteenth-century political machinations.[14]

Both these concepts are based on an original differentiation promoted by Friedrich Meinecke between *Staatnation* (nation-state) and *Kulturalnation* (cultural nation):

> We can divide nations into cultural and state-nations: into those which rest basically on a certain commonly experienced cultural possession and those which rest basically on the unifying power of a shared political history and constitution. Shared language, shared literature and shared religion are the most important and effective cultural goods that create and hold a cultural nation together.[15]

This differentiation has taken many forms including its most recent articulation between 'modernist' and 'traditionalist' approaches. Every theory, however, follows Meinecke's basic model of separation: modern-political nation or traditional-cultural/religious nation.

Although theorists prefer to promote one or another of these concepts, this research would ask if such a strict demarcation is really possible in the Bulgarian situation. Both theories have their place in the context of the Bulgarian nation: the modernist theory explains clearly the progression and development of nineteenth-century political machinations, while the traditionalist theory retains significance for what occurred prior to and to an extent simultaneously with the modern era. Therefore although contemporary nationalist debate surrounding 'nation-state' versus 'cultural nation' retains significance, in the context of this essay it would be profitable to speak of 'cultural-nation' and 'nation-state' in parallel, such as the 'cultural-nation state'.

Nationalism has political and cultural preconditions often rooted in the history of a nation. In Bulgaria both the idea and first forms of nationalism appeared before the nineteenth century and the so-called 'age of nationalism'. Although political nation-states began to manifest themselves simultaneous with the breakup of the Ottoman Empire, they still continued to be dominated by religious issues. In the Bulgarian situation the demise of Ottoman administration enabled the creation of a Bulgarian *millet*.[16] However, this cannot be deemed to have been as a result of Bulgarian nationalism per se, because a nation did not exist. It is therefore a problem of the language and terminology used. In Bulgaria's nineteenth-century struggle for church autonomy it may be better to speak, not of nationalism, but rather of *milletism*. Whichever term is preferred the concept of distinctiveness and separation from the 'other' remains the same. Undoubtedly the modern concept of nation-state has imposed itself as the dominant paradigm, but it is not the only one.

It is clear that Balkan and particularly Bulgarian nationalism have followed quite a different path from their West European counterparts. The precise geographical territory on which Balkan nations were to exist was unclear, unlike that of their Western counterparts. Therefore those first Balkan nationalists had to deal initially with the creation of a national identity within unspecified territorial borders. Religion and the specifics of local ecclesiastical eparchial borders lent themselves to the formation of Bulgarian identity as a nation. Each Balkan group in attempting to produce a history of its own pointed to the ecclesiastical traditions of its national church to emphasize its cultural and territorial difference from its neighbour. To comprehend the foundational links between church and nation we require looking back further still.

Formative links between Church and Nation/State

Georges Florovsky noted that Christianity is essentially a social religion whose point of reference is society. Christianity by necessity requires expressing itself in relation to society and state.[17] That association was reciprocated by the state for the first time in the Edict of Milan, pronounced by Constantine Augustus and Licinius Augustus in A.D. 313. This established Christianity as a *religio licita* thereby giving the Christian religion legal status and making the persecution of its followers illegal.[18] Subsequently, it became the favoured religion of the Roman Empire and later in A.D. 380 the official religion of the Empire, when Theodosius I (379–395) announced Christianity *cunctus populous* in the Edict of Thessalonica. This created a radically new situation which set the tone for the church's relationship with the state for the next 1,000 years: the church would serve the empire and the empire would protect the church. As the administrative centre of the Roman Empire moved eastwards it inclined towards Greek culture and language and Latin was discarded as the administrative language of church and state. Consequently religion and state became increasingly linked. As a result of the Great Schism of 1054 and later the sacking and occupation of Constantinople during the Fourth Crusade in the thirteenth century, Byzantine citizens identified the West as their enemy. Consequently bonds between Eastern Orthodoxy and the Byzantine State were reinforced so that Orthodoxy and Byzantine nationhood became intricately intertwined.[19] With Ottoman conquests in the fourteenth century and the establishment of the *millet* system, religion metamorphosed to become the sole determiner of cultural identity. This historical equation of religious and political unity equalling national identity was accepted by nineteenth-century nationalist movements as the framework in which they sought to develop increasingly secular concepts of the nation state.

The tension between the universal and the particular has been ever present within Orthodoxy. This can be identified clearly in the church's practical struggle to express itself as part of the wider catholic Church while simultaneously being part of an independent national or local church. All Orthodox Churches belong to the one universal Church, having the same liturgy, creed and canon; at the same time each local church requires to express its own cultural attributes, its historical peculiarities and its independence. Nevertheless, this expression of independence requires to be held in balance with the universality of the Church, and, in an effort to achieve this equanimity, the Ecumenical Patriarchate in Constantinople denounced nationalism as a negation of catholicity of the Church in 1904. Therefore any local Orthodox Church formed and based exclusively on nationalism, culture, class or ethnicity should regard itself not as a Church but rather as a purely nationalistic and cultural phenomenon, totally removed from the eschatological vision of the Kingdom of God.

Despite this denunciation, contemporary Orthodox theologians have expressed their dismay that every local Orthodox Church now exhibits nationalistic tendencies. According to John Meyendorff the Church became absorbed in nationalism during the nineteenth century.[20] Consequently the Balkan Orthodox Churches became deeply disunited, affirming their national identities at the expense of Orthodoxy's universal mission. National Churches treated each other with suspicion and hostility and submitted to what Vladimir Solovyov termed the 'provincialism of local traditions.'[21] This resulted in the sowing of unwanted division within the Churches of the Balkans which affects the region to the present day. Research undertaken during the spring of 1994 revealed that people from every Balkan nation confessed an aversion to their neighbour. For this reason Maros Mpegzos has called nationalism the enemy of the people.[22] Further research has suggested that the educational system within the Balkans may be at fault, as it has the propensity to instill a sense of national, cultural and spiritual superiority over its neighbours.[23]

The Bulgarian educational system has been heavily influenced by Paisii Hilendarski's *Slavo-Bulgarian History*.[24] His was the first national revival attempt to single out the Bulgarian national community from other Balkan communities by restoring the memory of a common past. In doing so he sought to implant in his reader's minds the concept that the Bulgarian nation was a fact of history, an existing reality within its own justifiable borders and not something to be created but rather re-established. In order to achieve the emancipation of the Bulgarian nation, through its separation and opposition to others, he set a number of goals before the Bulgarian people: First, he emphasized its religious distinction as an Orthodox community; then as a Slavic community he emphasized its distinctive language and culture; and last, as a separate ethnic group within the greater Slav community, he advanced the theory of its racial distinction, thereby maintaining the uniqueness of Bulgarians among the Slavic peoples. In this way he established a foundation for future national emancipation by creating a history which emphasized Bulgaria's uniqueness and superiority. Paisii's *History* also created within the Bulgarian educational system a model for proclaiming national superiority: 'There are many historical facts and phenomena which may help strengthen our sense of national dignity by bringing to the fore the advantages of our people over other peoples...'[25]

National segregation, although influenced by Paisii Hilendarski, was moulded in the struggle to establish modern secular education in Bulgaria. The struggle centred on the use of Bulgarian language in schools. Indeed, the efforts to restore the Bulgarian vernacular became one and the same as the effort for political emancipation. Thus, during the nineteenth century and in the birth of many of the Balkan nation-states language became a politicized tool. One of the entitlements for becoming a nation-state was justified by the existence of a culture's independent vernacular language.[26] For this reason the struggle for affirmation of the Bulgarian national vernacular became an important step in the struggle for national state sovereignty.

The development of Bulgarian nationalism in pre-Ottoman Bulgaria

The territory comprising of modern Bulgaria was first settled by the Slavs in the sixth and seventh centuries. However, it was not until the end of the seventh century that the region was invaded by the Proto-Bulgars and remained a loosely organized medieval kingdom until the ninth century. Following the ascension of Khan Boris I (852–889) the Bulgarian kingdom progressed from being a somewhat irrelevant and unorganized 'pagan' kingdom to become an independent sovereign Christian Empire. Under the rule of Boris an independent Bulgarian national and Christian identity was born, some ten centuries before the birth of the secular Bulgarian nation-state. Indeed, from that moment 'nationalism' or 'strong independent cultural identity' has been an integral part of the Bulgarian Church and nation.

In the eleventh century Bulgaria fell under the sway of the Byzantine Empire and in the fourteenth century was invaded by the Ottoman Empire, remaining under its administration until the late nineteenth century. Therefore, for the greater part of its existence Bulgaria has been under the jurisdiction of a foreign power and during this lengthy period of alien domination Bulgarian national and cultural consciousness almost disappeared. For this reason the year 1762 is cited as a definitive moment in Bulgarian history, for it was then that Paisii Hilendarski completed his *Slavo-Bulgarian History*. Driven by fervent national consciousness and by his fellow Bulgarians' abject lack of national awareness Paisii wrote his *History* to prevent the total disappearance of Bulgarian national territory, people, culture and history, which had almost been accomplished by means of Islamicization and Hellenization of the Bulgarian people over five centuries. Over time Paisii's *History* succeeded in sparking national consciousness in the Bulgarian people which in turn gave rise to the advent of the Bulgarian National Revival.

Orthodox Christianity and nation building in Ottoman Bulgaria

For Byzantine Christendom the fall of Constantinople in 1453 was a decisive turning point. In the article entitled '"Imagined Communities" and the Origins of the National Question in the Balkans' by the Greek historian P. M. Kitromilides, the author uses modern theories of nationalism to re-assess the traditional comprehension of Balkan scholars regarding the function of the Orthodox Church under Ottoman rule.[27]

Kitromilides argues that Balkan nationalist mythology has obscured a correct understanding of the relation between Orthodoxy and nationalism. Therefore if we are to re-assess this relationship, particularly in regard to Bulgaria, we must see through stereotypical nationalist interpretations which promote the view that the BOC played a major role in preserving the ethnic identity of Bulgarians under Ottoman rule and in guiding their national awakening. An explicit claim of this interpretation is the identification of Orthodoxy with nationality and the ensuing recognition of the BOC as a vanguard of Bulgarian nationalism. Kitromilides proffers general criticism of Eastern Orthodoxy as the preserver of collective identity under the Ottomans. However, his criticism is pertinent to Bulgarian historiography's 'continuity theory', which promotes the view that as preserver of Bulgarian collective identity, the BOC created the basis for future nation-building and political independence.[28]

First and foremost Kitromilides draws attention to the contradiction between religious and national communities. Basing his criticism on the biblical exhortation of Galatians 3.28 that in Christ 'there is neither Jew nor Greek, slave nor free, male nor female, for you are all one in Christ', he argues that Christianity's demand for universalism established the basis for Orthodox ecumenism, which in turn prevented the Patriarchate of Constantinople from being affected by nineteenth-century Enlightenment ideals which called for national identity and the establishment of separate nation-states. By this interpretation the nationalization of Balkan Church organization required a radical break from Orthodox canon and tradition that condemned nationalism as phyletism.[29]

Theological reasoning brings to the fore the fundamental and inescapable antimony between Orthodoxy and nationalism, between the incompatibility of the communities of religion and nation. Indeed, when nationalism raised its head the Church met the challenge with open hostility. One only has to recall the Bulgarian Exarchate's response to the nationalist rebels. The Bulgarian ecclesiastical hierarchy refused to support the Bulgarian nationalist cause, which threatened to ruin their relationship with the Ottoman Porte. Instead they handed the rebels over to the Ottoman authorities. Kitromilides claims therefore that one of the greatest anachronisms in Balkan historiography consists in its presentation of the Ottoman religious political system as being based on national difference; the difference he argues was based not on national but rather religious distinction. The only way in which the Orthodox Church could maintain a collective sense of identity among Christians in the Balkans was by emphasizing their religious unity. But under the Ottoman *millet* system the mixing of Orthodoxy and nationality implied a radical renunciation of biblical principle and Orthodox ecumenism. For this reason Kitromilides criticizes the way that Balkan historiography has uncritically accepted the link between Orthodoxy and national identity. Bulgarian national historiographical tradition has been premised on the assumption that the BOC played a major role in nation building by preserving collective identity under the Ottomans. The BOC in short is supposed to have created Bulgarian national identity through the years of captivity. According to Kitromilides' assessment, however, we must conclude that if the BOC did indeed contribute to the preservation of Bulgarian collective identity, this distinction was religious – not national – in content.

Despite Kitromilides' thought-provoking analysis, his article requires additional comment particularly in relation to the specifics of the Bulgarian situation. His presentation of the contradiction between Christian biblical foundations and the birth of national communities, although not incorrect, is utopian. It fails to recognize the complex inter-relation between political and ecclesiastical powers prior to the emergence of nation-states. Failure to do so creates a problematic historical vacuum, for since its recognition by the Roman Empire in the fourth century the Christian Church has maintained an intensely close relationship to the political powers of the day, a relationship articulated by the classic edict of Emperor Justinian (527–565) in 535: 'The greatest blessing of mankind are the gifts of God which have been granted us by the mercy on high: the priesthood and the imperial authority. The priesthood ministers to the things divine; the imperial authority is set over, and shows diligence in, things human; but both proceed from one and the same source, and both adorn the life of man . . .'[30] There can be no doubt that in Byzantine understanding the emperor and the church were intricately connected in a glorious concept of symphony: a sovereign empire required an autocephalous church. The Bulgars demonstrated that they had successfully adopted the Byzantine model by establishing the Bulgarian kingdom as a fully independent political power with its own self-governing church organization, albeit in theological and liturgical unity with the Constantinople Patriarchate.

This model entailed a major weakness; if political power collapsed so would the independence of the church. Therefore after the conquest of Bulgaria in 1393 its independent church structure disintegrated and after the fall of Constantinople in 1453 all Orthodox Christian inhabitants of the sultan were incorporated into a single church organization, under the authority of the Patriarch of Constantinople. The Ottoman *millet* system did not, however, create a radical break from former imperial religious tradition, rather it flowed in logical consequence for the Byzantine imperial Church, as it united in 'symphony' with its new political master. Indeed, the situation was viewed as providential, as the *millet* protected the purity of the Orthodox faith from the danger of Latin Christianity.

From his historical analysis Kitromilides claims that Orthodox Churches in the Balkans were neither ethnically nor nationally defined: 'The mediaeval churches were not national churches because their empires were not national; such an assertion is anachronistic.'[31] This researcher would disagree with that rejection of Orthodoxy as a synonym for national identification in the period prior to the nineteenth century. Kitromilides' anachronism lies again in the technical form of language used. Our historical preview revealed that Tsar Boris' goal for his Church was to be an instrument unifying Slav and Proto-Bulgar elements in the Bulgarian population resulting in the strengthening of his kingdom.[32] Therefore the Bulgarian medieval Church was founded and developed precisely on ethnic and nationalist foundations. History's generalized assumption that this relationship changed only with the advent of modern nationalism is clearly misconceived in the Bulgarian context. Nevertheless, the fragmentation of the Orthodox *millet* in Ottoman Europe into smaller national units during the nineteenth century did occur as the result of radical Western national ideological ideals which transformed the *millet* system and Orthodox tradition into the idea that nation-building must be accompanied by church institutional independence.

This critique of Kitromilides raises that most contentious question in the ongoing debate on the concept of nation and nationalism: Do nations have their origins in the modern political, social and economic conditions of the nineteenth century, or should these roots be sought in more ancient times? Kitromilides asks the same question in another manner: Did Orthodoxy become

politically instrumentalized in the nineteenth-century nation-building movement, or was the Church always an indicator of collective identity, before, during
and after the Ottomans? Although the latter view is generally closer to the relationship between church and nation in Bulgaria it would appear to be a matter
of degree: To what degree were national characteristics learned or acquired in
the modern national construction process, or were they continuations of medieval kingdoms?

Bulgaria during the period of state nationalism

The nineteenth century marked a new chapter in church–state relations for
Orthodoxy in Bulgaria. Disparate medieval Balkan societies had been politically unified by the Ottoman conquest, and with the advent of the *millet* system
they were ecclesiastically, culturally and psychologically bound together by the
traditions of Eastern Orthodoxy. However, with the import of Western Enlightenment ideals in the late eighteenth and early nineteenth centuries, modern
concepts of secular statehood threatened to subvert both Ottoman rule and
Orthodox unity. The work of national awakeners, such as Paisii Hilendarski,
although emphasizing Bulgaria's Orthodox history, actually succeeded in loos-
ening that ancient concept of Orthodox unity, which in turn gave impetus to
the gradual articulation of a secular historical interpretation of Bulgarian identity. Those secular-inspired patriots aimed to subordinate religion to state power.
By accepting the autocephaly of the Bulgarian Church the politicians hoped to
control it. Thereafter the Church was stripped of its authority and became, in
imitation of the Western model, an agency of the state.

Through the ensuing Bulgarian National Revival period the socio-political
process towards national independence passed through a number of stages.
The first affirmed the cultural and religious character of Bulgarian national identity, then organizations were formed which championed the national cause and
finally elite concepts of nationalism were espoused by the masses in the formation of the secular Bulgarian state in 1878. After the first great victory of Bulgarian
nationalism, the establishment of the Bulgarian Exarchate (1870), the Bulgarians turned their attention to agitating for their separation from the Ottoman
Empire. Thus towards the end of the nineteenth century the concept of 'nation'
became tantamount to Bulgaria. The national revival era spawned a new class
of Bulgarians: artisans, merchants, intelligentsia and priests, who guided the
Bulgarian people, informing them of who they were and, perhaps more impor-
tantly, who they were not. National awareness served to differentiate ethnic
Bulgarians from ethnic Turks. National consciousness rose to such levels that
many Bulgarians were willing to defend the sovereignty of their land. Thus alongside the struggle for and introduction of an independent national state, including church institutions, army, schools and a state constitution, arose a spontaneous

wave of violence against former symbols and reminders of Ottoman–Muslim power. Muslim families were forced to flee, houses were burned and mosques destroyed as the Orthodox Christian population sought to obliterate the characteristics of previous domination.

Once the San Stefano borders of Bulgaria had been reversed by the Berlin Treaty (1878), the re-incorporation of lost territories became the goal of the nationalists. Bulgarian nationalism therefore did not only express a pride in the borders agreed by European politicians, but demanded the recognition of lands that historically belonged to Bulgaria and were now, it was argued, populated by ethnic Bulgarians. Therefore as early as 1878 during debates within the Constitutional Assembly it was proclaimed that, '...we who are part of this nation shall never rest . . . We shall always support the wishes and attempts, of those, who are flesh of our flesh and blood of our blood...'[33]

In this sense the Balkan Wars, and to an extent the two World Wars, demonstrated the people's commitment to the Bulgarian nationalist cause. Those wars were not fought to fulfil someone else's greater European or global objectives but were undertaken to accomplish the national unification of Bulgaria's dispersed ethnic population within her historically justifiable borders: 'Bulgaria has always united in a single entity only the Bulgarian people; the waged wars, in general, were aimed at the unification of the people.'[34] However, the liberation of Bulgarians outside Bulgaria's recognized borders was not the only goal of the nationalists; they called for the enlargement of the state to include regions that belonged to Bulgaria in the past. Thus the development of the nation and the desire to establish a Greater Bulgaria were presented as the finest Bulgarian virtues, as the ultimate justice crowning the people's movement towards happiness.[35] Only by achieving this goal would the Bulgarian people be enabled to 'grow and improve on the basis of the values which incorporate them into spiritual entities'.[36] By this interpretation anything which stood against national unification and the expansionist efforts of the Bulgarian state was deemed unfair and unjust. Hence, the findings of the Berlin Congress were 'unfair' because they cut off parts of the nation, but war on the other hand was viewed as being 'liberating and legitimate'.[37] This value system was structured around two teleological theories: progress is compulsory for humanity and humanity's progress is conditioned upon the progress of nations, which, in Bulgaria's situation, was feasible only under national unification. Symbolically then 1870 marked the transition from church-nationalism to state-building nationalism and 1878 the passing from state-building to irredentist nationalism, a stage which would last until 1944.

Nationalism, internationalism and communist Bulgaria

The communists initially considered Bulgaria's xenophobic concentration on nationalist issues to be a debilitating obstacle in the establishment of their global and domestic policies. Steered by Moscow, the authorities of the Fatherland Front sought to remove the hindrance through the creation of a Balkan Federal Republic. This would be built upon the principles of internationalism rather than on the right of the nation. One of the first indicators of this new direction appeared in a school textbook from 1946, which talked about the 'emancipation of the people' and the 'possibility to realize people's interests'. The realization of people's happiness, it was stated, could be achieved only at an international level and therefore the historical narration of the book attempted to diminish Bulgarian national identity and engender a greater sense of Balkan détente. The textbook implied that continuing on a path of inward national self-absorption and claiming superiority over fellow communist neighbours would lead to 'catastrophe'; whereas internationalism was linked with the concept of 'salvation': 'The new path [communism] which Bulgaria takes on – the path of the people's welfare, Slavic brotherhood and unification – is a path traced by our history, by our historical development. Each deviation from this path has led to national calamity.'[38] Through this historical interpretive lens of Stanev's view of Bulgarian history, the praise of war and struggle for unification, were understood to be 'aggressive and catastrophic'. Nationalist ideals were to be replaced with an internationalist identity based no longer on universal Orthodoxy but communist internationalism.

From the 1970s, however, the communist credo changed substantially. The emphasis became nationally focused once again with the authorities claiming that all citizens of Bulgaria were Bulgarian. The socio-political reasoning behind this emphasis was to affirm the ethnic identity of Bulgarians, to the exclusion of any religious reference. Bulgarians were treated as one non-religious ethnos.[39] Thus, the xenophobic nationalism of previous Bulgarian generations continued even within this appeal to international communism. The Bulgarian Communist Party (BCP) followed its own nationalist programme which aimed at assimilating every Bulgarian Pomak and Turkic Muslim into one homogeneous Bulgarian population.[40] The BCP used every means at their power, including educational and ecclesiastical resources, to prove that there were no Turks in Bulgaria. Even Bulgarian Orthodox Church history was re-interpreted to justify the government's confrontational policy to separate Muslim religious and national identity.

So why did the BCP undertake this assimilation process? The Bulgarian press suggested that the government had been attempting to defuse virulent Islamic separatist movements.[41] However, a contemporary report on Bulgarian ethnic groupings appears to provide an answer closer to reality. The study reported that Bulgaria's Turkish-Muslim population had grown alarmingly, while Christian Bulgarian numbers were on the decrease.[42] The Politburo suggested that in this Muslim growth lay the possibility of eventual Ottoman-cum-Turkish revanchism, which if unchecked would lead to the Muslims outnumbering the Orthodox Slav population. In this manner the communist authorities revealed their national policies to be on par with both post-Ottoman and wartime Bulgarian governments, particularly in their attempts to obliterate any remaining vestige of Ottoman rule in Bulgaria.

Religion and nationalism in post-communist Bulgaria

This research has revealed that during the eras of Byzantine, Ottoman, and even to an extent communist control, the Orthodox Church has been recognized and protected as the traditional religion of the Bulgarian people. However, whenever Bulgaria has entered into periods of independence, democracy, cultural pluralism and/or religious diversity, the discourse on religion, or more precisely the place of the BOC in society, has become increasingly prominent.

This discourse, prevalent in post-communist Bulgaria, has articulated itself through the introduction of new religious statutes. Immediately after the fall of communism one of the first steps of the new government was to introduce revised laws on religion. As Paul Mojzes remarks, 'Throughout the region, constitutions and laws were written that contained guarantees for human rights and religious liberties, bringing Eastern European states in line with the Western democratic civil rights tradition.'[43] Initially these new laws guaranteed freedom of conscience and religious liberty, replacing former restrictive laws. In 2003, however, a new bill was introduced favouring the traditional role of the BOC as an 'inseparable part of Bulgaria's historical, spiritual and cultural heritage.'[44] This decision met with sharp criticism from human rights activists, politicians, minority religious groups and the European Union. Its adoption was considered retrograde, particularly for the development of democratic civil society.

By taking this decision Eastern Orthodoxy has been advanced as the 'traditional' and 'national' religion in Bulgaria, and all other religious groups have been deemed alien to the prevailing national ethos. As a result of political and ecclesiastical activity they have been accused of betraying national interests and have become objects of societal intolerance.[45] However, this development is not specific to Bulgaria; it has been a general repercussion which has arisen across post-communist Europe where nations have searched for symbols and myths to provide orientation and identity during a period of radically changing circumstance. There has been a return to the values of an 'imagined community' that existed in the past. In this sense nationalism has worked as an anti-modern factor in which the nation becomes a transformation of traditional pre-modern realities. While accepting the need to maintain stability in the midst of socio-political chaos, genuine religious freedom can never be achieved through abstract legal and governmental provision for the traditional Church:

Experience shows that the framers of the post-communist constitutional provisions for religious liberty generally tended to interpret the notion of religion in Christian terms and even in the terms of the Christian churches traditions for a particular country. This trend nurtured by the common lack of religious culture, not to say ignorance in religious matters. . . is hardly justifiable at the level of state policy.[46]

Father Innokenti Pavlov, in analysing the preferential treatment of the Orthodox Church, has suggested that these actions are attempts to endorse a new state ideology to replace the spiritual void after the collapse of communism. In addition he identifies an ambition within particular political circles that attempts to promote the Orthodox Church as the new compulsory 'national' ideology in the place of the old.[47] For this reason other religious movements are considered to be an alien threat to the state, and restrictions can therefore be legitimately placed on them. Father Pavlov's argument is open to the criticism that it fails to consider the constitutional provisions which explicitly favour a model of separation between church and state. Yet the Bulgarian church-state separation has clearly articulated itself within the terms of the 'accommodationist' approach, or to quote Mark Howe, the 'liberal principle of tolerance' as opposed to the 'radical principle of religious liberty.'[48] This explains why Bulgarian governmental preference is still given to the traditional Church of the state. In other words, constitutionally defined separation signifies neither neutrality, indifference nor neglect. A contradiction had arisen, however, in that post-communist Bulgaria's support of the BOC did not equate with her leaning towards European integration. This inconsistency would not remain silent within the religious pluralism of multi-cultural European existence.

The contemporary evolution of Bulgarian nationalism

On 1 January 2007 Bulgaria became a full member of the European Union. For a number of years prior to its accession the Bulgarian government had been forced to re-assess its traditional historical relationship with the BOC. Having signed the Agreement for Accession to the European Union on 25 April 2005 Bulgaria was instructed that one of the stipulations of its acceptance would be a required change in relationship between state and church. This would involve a democratization of relationships, a harmonizing of legislature on religion with European legal standards and the formation of a favourable social context from which to work these new laws.

This action was deemed necessary as the Bulgarian parliament had, as previously mentioned, adopted a new Law on Religions (2003) which granted preferential treatment, official status and automatic registration to the BOC. Widespread protest against the 'unjustness' of this new law had shaken the political establishment. Eighteen legally registered religious organizations voiced their concern, the basic premise behind their protest being that all religious bodies in Bulgaria were to be subject to restrictions which did not apply to any other non-government organization. They were particularly aggrieved because the BOC had been granted complete immunity from these state restrictions.[49] Article 9 of the new law stated that non-Orthodox religious communities had to register with the courts; if they did not, they could be legally banned and their leaders punished. It also allowed courts to punish non-Orthodox religious organizations for a wide variety of offences including banning their activities for up to 6 months; restricting the distribution of religious literature; cancelling an organizations registration and these punishments could also incur fines of up to 5,000 leva (2,600 Euros). While accepting the Bulgarian Constitution's affirmation describing the BOC as the nation's traditional religion, the protest-ers objected to its being granted extra judicial rights which discriminated against other religious organizations. They condemned these as being com-pletely unjust, contravening not only the Bulgarian Constitution but also the Constitution of the European Court of Human Rights.

Bulgaria's religious minorities were not alone in criticizing the 2003 Law on Religions; the Organization on Security and Cooperation in Europe (OSCE) also raised its concerns.[50] In a report published in the same year the OSCE voiced alarm that Bulgaria's commitments to religious freedom were out of step with the requirements needed to satisfy entry into the European Union. For example, in its haste to pass the Law on Religions, the Bulgarian government neglected to consult with religious communities other than the Orthodox dur-ing the drafting process. Also during the review stage of the bill it refused to respond to complaints brought by 50 parliamentary representatives regarding this issue. The OSCE also criticized the Sofia City Court, mandated to deal with all religious re-registration, for its stalling tactics on issuing registrations. The major concern raised by the OSCE report regarded the Bulgarian government's recognition of the BOC as the 'traditional church of Bulgaria'. The apprehen-sion being that the positive assessment given by the State to one religion and one creed would explicitly influence the choice of public religious opinion and also automatically give the BOC legal advantage over other religious groups. The registration process clearly favoured Orthodox organizations and discrimi-nated against non-Orthodox religious bodies. It was apparent that this system was open to arbitrary and non-transparent decision making by pro-Orthodox civil servants. The OSCE report concluded by stating that the Bulgarian Law on Religions curtailed fundamental freedoms of religious minorities in Bulgaria and should therefore be amended and brought into line with decisions of the Constitution of the European Court of Human Rights. This resulted in the Par-liamentary Assembly of the Council of Europe, along with the European Court of Human Rights, condemning the Law on Religions (2003). They concluded that the Bulgarian government had interfered with religious freedom: '. . . the right to freedom of religion excludes any discretion on the part of the State to determine whether religious beliefs or the means used to express them are legitimate.'[51] Thus the entry of Bulgaria into the European Union involved an important national challenge, namely, the reassessment of the relationship between church and state and the creation of democratic standards vis-à-vis religion.

With an evolving Euro-centric identity the present Bulgarian government has been forced to re-assess its historical relationship with the Orthodox Church. The present hierarchy of the BOC has been unwilling to alter its traditional stance, indeed the Church itself appears to have exacerbated the problem. The BOC's inextricable link with national identity has led it to forge new political relationships. As the leading political parties have refused to openly place the BOC in a position of pre-eminence, the hierarchy of the Church has sought a new political alliance, with the 'Attack Coalition' (Ataka) which recognizes the ancient role of the BOC.[52]

On Monday 27 March, 2006 representatives from the Holy Synod of the BOC met with the leader of the 'Ataka' Party, Volen Siderov.[53] Afterwards Siderov notified reporters that an agreement had been reached whereby his party would now provide a political voice for the BOC lobbying on their behalf in parliament. He later added that the task of representing the BOC would be one of the main political causes for 'Ataka'.[54] Siderov's willingness to assist the BOC led to his 'Ataka' party and its activities being officially blessed by representatives from the Holy Synod.

This new religio-political coalition has set a disturbing precedent. 'Ataka' openly present themselves as an ultra-nationalist party who systematically use aggressive racist, anti-European and xenophobic propaganda.[55] Its propaganda targets the country's minority groups including Roma, Turkish, Jewish, Muslim and non-Orthodox Christian communities. The party's two manifesto documents, the '20 Principles' and the 'Program Scheme' feature a number of nationalistic characteristics.[56] They define Bulgaria as a one-nation and one-religion state and ignore issues regarding ethnic and religious diversity. They demand that the national Constitution be rewritten thereby recognizing Eastern Orthodoxy as the only official religion of the Bulgarian State. They desire to see Holy Synod representation at governmental decision-making levels and they wish only Orthodox doctrine to be taught at school. They have also formulated and proposed a new crime of 'national betrayal', which would incriminate non-BOC members and human rights and minority rights activists.

The charge of 'phyletism' was raised against the BOC in 1872. Regrettably it appears that the Bulgarian Church is guilty of this once again. By blessing the activities of 'Ataka' the BOC hierarchy communicates the impression of supporting its ultra nationalistic goals. This provides justification for supporters of the 'Ataka' Party and Orthodox believers to hold racist attitudes. It deems acceptable the establishment of a triadic xenophobia within predominant Orthodox societies whereby 'others' who disagree with their policies will be perceived as non-Bulgarian, non-Christian and non-Orthodox. This can only lead to an increase in feelings of resentment and negativity towards minority non-Orthodox communities. Indeed by the summer of 2006 'Ataka's' aggressive attitude had extended from the debating chamber onto the streets of Sofia. Party representatives began a campaign against the use of loudspeakers for the call to prayer at Muslim places of worship.[57] They installed their own loudspeakers outside the sixteenth-century Banya Bashi mosque in Sofia and played loud nationalistic music during every call to prayer. Volen Siderov suggested live on national television that the call to prayer was actually 'an invitation to jihad'. He also alleged that the Chief Mufti, Mustafa Alish Hadji, was linked to radical Islam.[58]

Far from distancing themselves from these volatile actions, the BOC hierarchy has continued its support of 'Ataka'. After further success in winning a small number of seats in the European Parliamentary elections, Ioanniky, the Metropolitan of Sliven, again blessed the actions of the party. Indeed, in a national newspaper the Metropolitan announced how impressed he had been by Siderov and especially by 'Ataka's' election promise that they intended to build an 'Arch of Orthodoxy' on the borders with Turkey, so that Muslims would know upon entering Bulgaria's borders that it was an Orthodox Christian state.[59] Neofit, the Metropolitan of Ruse added his praise explaining that the Holy Synod had called on 'Ataka' to 'defend the faith of Bulgaria and the Bulgarian people from any aggression'.[60]

Conclusion

This essay has exposed the central preoccupation of 'nation' and 'religious tradition' in Bulgaria, both of which have succeeded in creating a powerful unifying effect within society. Ecclesiastical nationalism has been underpinned by the conviction that the Church is deeply rooted in the national ethos, so much so that it considers Bulgarian national culture to be unsustainable without the BOC: 'It is not the Church which should fear separation from the State, but the State which should fear separation from the Church, as this would separate Bulgaria from her soul.'[61] However, as modern civil society has evolved and particularly since Bulgaria has become a full member of the European Community, many have come to question this traditional stance. The re-invention of South-eastern European society is attempting to mirror patterns of Western democracy; it is no longer based on principles of ethnic and religious uniformity, but is founded on notions such as democracy, pluralism and tolerance. The BOC therefore finds itself in a complex situation. On the one hand it still needs to recover from the spiritual stagnation it experienced under communism, while on the other it must come to terms with new social realities, the greatest of which is religious pluralism.

This is a major reason why the BOC has found it difficult to function in contemporary Bulgaria and why it struggles, by whatever means, to maintain the patterns of the past and reinterpret its history towards a future in which the Church will once again take its place at the head of nation and society. That ultimate desire is best expressed in the words of Dostoyevsky's *The Brothers Karamazov:*

> 'The Church is not to be transformed into the State . . . On the contrary the State is transformed into the Church, it will ascend and become a church over the whole world – which is the glorious destiny ordained for the Orthodox Church.'[62]

In this vision the Orthodox Church attempts to supplant the State altogether, reflecting the true *orthos* project of the Church, not to exist with the State, but to strive to reconstruct the world on Orthodox Christian principles. Dostoyevsky articulates the implicit vision shared by Bulgaria's Orthodox hierarchy, which explains the intense struggle to maintain the BOC's traditional role within society.

This 'fortress mentality' is stereotypical of the behaviour of a Church seeking to protect itself after enduring the oppression of totalitarianism. It is the reaction of a Church which cooperated with the communist regime, initially in order to survive repression and later because it was assured particular privileges. It must be stressed, however, that despite 'survival' the BOC has been systematically and politically used, not only by communism, but also by Byzantine and Ottoman powers, so much so that the BOC now perpetuates a model of 'functional religion'. The BOC has never experienced another model and therefore follows this *modus operandi* as its benchmark. This 'fortress mentality' has tended to express itself socially in negative terms, exposing the BOC's unwillingness or inability to interact with contemporary society. Although this situation is largely due to the BOC's refusal to accept cultural plurality and religious diversity, it is also strongly based on Orthodox theology which focuses on the soteriological role of the Church in terms of eschatology. David Martin forewarned that any Church incorporated within a political power structure would eventually be involved in the ruins of that structure.[63] Ina Merdjanova fears that the BOC has become a visible illustration of that omen and has declared that the Church must develop relevant theological understandings, practical social explanations and *modus operandi* for a new democratic, pluralistic and diverse European era.[64] The failure to do so could have grave consequences for the Bulgarian Orthodox Church.

Bulgaria's national consciousness, built upon historical, cultural and religious kinship has steered the Bulgarian nation throughout the centuries. In the nineteenth century Bulgarian nationalism achieved two important and positive goals: the creation of an independent Church in the form of the Bulgarian Exarchate and the establishment of the Bulgarian Principality. Once these goals had been accomplished Bulgarian nationalism took on negative xenophobic and irredentist qualities, features which the BOC has promoted to the present day. These xenophobic features of Bulgarian nationalism have cloaked ethnic and religious discrimination in patriotic wrappings, placing membership in the Bulgarian Orthodox Church and devotion to the Fatherland above all. This nationalism is grounded in the events of the National Revival period, in a national inferiority complex, which views the Ottoman era as a catastrophic period in Bulgarian history. Xenophobic nationalism also masqueraded behind the communist credo of 'internationalism', as it sought to enforce an ethno-political homogenization programme in an attempt to submerge the Turkish-Muslim minority into the Bulgarian-Christian majority.[65]

Today, as Bulgaria strives towards a new Euro-centric existence the BOC is struggling to maintain its traditional links with the past, indicating that the hierarchy of the Church are unwilling to put their mythological past behind them. In its quest for relevance and survival the BOC has actively promoted the Bulgarian nationalist cause. In the twenty-first century the Church has discovered in ultra-nationalism its latest refuge for survival. This is the reason why Raikin, with whom this essay began, could claim that nationalism has become a deeper faith for the BOC than the Gospel. By espousing this philosophy the hierarchy of the Bulgarian Orthodox Church believes it can continue to stand with dignity.

Notes

[1] S. Raikin, 'Nationalism and the Bulgarian Orthodox Church' in P. Ramet (ed.) *Religion & Nationalism in Soviet and East European Politics*, (Durham, 1984), p. 371.
[2] Bishop Basil of Sergievo, 'Orthodoxy in a United Europe: The Future of our Past' in J. Sutton and W. van der Bercken (eds) *Orthodox Christianity and Contemporary Europe*, (Leuven, 2003), p. 3.
[3] S. Huntingdon, *The Clash of Civilizations and the Remaking of World Order*, (New York, 2002).
[4] T. Sabev, *The Orthodox Churches in the World Council of Churches: Towards the Future*, (Geneva, 1996), p. 16.
[5] P. Kuzmić, 'Christian Mission in Europe', *Themelios*, 18(1992) 23.
[6] Letter from Patriarch Maxim and the Holy Synod of the Bulgarian Orthodox Church addressed to Mr. Stanko Todorov, Chairman of the National Assembly of the People's Republic of Bulgaria (18 December 1989).
[7] Raikin, (1984), p. 201.
[8] P. Nikov, *Revival of the Bulgarian Nation* (Sofia, 1929), p. 41.
[9] P. Ramet, 'Autocephaly and National Identity in Church-State Relations in Eastern Christianity', *Eastern Christianity and Politics in the 20th Century*, (Durham, 1988), p. 6.
[10] J. G. von Herder, *Auch eine Philosophie der Geschichte der Bildung der Menschheit*, (Riga, 1774).

11 M. Velikonja, 'Historical Roots of Slovenian Christoslavic Mythology', *Religion in Eastern Europe*, 19(1999)17.

12 E. Lemberg, *Nationalismus*, (Hamburg, 1964), p. 52.

13 R. E. Park and E. W. Burgess, *Introduction to the Science of Sociology*, (Chicago, 1924), p. 931.

14 E. Hobsbawn, *Nations and Nationalism since 1780: Programme, Myth, Reality*, (Cambridge, 1992), pp. 9–11.

15 F. Meinecke, *Weltburgertum und Nationalstaat: Studien zur Genesis des deutschen Nationalstaates*, (Munich, 1919), pp. 2–3.

16 *Millet*: A community defined by religion recognised by the Ottoman state.

17 G. Florovsky, *Christianity and Culture* (Belmont, 1974), p. 132.

18 For the full text of the Edict of Milan in English see: http://gbgm-umc.org/umw/bible/milan.stm. Accessed 9 March 2008.

19 D. J. Geanakoplos, 'Religion and Nationalism in the Byzantine Empire and After: Conformity and Pluralism', *GOTR*, 22(1977)98–116.

20 J. Meyendorff, *The Orthodox Church: Its Past and its Role in the World Today*, (Crestwood, 1996), pp. 131–132.

21 A. Schmemann, *The Historical Road of Eastern Orthodoxy*, (London, 1963), p. 281.

22 M. Mpegzos, 'Ethnikismos: ho echthros tou ethnous', *Kath' Hodon*, 1(1992)18–26.

23 The Greek Helsinki Committee, *Ratismos, antisemitismos, xenophobia kai misallodoxia sten hellenike koine gnome*, this report was forwarded to various newspapers in June 1995.

24 The full title of Hilendarski's work is *Slavo-Bulgarian History of the Bulgarian People and Kings and Saints and of all the Bulgarian Acts and Events. Collected and Arranged by the Ordained Monk Paisii, who lived on Athos and had come from there from the Diocese of Samokov in 1745 finishing this History in 1762 for the Benefit of the Bulgarian People.* An English translation can be found in Paisii Hilendarski. *A Slavo-Bulgarian History. A Facsimile of the Original Zograph Manuscript Draft (1762)*, (ed.) B. Atanasov (Sofia: St.Kliment Ohrodski University Press, 2000).

25 I. Kepov and V. Kepova, *Brief Instruction for the Teaching of History in Junior High Schools*, (Sofia, 1932), p. 6.

26 S. Dimitrova, 'Bulgarian Historical Education and Perspectives of the National Identity', *Balkanistic Forum*, (Blagoevgrad, 1999), p. 57.

27 P. M. Kitromilides, '"Imagined Communities" and the Origins of the National Question in the Balkans', *European History Quarterly*, 19(1989) 149–192.

28 P. M. Kitromilides, (1989), p. 178.

29 Phyletism: the national or ethnic principle of church organisation – commonly referred to as ecclesiastical racism.

30 D. J. Geanakoplos, *Byzantium: Church, Society and Civilisation Seen through Contemporary Eyes* (Chicago, 1984), p. 136.

31 P.M. Kitromilides, (1989), p. 178.

32 For further information on this area of research see, J. Hopkins, *The Bulgarian Orthodox Church: A Socio-Historical Analysis of the Evolving Relationship Between Church, Nation, and State in Bulgaria*, (New York: Columbia University Press, 2008), Chapter 1.

33 S. Radev, *The Construction of Contemporary Bulgaria*, (Sofia, 1911), p. 69.

[34] I. Ormandzhiev and M. Velkova, *General and Bulgarian History for III Grade of the National Junior High School. Approved from 1937 to 1941,* (Sofia, 1941), p. 123.

[35] N. Stanev, *The Most Recent History of Bulgaria 1878-1941,* (Sofia, 1943), p. 295.

[36] P. Enev, 'Nationalism, Internationalism and Education', *School Review,* 5–6(1938)607.

[37] I. Kepov & V. Kepova, *Universal and Bulgarian History for III Grade of Junior High Schools,* (Sofia, 1940), p. 115.

[38] B. Bozhikov, *Bulgarian History for VII Grade of High School,* (Sofia, 1946), p. 434.

[39] Census statistics between 1965 and 1992 provide no information on national minorities, they simply provide a population figure of Bulgarian inhabitants.

[40] S. Trifonov, 'The Muslim in the Politics of the Bulgarian State', *Pages from Bulgarian History,* (Sofia, 1993), pp. 212–213.

[41] *Nova Svetlina,* 5 April 1990.

[42] I. Ilchev and D. Perry, 'Bulgarian Ethnic Groups: Politics and Prospects', *RFE/RL Research Report,* Vol.II, No.12, pp. 35–41.

[43] P. Mojzes, *Religious Liberty in Eastern Europe and the USSR before and after the Great Transformation,* (Boulder, 1992), p. 383.

[44] *Law on Religions,* December 2002.

[45] H. Grymala-Moszczynska, 'Established Religion vs. New Religion: Social Perceptions and Legal Consequences', *Journal of Ecumenical Studies,* 33(1996)69–73.

[46] I. Merdjanova, 'In Search of Identity: Nationalism and Religion in Eastern Europe', *Religion, State & Society,* 28(2000), p. 233.

[47] I. Pavlov, 'The Imperial Revanchism and the Freedom of Conscience', *The 1997 Law on the Freedom of Conscience: The International Norms and the Russian Tradition,* (Moscow, 1998), pp. 48–51.

[48] P. Hammond, *With Liberty for All. Freedom of Religion in the United States,* (Louisville, 1998), p. xi.

[49] *Law on Religions,* Article 11(2).

[50] *Bulgarian Law on Religions: Problematic Law Out of Step with OSCE Commitments,* a report prepared by the OSCE, 108th Congress, 1st Session, Washington, DC, 2003.

[51] A. Amicarelli, 'The European Union Enlargement: Human Rights Perspectives', a paper presented at the *Globalization, Immigration, and Change in Religious Movements* International Conference, June 7–9, 2007, Bordeaux, France.

[52] At the general election on 25 June 2005 'Ataka' won 9.0 per cent of the popular vote. By March 2006 it was claimed that 25 per cent of the electorate now supported 'Ataka', *SKAT,* 3 March, 2006.

[53] 'Ataka will lobby for the Bulgarian Orthodox Church in Parliament', *Focus,* 27 March, 2006.

[54] 'Blessings of the Holy Synod on the BOC's Party Ataka', *Focus,* 29 March, 2006.

[55] 'Human Rights in the OSCE Region', *International Helsinki Federation for Human Rights,* (2006), p. 100.

[56] See the 'Ataka' web site for further information (in Bulgarian language only), www.ataka.bg. Accessed 8 April 2008.

[57] 'Bulgaria's Ataka Campaigns against Mosque Loudspeakers', *Sofia Echo,* 24 July 2006.

[58] Volen Siderov being interviewed by *Nova Television,* 17 July 2006.

[59] 'The Metropolitan of Sliven is Touched by the Attention of the Nationalists', *Focus*, 27 May, 2007.

[60] Metropolitan Neofit of Ruse interviewed by Velislava Dureva for *Vseki Den*, 29 March, 2007.

[61] Personal interview with Father Boyan Stanimirov, 2 September 2003.

[62] F. Dostoyevsky, *The Brothers Karamazov*, (New York: New American Library of World Literature, 1960), pp. 61–63.

[63] D. Martin, *A General Theory of Secularization*, (Oxford: Blackwells, 1978), p. 96.

[64] I. Merdjanova, *Religion, Nationalism, and Civil Society in Eastern Europe*, (Lampeter, 2002), p. 43.

[65] Amnesty International, *Bulgaria: Imprisonment of Ethnic Turks*, (Lasa, 1956), pp. 4–5.

Part Five

The Asian Context

Chapter 11

Baptism and Inter-Religious Dialogue

Kenneth Fleming

Unnecessary fears

To the uninitiated, 'methodology' is a word that can send shivers down the spine. Some years ago, like other new doctoral students, I was greatly concerned about it. Possessing the right methodology, it was stressed, is of crucial importance for the development and defence of a thesis in academic circles. Having recently returned from working as a pastor in a poor rural context in northern Thailand, where the needs, desires and concerns were quite different, I became worried and fretted over finding the correct methodology. David Kerr came to my rescue. He demythologized the word and explained, in simple terms, what was required. This was an indication of one of David's gifts – the unpacking of unnecessarily complex thoughts and *angst*-ridden structures of meaning.

In this essay I want to return, hesitantly, to the issue of methodology. This time, however, not in relation to writing a thesis, but on what approach to take as a Christian when it comes to inter-religious dialogue. Methods are of course, in great part, shaped and determined by contextual realities. The relative comfort of Freiburg, Germany, where I now live, with its influential democratic and Catholic institutions, imparts a different atmosphere for dialogue than that say of Yangon/Rangoon, with its background of totalitarian government and strong Buddhist culture. The realities of dialogue – opportunities, priorities, agendas, meeting places, conflicts, etc. – will differ greatly from place to place. No one method, I am aware, will suit all circumstances. Here then I will look for a method that can count as a general help in approaching other religions; one that is worthy of deliberation for use in various contexts. Particular reference is made to Buddhist–Christian dialogue in the Asian context, wherein lies my experience and theological interest, and to the work of Christian theologians in Asia. As a well-spring for finding the right method for Christians in dialogue, I turn to what might at first seem an unlikely source – the sacrament of baptism.

Baptism

In 1982 the World Council of Churches (WCC) published a groundbreaking document entitled *Baptism, Eucharist and Ministry (BEM)*.[1] It was the fruit of over

50 years of theological consultation that had involved the Orthodox, Roman Catholic and WCC Protestant churches. It presented an ecumenical understanding of these three highly contentious areas, and was sent out to the churches for study and responses. Like few others before it, *BEM* gave rise to much discussion and debate across the world. There was, as one would expect given the history of schism and current theological pluralism in Christianity, much disagreement on the details. Many questions were raised and requests for further research made.[2] Nonetheless, *BEM* was seen as an ecumenical milestone, warmly welcomed for its courage in tackling serious issues, concise style and theological depth.

   BEM made statements on the institution, meaning, practice and celebration of baptism, and also commented on the relationship between baptism and faith. Baptism, it was explained, contained a rich assortment of meanings: (1) as participation in Christ's death and resurrection, (2) as involving confession, pardoning and conversion, (3) as intimately connected with the gift of the Holy Spirit and (4) as incorporation into the body of Christ. The document did not heal the divisions nor bridge the theological differences between those who practise infant baptism and those who practise only adult or believer's baptism, or indeed those Christians who do not baptize at all. Yet the text was heralded for the way in which it highlighted the vivid imagery of baptism and succinctly described its rich meanings, weaving together biblical quotes and theological interpretation. It remains today a key theological document in intra-religious dialogue.

Baptizing Buddhists

In the history of Christian missions in Asian Buddhist lands the numbers of those being baptized has been used as a gauge to measure success or failure in the missionary enterprise. The aspects of baptism that have received most emphasis are perhaps those related to confession, pardoning and conversion, and incorporation into the body of Christ, the Church. Through baptism the convert became a new person and associated with a new community. It also symbolized the giving up and renouncement of the convert's previous religion and many associated aspects of the culture. As the convert died symbolically with Christ in baptism, their former religious beliefs and practices died with them – only these would never rise again. The move away from the previous religion often gave rise to difficult and painful personal and socio-cultural repercussions. The relative newness and foreignness of the Christian religion reinforced this. Christianity was, and still is in many parts, seen as a Western import that sits uneasily in Buddhist lands. This view is underlined by the adoption of Western approaches to church architecture, liturgies and vestments, educational materials, and theological viewpoints. So the Indian Catholic theologian, Michael Amaladoss SJ, like many other Asian Christian theologians, laments:

Jesus was born in Asia. But his disciples spread mostly westward. Jesus was appropriated by Graeco-Roman and later European cultures and has come back to us in that garb.[3]

This Western garb has also been associated and, in the eyes of the people, tainted by the West's history of colonialism in Asia.

From the perspective above, then, baptism can be viewed as a rite that fits well with the exclusivist theologies of religion and culture that have dominated much of Christian history in Asia. It would seem an improbable candidate upon which to develop a more open approach to other religions.

Baptizing Buddhism

While baptism has been associated with a turning away from other religions, it has also been utilized in more recent times to indicate a move towards them. This has happened in the field of inculturation/contextualization. The religions have been viewed as an important source of meaning and value to be mined for presenting Christian faith anew. In the Thai context, John Davis, an evangelical missionary who has spent many years in Thailand, has written an important book on contextualization, *Poles Apart?* Among other sources, he highlights the practice of baptism, by John and by the disciples of Jesus, as providing biblical warrant for selecting Buddhist concepts and practices in order to mould them for Christian use.[4] Davis views baptism as a former 'pagan' rite that John and later Jesus invest with new meaning and significance. In the Thai context he suggests a variety of new Christian rites and theological formulations that take over and transform elements from Buddhism. So, for example, he and some Thai Christians have worked on a new creed that presents a Christology using the Buddhist concept of merit making.[5] The underlying motivation here is the desire to make the Christian faith more understandable and attractive to Buddhists, who make up some 94 per cent of the population. Buddhism, here, is used as a tool of evangelism.

Earlier, the Japanese theologian Kosuke Koyama, who spent 8 years as a missionary in Thailand, spoke about baptizing elements from Buddhism. He draws consistently on Buddhist ideas and practices in his theological works.[6] In a classic text in Asian contextual theology, *Waterbuffalo Theology*, for example, he carefully examined the meaning of the Buddhist 'three marks of existence'– *anatta* (no-soul), *anicca* (impermanence) and *dukkha* (suffering) – and then went on to recast them to fit with Christian categories and perceptions.[7] Attempts like this he described as 'participation of the insights of the Buddha in the Christian understanding of history.'[8] Such things, he claimed, could operate as 'baptized servants'[9] in the quest for the contextualization of Christian faith in Asia. The motivation for Koyama is not simply to *use* Buddhism in service of the Christian faith, as Davis seems to do, but he also emphasizes that Buddhism can offer insights that enrich Christian faith. It is not now the case of the convert denouncing and rejecting their old religion through baptism, but elements of that religion become incorporated – baptized – into Christian theology and practice.

Such attempts at contextualization are of course not new in Asia. Persian Christians, often called Nestorians, had since before the Christianization of Europe engaged in a significant dialogue with Buddhism. In China they purposefully employed Buddhist terms, such as *sunyata* (emptiness), and Buddhist images, such as the cross resting on a lotus flower, in order to present better the Christian Gospel to the people.[10] There are of course many challenges and dangers in such attempts at contextualization. One oft-repeated charge is that it leads to syncretism, to a confusion of Christian beliefs and eventual denial of them. The Nestorians were accused of this (unfairly so according to more recent research). Another criticism is that such contextualization is nothing more than a form of religious sabotage, which will only provide results that are artificial and temporary and, moreover, lead to hostility. This is not the place to debate in full the merits of such arguments concerning contextualization. There is, no doubt, some truth in both the above objections, though contextualization is not an exact science. An ongoing discussion I had with a local Buddhist monk in Thailand over the course of 3 years was instructive for me in this regard. He was dismissive of Catholic attempts in Thailand to inculturate the Christian faith through the adoption of Buddhist styled architecture in church buildings, and through the adoption of Buddhist terms in the translation of biblical and theological ideas. He viewed it as a form of religious plunder. On the other hand, the monk was even more scathing of churches and missions of evangelical and protestant background that strongly maintain a Western style of religion. This reinforced the sense of Christianity as being essentially a foreign religion, which acted dismissively and arrogantly towards the indigenous cultures and religions. It seemed like a no win situation! If we take the context seriously and see value in the other religions, I believe there is little alternative but to engage in the patient, careful, and difficult task of contextualization. This is after all what Buddhism itself has done so successfully throughout its history in many Asian countries.[11] The necessary task of contextualization confronts all religions.

Buddhism baptizing

In the above examples there is little in the way of a detailed reflection on baptism's relevance to inter-religious dialogue. Baptism is appealed to in order either to build a theological case for contextualization or to speak figuratively and generally about incorporating aspects of other religions into Christian thought and practice. Koyama, however, went a step further when he spoke of himself undergoing a 'second spiritual baptism' through the experience of learning the Thai language.[12] This relates more directly to the Christian meaning of baptism. Through learning Thai, Koyama was profoundly exposed to Thai Theravada Buddhism and the immense influence it has on the culture and ways of the people. He was deeply impressed. A conversion of sorts is implied here: away from an exclusivist theology of other religions to being more open and appreciative of them. This confrontation and engagement with Thai Buddhism taught Koyama to be more humble and self-critical.

Koyama, here, is using baptism not only in a metaphorical sense. The Christian symbolism of baptism has deeply influenced Christian faith and Western cultures, and is capable of being employed in various ways. In secular society and literature it is employed in a general sense, as a metaphor for undergoing radical change or confronting a very testing situation. Koyama is speaking about more, however, than just learning a difficult language. The implied conversion he speaks of is full of religious significance, and this has greatly influenced his subsequent theological work. This is challenging in itself for theological reflection in relation to other religions. His reference to a second baptism may inspire some Christians towards a more generous and committed dialogue. It leads us towards our searched for methodology, but we require something with more substance. For that we need to turn to another Asian theologian, the Sri Lankan Jesuit, Fr Aloysius Pieris.

Pieris is a Christian priest, liberation theologian and a recognized scholar of Buddhism. He speaks about the need for a *communicatio in sacris* between Buddhism and Christianity – a sharing in sacred things – that can lead to mutual enrichment. Such a desire is shared by many Christians today. In recent decades, Christian theologians have developed theologies of religions that are more open and appreciative of the 'other' than at almost any time in history.[13] Good theological arguments are presented for such an in-depth encounter, but an appeal based on biblical texts often trails behind. This is not the case with Pieris, whose theological discourse develops with constant reference to biblical texts. Central to his development of an 'Asian Theology of Liberation' are his reflections on baptism. He speaks of the need for Christians in Asia to undergo a 'double baptism' in Asia: to be baptized into the lives of the poor and oppressed in Asia and to be baptized into the liberative strands of Asian spirituality represented in its great religions.[14] In the first of these Pieris refers to following Christ's self-giving love for others – especially the poor – that culminated in crucifixion. For developing his understanding of baptism in Asian religions, he refers to Christ's baptism in the Jordan. This latter source is what concerns us most in this essay.

The baptism of Jesus under John, who preached a baptism of repentance, has been a theological problem for Christianity and a source sometimes of embarrassment. How could Jesus, pure and without sin, submit to such a baptism? For Pieris, however, it represents a key theological source for an approach to other religions in the Asian context. He deciphers four 'missiological principles' from the baptism of Jesus under John. First, he argues that Jesus' ´submission to baptism was a way for him to affirm the spirituality of John. There were other forms of spirituality around that Jesus could have chosen to support, such as that of the Pharisees or Zealots, but he opted for the prophetic stance of John. Here, Pieris stresses the ability of Jesus to discern between good and bad religion – between what constitutes a liberative form of religion and a religion that only serves for selfish or violent ends. It is this ability, Pieris says, that Christians must develop in Asia, to discern the liberative ideologies and spiritualities within the Asian context of different religions. Second, Pieris notes that it was the rural poor who were drawn to John. They were attracted, in part, by his ascetic life-style which provided him with authority in the eyes of the people. Through baptism, then, Jesus shows solidarity with the poor and affirms the value of John's asceticism. Likewise, Pieris argues, the churches in Asia have to appreciate the ascetic traditions found in Buddhism and elsewhere, as well as show solidarity with the poor. This is a particular feature of Pieris' liberation theology; solidarity with the poor and inter-religious dialogue go hand in hand. Third, he stresses that the authority and holiness of Jesus, revealed through baptism, are linked with Jesus' act of submission and humility before John. To follow Jesus in Asia, argues Pieris, is to possess this humility and so submit oneself before the poor and before the liberative strands of other religions. He says in comment:

> The 'fulfilment theory' of the church fathers now revived by Vatican II – which I have repeatedly criticized in the past – relegates other religions to a 'pre-Christian' category of spirituality to be 'fulfilled' through the church's missionary enterprise. It is on the basis of this theory that some (Western) missiologists speak of the need to 'baptize' pre-Christian religions and cultures rather than of the prophetic imperative to immerse oneself in the baptismal waters of Asian religions that predate Christianity. The local church *in* Asia needs yet to be 'initiated' into the pre-Christian traditions under the tutelage of our ancient gurus, or it will continue to be an ecclesiastical complex full of 'power' but lacking in 'authority.' It is only in the Jordan of Asian religiousness that it will be acknowledged as a voice worthy of being heard by all: '*Hear ye him.*'[15]

Fourth, Pieris explains that Jesus' submission before John did not lead to a simple regurgitation of John's spirituality. In important ways Jesus' message and lifestyle differed from John. Pieris thus says that Christians engaged in in-depth dialogue in Asia should not worry about losing their identity. It is precisely through such engagement that understanding is sharpened and differences highlighted. The religions do not necessarily merge even if there is much to learn from one another.

Pieris presents us here with a rich and challenging biblical reflection. *BEM* said little about the baptism of Jesus by John. Before emphasizing the Church's rite of baptism, Pieris calls upon Christians to take a step back and consider what was happening in Jesus' own baptism. Buddhism contains no rites of baptism[16] as in Christianity but, following the explanation of Pieris, it could be indeed argued that Christians need to undergo a baptism in its metaphorical waters. The tables have in a sense been turned, instead of trying at every turn to baptize, Christians must first of all learn to be baptized anew.

A step too far?

With these four missiological principles Pieris presents us with a methodology, a way of approaching other religions. But what are we to make of his understanding and use of baptism? One possible criticism that could be raised relates to religious context. Jesus and John were Jews; despite their differences, they did not come from different religions. Their disciples could converse on common themes and relate directly to the spiritualities of both. We could, therefore, dismiss Pieris's interpretation of baptism as fanciful. Furthermore, we could pick up a criticism often repeated by evangelical scholars of those engaged in dialogue, to say that Pieris is using biblical texts in order to justify his prior theological position. There is no doubt that Pieris is creative in linking ancient texts with the contemporary context. However, this is an essential task of theology for all Christians. The overwhelming reality for Christians in Asia is one of religious pluralism; they find themselves living alongside ancient religious traditions, tested and renewed throughout history. The biblical interpretation of Pieris appears measured and reasonable both in consideration of the primary context in Israel and the applied one in Asia. He does not use baptism simply as a metaphor but takes its biblical context seriously, and his exegesis goes further than that of many missiologists. In view of this, it seems reasonable for Pieris to adopt and adapt the biblical insights he has done in the light of the realities faced.

   Pieris, here, presents us with, I believe, a basic methodology for inter-religious dialogue. It is a methodology, however, that may make many Christians nervous and fearful, especially in relation to a loss of identity. Who can submit to a guru or sage from the 'other' without at the very least compromising their own Christian identity? Will this not lead to a confusion of identity, or worse to a dual or multiple religious identity? This is an important and difficult issue in contemporary theology, where a small but increasing number of people are claiming such a dual or multiple identify.[17] Without getting into this debate in detail, it seems to me that Pieris' approach does not necessarily put Christian identity in danger. His basing of the missiological principles in the Bible and in the ministry of Jesus reinforces the sense of identity created in and for Christ. The commitment to being open to the 'other' religions and to dialogue is presented as an issue of Christian discipleship rather than philosophical fancy. The crucial question concerns the demands of radical humility: to what extent should we submit ourselves before the great religious traditions of wisdom and compassion outside Christianity? It should be remembered also that not so long ago Christians from different denominations largely ignored one another or violently disagreed with each other. Intra- and inter-religious dialogues are closely related. It will of course depend on our basic theological beliefs – do we still deny that there is truth and good in other religions or are we more open to the workings of God outside our own traditions? My sympathy is with the latter.

It has to be acknowledged also that Pieris emphasizes the need for discernment. The ability to discern between good and bad religion is a crucial factor. For the process of discernment in such a challenging field of theology and life, the Christian will need to draw on the classic sources of the Bible, church tradition and experience/reason. The discerning Christian community has also a crucial role to play in debating questions, testing new understandings and insights and offering pastoral support. Pieris has himself relied greatly on the Jesuit community for such criticism and support. He makes no claims to having arrived at final answers.

There will of course be contradictions and impossibilities. How can one reconcile the non-conceptual wisdom and compassion of the ultimate in Buddhism with the personal love of God in Christianity? There are significant differences between religions. The approach to dialogue proposed through the four missiological principles of Pieris teaches us to expect these differences and not to gloss over them. Pieris does not provide us with an agenda, timetable or programme for dialogue. However, the general approach suggested has a sound biblical and theological basis. With this the Christian can move confidently and lovingly into the world of the 'other'. To travel down such a bumpy path may not be a calling felt by all Christians, in Asia or elsewhere. Yet those with the desire and ability for such dialogue deserve the necessary critical and caring support of the churches. Here stands a methodology for discipleship in today's pluralistic world.

Notes

[1] The agreed text can be found online at: http://www.oikoumene.org/en/resources/documents/wcc-commissions/faith-and-order-commission/i-unity-the-church-and-its-mission/baptism-eucharist-and-ministry-faith-and-order-paper-no-111-the-lima-text.html. Accessed 12 June 2007. It has been translated into several languages.
[2] Six volumes of official church responses to *BEM* from around the world were edited by the WCC. Some major denominations published their own responses and reflections separately also.
[3] Micahel Amaladoss, 'The Asian Face of the Good News', *East Asia Pastoral Review* 37, no. 4. (2000). Available also online at http://eapi.admu.edu.ph/eapr00.htm. Accessed 12 June 2007.

[4] John R. Davis, *Poles Apart? Contextualizing the Gospel* (Kanok Bannasan: Bangkok, 1993), p. 92.

[5] *Ibid.*, pp. 146–148.

[6] For a study of Koyama's work and that of Aloysius Pieris, mentioned later, see Kenneth Fleming, *Asian Christian Theologians in Dialogue with Buddhism* (Peter Lang, 2002).

[7] Kosuke Koyama, *Waterbuffalo Theology* (London: SCM Press, 1974), pp. 154–155.

[8] *Ibid.* 156.

[9] Kosuke Koyama, *Theology in Contact* (Madras: Christian Literature Society, n.d.) p. 61.

[10] *Sunyata* is a key Mahayana Buddhist concept, related to that of *anatta*, and used to describe the nature of all reality. The lotus flower is a powerful image in Indic iconography and is used as an offering to the Buddha in temples. See John C. England, *The Hidden History of Christianity: The Churches of the East before the Year 1500* (Delhi: ISPCK, 1996) and David A. Scott, 'Christian Responses to Buddhism in Pre-medieval Times' in *Numen* 32, no. 1 (1985), pp. 88–100.

[11] For example, Buddhism in China adopted key ideas from the indigenous religious and philosophical thought in the development of Ch'an (Zen) and other Buddhist traditions. In Japan, Buddhists adopted and adapted many Shinto ideas and beliefs. There is much current debate on the different forms that Buddhism is now taking in the West.

[12] Kosuke Koyama, 'My Pilgrimage in Mission,' *International Bulletin of Missionary Research* 21, no. 2 (1997), p. 56.

[13] For a comprehensive overview of theologies of religion, see Paul F. Knitter, *Introducing Theologies of Religion* (Maryknoll, NY: Orbis Books, 2002).

[14] Aloysius Pieris, *An Asian Theology of Liberation* (Maryknoll, NY: Orbis Books), p. 45–50.

[15] *Ibid.*, p. 47.

[16] Water is however used to bless and purify Buddhist images and, occasionally, monks and elders.

[17] See for example some of the contributions in John D'Arcy May, ed. *Converging Ways? Conversion and Belonging in Buddhism and Christianity* (Munich: EOS Klosterverlag Sankt Ottilien, 2007).

Chapter 12

The Immediacy of Presence in the Experience of God: An Indian Christian Perspective

Geomon Kizhakkemalayil George

Introduction

In his book *An Introduction to Indian Christian theology* R. H. S. Boyd writes, 'The Indian tradition demands direct experience in religion, whether this be the experience of devoted self-surrender to a chosen deity or of calm and blissful abortion in *nirguna Brahman*.'[1] The goal of this essay is not an attempt to survey Hindu experiences of God. Rather, the goal of this essay is to examine Boyd's question 'What has Christianity to offer to the Hindu seeker who comes wanting realization or immediate experience of God' as developed in Indian Christian theology.

The essay will survey different streams of Indian Christian theology relating to the immediacy of the presence of God. Specifically, it will argue that there is a diversity of approaches emerging in the Indian Christian theology in relation to understanding the presence and activity of God. The principle Christian theologians who will be considered in this essay are V. Chakkarai and his apprehension of experiential Christology; Stanley Samartha and his understanding of the presence and activity of God in the people of other faiths; Samuel Rayan and his interpretation of God actively participating in the life of the poor people. Building upon this precedence, the author will offer another approach from the Pentecostal experience of God.

V. Chakkarai: Christology of experience

The Church in India at the turn of the twentieth century had a distinctively Western characteristic, reflecting the impact of the missionaries during the previous 100 years. Western in structure and worship, many Indian Christians were repulsed by what they saw as a transposition of Western theology with its theological formulae and liturgy. Some argued that the only solution to this problem was to set the Church in India free from the control of the Western churches and Western political power, so that it could find its own identity as an Indian

church. A group of young Indian Christians in Bangalore started a club called
'The Young Liberals Club', the purpose of which was to contextualize Christianity in India and draw Indian Christians into the freedom struggle for an India
independent of the British *Raj*. Parallel with this development, a similar development in Madras saw the rise of 'The Rethinking Group', dedicated in the
words of D. A. Thangasamy to 'questioning doctrines and the need of the Church
itself'.[2] V. C. Rajasekaran explains the group's purpose thus:

> The 'Rethinking Group' through various means endeavored to give a new
> expression to Christian way of life and thought in India and to slowly trans-
> form the Indian Christians to think and act for themselves independently.[3]

The group consisted of laymen from various secular professions and pursuits,[4]
whose basic premise was that the Indian Church should think and act for itself and
make Christianity an indigenous movement. The theological task of the Indian
Church was not to translate or re-state Western Christian doctrines but to develop
an Indian Christian theology 'as a truly creative act in the Indian situation.'[5]

One of the prominent individuals among the Re-thinkers was V. Chakkarai who
wanted to escape the captivity of Latin and Greek theology in favour of a critical
usage of Hindu concepts and terminologies for an indigenous expression of
Christian faith.

In his article 'Jesus of history and Christ of experience' Chakkarai explored
the relationship between the historical Jesus of Nazareth and the risen Christ
whom the Apostles preached and whom we know in our experience. Chakkarai
believed if we only focus on the history of Jesus then he is just a man and we
have no living relationship with him today.[6] On the other hand if we over-
emphasize the risen Christ as the second person of the trinity then, according
to Chakkarai, we deny the core of Christianity which is the incarnation.[7]

For Chakkarai, the living experience of Christ is central to having a living
faith, the beginning of Christianity starts with the direct experience of Jesus
Christ.[8] He said,

> our knowledge of God must be founded on the experience and conscious-
> ness of Jesus and not on a priori speculations like those of Anselm in Europe
> and Saṅkara in India If there is a God or if there are elements in Him unre-
> lated to Jesus and existing outside Him, they are simply non-existence to us.[9]

Therefore, the real knowledge of Jesus Christ is not through intellectual
exercise but with personal experience of Christ.

While affirming Jesus in terms of *avatar*, Chakkarai challenged the Hindu concept of plural *avatars* by insisting that the incarnation of Jesus Christ is permanent,
dynamic and advancing. Jesus is thus Christ, the unique incarnation of God,[10]
in whom there was the real descent of God. As *avatar*, Jesus Christ is therefore
the revealer of God, God being fully present in Jesus as a historical person.

But, with respect to the Hindu notion of repeated *avatar*s, Chakkarai argued that the real incarnation of God in Jesus did not end on the cross, but is repeated through incarnation of the Holy Spirit. This is also the real presence of God in Christ, as distinct from the Hindu mythic concept of *avatar*, but it is historical and continuing in its effect, as Jesus Christ reincarnates in the hearts of believers. 'Jesus Christ is the incarnation or avatar of God; the Holy Spirit in human experience is the incarnation of Jesus Christ.'[11] As such it is permanent and continues to provide in-depth meaning. Thus, the Christian understanding of Incarnation, mediated through Hindu understandings of *avatar*, is that it does not cease with the crucifixion or ascension, but continues as God in Christ continues to be man, living and working in the lives of believers.

Stanley Samartha: God as present and active in the traditions of people of other faiths

In examining the work of Samartha, Eeuwout Klootwijk describes his approach to Christian theology of religions as one of 'commitment and openness'. Samartha has published widely in India and abroad. He championed writing a contextual theology, particularly in developing a Christian approach to other religions and ideologies. He was the Director of the WCC's sub-unit on 'Dialogue with People of Living Faiths and Ideologies'.

When Samartha refers to God, he often uses the term 'mystery'. He observed that Greeks thought of God as the unmoved mover, the absolute being and uncaused Cause. Many Hindus on the other hand think of God as truth, as the highest Spirit and in the Bible God is known as the living God, God of hope. The theme of God as mystery first appeared in 'the Mystery and Meaning of God'. In this article he referred to biblical, patristic and Upanishadic texts, and commented that one should not forget the 'inexhaustible Mystery of God' in relation to God's revelation.[12] In *The Hindu Response to the Unbound Christ*, Samartha wrote about the 'mystery and depth in God' referring to God's love.[13] According to his understanding God's activity in the world is like 'groping after a mystery'. In *Courage and Dialogue*, he used the term 'mystery' in order to understand the Hindu and Christian responses to the truth.[14]

It is evident from his works that Samartha's idea of 'mystery' derived from the *advaita* tradition of Hindu philosophy which provides the ontological basis of the divine reality. According to Samartha, *Advaita Vedanta* tradition described mystery as Brahman, which provided a 'point of unity to all plurality'. Samartha defined Mystery as:

> This mystery, the Truth of the Truth (Satyasa Satyam), is the transcendent Centre that remains always beyond and greater than apprehensions of it or even the sum total of those apprehensions. It is beyond cognitive knowledge

(tarka) but it is open to vision (dristi) and intuition (anubhava). It is near yet far, knowable yet unknowable, intimate yet ultimate . . . .[15]

What this means is that human rationality cannot fully express or grasp the Mystery. Samartha did however argue the limited nature of humans to fully grasp the 'mystery'.

Furthermore, in reflecting and experiencing the 'mystery' no one religious tradition has fully understood it. Samartha argued that different religious traditions are different responses to the 'mystery.' Each tradition is neither the same nor one tradition better than the others. Each tradition contributes to others in a way that would benefit the whole community. In this connection, Samartha can write that Jesus Christ is the way for Christians in the sense that there is something in Christianity that is unique which no other religions have. This is the 'uniqueness' of Christ, but at the same time, Christians need to acknowledge that other religious traditions have 'uniqueness' which Christians need to listen to. In terms of religious language, different religious expressions are different responses which are culturally and historically conditioned. Therefore, one may designate Mystery as God or Brahman without denying the experiences of the ultimate reality. Samartha wrote:

> Both the terms 'Brahman' and 'God' are culture-conditioned. One could as well use the term mystery, which may be more acceptable. In this case the two statements – namely, that 'Brahman is sat-cit-ananda' and 'God is triune, Father, Son, and Holy Spirit' – could be regarded as two responses to the same Mystery in two cultural settings.[16]

Therefore neither claim has any inherent right to be 'the truer' representation of the mystery.

This understanding of the mystery notably raises the question of the Lordship of Christ in the context of religious pluralism. The challenge for Samartha was how to affirm the Lordship of Christ in a religiously pluralistic context:

> Does universality mean simply the extension of Christian particularity? What happens if our neighbours of other faiths also have similar notions of universality, that is, of extending their particularities?[17]

Samartha revised the traditional Christology of the Church and emphasized the universality of Christ which is not bound to the Church. He wrote, 'Christianity belongs to Christ. Christ does not belong to Christianity.'[18] He replaced the 'exclusive' understanding of Christ with 'relational distinctiveness'. He defined this new term as follows:

> It is relational because Christ does not remain unrelated to neighbours of other faiths and distinctive because without recognizing the distinctiveness of

the great religious traditions as different responses to the Mystery of God, no mutual enrichment is possible.[19]

Samartha, then, preferred the term 'distinctiveness' as being helpful for him to embrace other responses to the Mystery. In Jesus Christ an 'icon' of salvation is seen. Christians know this and must witness this. However this does not mean Muslims or Hindus need to accept Christ in order to be saved.

By appealing to 'Mystery of God', Samartha was able to utilize the Indian philosophical tradition of *Advaita Vedanta* and thus providing a contextual ontological basis for dialogue in that it recognized various ultimate realities without reducing it to a common denominator. The Mystery of God represented by Samartha raises various theological issues. Samartha's identification of the 'mystery' with a particular *Advaitic* Hindu tradition needs close scrutiny. According to Jathana, professor at the United Theological College, Bangalore, interpreting the 'mystery' from within the framework of *Advaita Vedanta* results in a Christianity that is 'reduced to a sub-species of Advaita Vedanta . . . and a Christianity that 'loses all its distinctive and decisive characteristic features.'[20] Furthermore, when Samartha writes God's presence can be discerned in India, he meant God is active in the history of India. However, the question needs to be raised as to whose history. There are many who recognize the activity of God not in the national history of the hegemonic cultures of the nation but the 'counter cultures' and grassroots movements which are largely suppressed by the mainline cultures.

Samuel Rayan: God as present and active in the historical situation of the poor

Another great Indian Christian interpreter of Christian faith in the Indian context is the Catholic theologian Samuel Rayan, who through his work with the Indian Theological Association (ITA) and the Ecumenical Association of Third-World Theologians (EATWOT) became the spokesperson for Indian theologians and for third-world theologians in general. At the heart of Rayan's theology is the understanding that God works through the poor people. The poor exist within every religion, and as the people through whom God's action is most decisively effective, they must be validated as theologically significant in themselves, rather than being divided among and obscured by divisive religious definitions. He writes:

> The concern of the Church is not Christians but the poor; its struggle is not for itself but for the liberation of all men and women who are held captive . . . The task of the Church is to champion a whole new social order.[21]

This is illustrated by the narrative of the Good Samaritan (Mat. 25.31–46), the meaning of which he interprets as a concern for the 'neediest, irrespective of religious affiliation'.[22] While in no sense ignoring religion, Rayan sees the poor within all religions as God's option for being present within all religions, uniting those in whom God's action is most dynamically embodied – that is, the poor – across the divisions of institutional religion. Here Rayan most evidently moves away from the secularized approach to Latin American liberation theology. He takes seriously the cultural and non-Christian religious realities of the task of liberation in the Indian context. The critical reflection from within the religious pluralism of India cannot transcend particular faith communities in the search for a national identity, except that it first integrates the experience of the poor across all religions.

As the locus of God's salvific action, the poor in each religion experience the solidarity of forced poverty that unites them across the boundaries of institutional religions. The Gospel is the criterion by which Christian theologians engage this task, but their interpretation of the Gospel is now transformed by the insights of the poor in all religions as they stand in solidarity with them.

Christian mission is to discern God's presence among the people and to sense what God has been doing in the past and continuing to do. Evangelization becomes more than just verbal proclamation. Rayan interprets Luke 4.18–19 as mission addressing exclusively towards the poor, oppressed and the hopeless.[23] The mission, therefore, is to witness to these people 'the glad tiding', that they have rights, dignity, that God wishes everyone the possibility and the hope of a fuller, more human life and that God is present and active with them in their struggle against injustice.[24] In this context, other religions have inherent value as opposed to acquiring 'revelatory' values when but only when it is read in light of Jesus Christ.

Jesus takes oppression upon himself to set people free. To follow Jesus Christ in the modern world is to serve Christ who is calling human beings to be on the side of the poor and the oppressed. Rayan writes:

> The only adequate response to God's unconditional love in Jesus Christ is to make our own God's concern for people and to give all we have for their total liberation and wholeness as God gave the Son for the world's salvation.[25]

According to Rayan, the justice of God is reflected in the faithfulness and provision for every creature that ever came into existence. He refers to biblical passages such as liberation of slaves from Egypt, freedom and fellowship for outcasts and sinners in the ministry of Jesus to show the 'concrete and contextual nature of the justice of God'. Thus, through social analysis, teaching and praxis, the Church in India must fight in order to fulfill the 'historical realization of God's fidelity – justice'. In other words, just as God was active in the incarnation of Christ, Christians ought to be active in the Kingdom of God that is inaugurated with creation.

For Rayan the Kingdom of God is not a general or an abstract idea.[26] However, the question for Rayan is whether non-Christian religions are preparations for the Kingdom of God, or is the Kingdom of God somehow already present in all religions? People of other faiths are not only already in the Kingdom but are also promoting the same kingdom through their faith commitments. In this view, God is understood to be leading everything and everyone to the final consummation to which all are summoned. In this perspective, different religions provide a common spiritual foundation to a common commitment to the task of liberation. The task therefore is to work as partners in building this kingdom. In this task, social justice concerns provide a common basis for inter-religious understanding. People of other faiths responding to their religious traditions become participants in the Kingdom.

While Rayan's distinctive liberationist understanding of God as the liberator who works in history is helpful, the manifestations of the gifts of the Holy Spirit which testify to apostolic power are ignored. For Rayan 'powers' and 'spirits' are the social structures against which liberation is to be waged. In this regard, Rayan's criteria for discerning the mission of the Spirit are socio-economic.

A Pentecostal contribution

The heart of Pentecostal experience is the presence and activity of the Holy Spirit. The Pentecostal vision of *Shakti* is influenced by the account in the Book of Acts chapter 2, where the Spirit appears in the form of wind and flame regenerating and renewing the disciples to carry on the work of the Kingdom of God. The Pentecostals believe that the gifts of the Holy Spirit – speaking in tongues, prophesying, healing, dreams and visions among others – were not meant for the early Christians alone. This experience in the divine outpouring of the Spirit points to the various ways in which the Spirit of God is being manifested in the life of the believers individually and corporately. Pentecostals associate these manifestations of the Spirit with the powerful work of the Holy Spirit. In this there is the sense that the divine is not transcendent but active in the everyday life of devotees. In the Pentecostal community God is seen as actively participating in the life of His children. In this sense, the troubles and trials of the sick and the needy are at the heart of God's concern.[27] Consequently, Pentecostals were able to experience the immediate presence of God in everyday life. Therefore, it is no surprise that Pentecostals emphasize that through the Holy Spirit God is actively involved in the events of human history. Thus, Caplan writes:

Unlike the liberal Christianity imported by late nineteenth and early twentieth century missionaries of the principal denominations, and inherited by their successors in the hierarchy of the Indian Church, which denied the 'reality' of evil forces in the everyday lives of the followers and potential converts, Pentecostalism not only acknowledges their existence but continuously demonstrates the power of the Holy Spirit to vanquish them.[28]

From a Pentecostal perspective, the Holy Spirit is active in the present struggle of the oppressed by giving people strength to face up to the struggle for their own survival and the hegemony of a socio-economic system. Pentecostals believe that the emergence of the Pentecostal community is the result of the action of the Spirit. This Pentecostal community is more than an institution. It is the continuation of the movement started by Jesus who committed himself to the justice of the Kingdom of God. The Church then becomes a sign and a vehicle for liberation. In this regard, the poor become God's poor. However, liberation of the poor and eradication of poverty is not reduced to social and political structures. Rather, since evil spirits are at work in human history, the reality of spiritual oppression must be taken more seriously. Pentecostals have a way of dealing with this on the basis of the reality of the Holy Spirit. They know good as well as evil among spirits. It is in this realm of spiritual oppression that inflicts the life of many people that Pentecostals are able to engage through the gifts of the Spirit. The Spirit related to Jesus Christ is able to distinguish between the good from the evil in the spiritual world. Pentecostals take account of the 'principalities and powers' found in religions, including Christianity that opposes the purposes of God. In this framework, the presence and power of demonic forces operating in history are not neglected. This enables Pentecostals to avoid the pitfalls of Samartha by recognizing that it is Jesus whose apprehension of God in faith is reflected in the Bible and enrich Rayan's theology by bringing to it an awareness of a spirit world that has the potential for spiritual oppression.

The Spirit of God is not just a universal Spirit but is identified with the immediate presence of God through the manifestations of the Spirit in the life of the believers. This opens up the possibility of discriminating between the Spirit and oppressive spirits and acknowledges the gifts of the Spirit wherever they may be found. The Spirit, who in the past empowered the disciples to witness of the Kingdom of God, empowers us to discern the presence and action of the Spirit within the culture and history of India today.

Conclusion

The evidence examined in this essay confirms the hypothesis that there is a diversity of approaches in understanding the immediacy of the presence of God in the Indian Christian theology. Situated within the Indian religious and social context, these Indian Christian theologians attempted to interpret the presence and activity of God. Chakkarai argued that through the experience of Christ one can have the immediate presence of God because he does not cease with the crucifixion or ascension, but continues as God in Christ continues to be man, living and working in the lives of believers. Samartha argued that God's presence is not limited to the Church, but is offered to persons of all traditions. This raised the issue of the relationship between God's saving presence in all cultures and the Christian understanding of the salvific event which occurred in Christ. Rayan's theology originated as faith confronted the injustice of the poor in the social context of India. In this understanding, God is present and active through human beings of all faiths in the fight against oppression and injustice because it disrupts God's purposes in this world. This theology seemingly cannot address the realm of spiritual oppression that inflicts the life of many people. It is in this area, Pentecostals have the spiritual gifts to be able to engage.

As Pentecostals welcome mainline theological positions in that the God of the Bible is not just for Christians but belongs to all of creation, Pentecostals know this God through Christ and the presence and activity of the Holy Spirit as experienced through the manifestations of the Spirit. This life in the Spirit provides an experiential reality of the presence of God. Subsequently, there is a sense of the immediate presence of God. This enables Pentecostals to answer Boyd's question 'what has Christianity to offer to the Hindu seeker who comes wanting realization or immediate experience of God' in an affirmative way, while holding to biblical fidelity.

Notes

[1] R. H. S. Boyd, *An Introduction to Indian Christian Theology* (Delhi: CLS, 1975), p. 229.

[2] Quoted in T. V. Philip, 'Chakkarai and the Indian Church', Taylore, R. W. (ed.), *Society and Religion* (Bangalore: CISRS, 1976), p. 153.

[3] V. C. Rajasekaran, *Reflections on Indian Christian Theology* (Madras: CLS, 1993), p. 121.

[4] The Members of the Rethinking Group were V. Chakkarai, Justice P. Chenchiah, Eddy Asirvatham, G. V. Job, A. N. Sudarisanam, D. M. Devasahayam, and S Jesudason.

[5] Philip, p. 153.

[6] V. Chakkarai, 'The Historical Jesus and the Christ of Experience', in P. T. Thomas, ed., *The Theology of Chakkarai* (Bangalore: CISRS, 1968), p. 82–85.

[7] *Ibid.*, p. 87–89.

[8] In the West, James Dunn, *Christology in the Making: A New Testament Inquiry into the Origins of the Doctrine of the Incarnation* (London: SCM Press, 1989). Larry Hurtado, *One God, One Lord: Early Christian Devotion and Ancient Jewish Monotheism* (Edinburgh: T&T Clark, 1998), writes an account of how experience influenced early Christian devotion to Christ.

[9] V. Chakkarai, *Jesus the Avatar*, (Madras: CLS, 1932), p. 210.

[10] V. Chakkarai, 'My Credo' in T. P. Thomas, ed., *The Theology of Chakkarai* (Bangalore: CISRS, 1968), p. 44.

[11] Chakkarai, *Jesus the Avatar*, p. 121.

[12] E. Klootwijk, *Commitment and Openness: The Interreligious Dialogue and Theology of Religions in the Work of Stanley J. Samartha* (Zoetermeer: Uitgeverij Boekencentrum B.V., 1992), p. 225.

[13] S. J. Samartha, *The Hindu Response to the Unbound Christ* (Bangalore: CISRS, 1974), p. 191.

[14] S. J. Samartha, *Courage for Dialogue: Ecumenical Issues in Inter-Religious Relationships* (Geneva: WCC Publications, 1981), p. 149.

[15] S. J. Samartha, 'The Cross and the Rainbow: Christ in a multireligious culture' in *The Myth of Christian Uniqueness*, John Hick and Paul F. Knitter, eds. (Maryknoll, NY: Orbis, 1987), p. 75.

[16] *Ibid.*, p. 76.

[17] S. J. Samartha, 'The Lordship of Christ and Religious Pluralism' in *Christ's Lordship and Religious Pluralism*, Gerald Anderson and Thomas Stransky, eds. (Maryknoll, NY: Orbis, 1980), p. 19.

[18] Samartha, *The Hindu Response to the Unbound Christ*, p. 10.

[19] S. J. Samartha, *One Christ - Many Religions: Toward a Revised Christology* (Maryknoll, NY: Orbis, 1991), p. 77.

[20] O. V. Jathana, 'Indian Christian Theology: Methodological Reflections' in *Bangalore Theological Forum*, vol. 23, No.2–3, April–September 1986,' p. 67. See also, M. Amaladoss, *Theologizing in India*, p. 53; S. Kappen, 'A New Approach to Theological Education' in *Theologizing in India*, p. 58; Chethimattam, 'Problems of an Indian Christian Theology' in *Theologizing in India*, p. 199.

[21] S. Rayan, 'The Justice of God' in *Third World Liberation Theologies: A Reader*, Deane William Fearne, ed. (Maryknoll, NY: Orbis, 1979), p. 354.

[22] S. Rayan, 'Reconceiving Theology in the Asian Context' in *Doing Theology in a Divided World*, V. Fabella and S. Torres, eds. (Maryknoll, NY: Orbis, 1985), p. 140.

[23] Rayan, 'The Justice of God', p. 95.

[24] *Ibid.*

[25] S. Rayan, 'Asia and Justice' in *Vidyajyoti Journal of Theological Reflection*, 50/7 August 1986, p. 349.

[26] S. Rayan, 'The Kingdom of God: Blueprint for a New Society,' www.geocities.com/orthopapism/samrayan.html., p. 2. Accessed July 2007.

[27] See M. S. Joshua, *Spadika Samudram, (Ocean of Blessings)*, (Kottayam: International Gospel Church, 2001); G. F. Fee, 'Baptism in the Holy Spirit: The issue of Separability and Subsequence' in *Pneuma*, 7/2, 1985, pp. 87–99.

[28] L. Caplan, 'Popular Christianity in Urban South India' in *Religion and Society*, 30/2, 1983, p. 42.

Chapter 13

Reading John Through *Bhakti* Eyes: The Hermeneutic of A. J. Appasamy

Sean M. Doyle

Introduction

Writing a chapter for a volume dedicated to Professor David A. Kerr is a great honour for me. He was my doctoral supervisor at the University of Edinburgh. His precision in thinking theologically and critically about issues related to contextual Christianity and inter-religious dialogue is unrivalled, and his ability patiently to develop these scholarly skills in his students is impressive. I am deeply appreciative of his professional investment in my life.

Christianity has been present in the Indian subcontinent from at least the third century C.E. in the form of the ancient Syrian Church. It is significant that this nascent community did not attempt to develop a theological voice that was Indian in terminology or conceptuality; the liturgy remained fixed in the Syriac language. This non-indigenized expression of faith was by no means an exception to the general historical pattern that characterized south Asian Christianity until the nineteenth century. Theological articulation was dominated by Western thought-forms and methodologies, far removed from the Indian cultural context and philosophical categories.

In the nineteenth and early twentieth centuries, numerous theologians began self-consciously to interact with their intellectual and spiritual heritage in order to rethink the character of Christian faith that had taken root in Indian soil. Some important figures of this era were Krishna Mohan Banerjea, Nehemiah Goreh, Brahmabandhav Upadhyay, P. Chenchiah, V. Chakkarai, Sadhu Sundar Singh and A. J. Appasamy. These seminal thinkers have been compared with Origen, Tertullian, Clement and Augustine, who helped lay the foundation for the indigenization of Christianity in Greco-Roman culture. Just as many of the Fathers actively engaged with currents of thought in the Hellenistic milieu, these Indian theologians wrestled with particular Hindu traditions, such as Vedanta, yoga and Vedic ritual.

Bishop A. J. Appasamy (1891–1975) is generally regarded as one of the most prominent contributors to indigenous theology in the subcontinent; he is especially remembered for his unique efforts to relate the Christian message to popular, devotional Hinduism.[1] The personalist tradition of Indian theism is known as the *bhakti* movement. The essence and appeal of *bhakti* was expressed by Appasamy in the following manner: 'personal faith in a personal God, love for Him as for a human being, the dedication of everything to His service, and the attainment of *moksha* (final bliss) by this means, rather than by knowledge, or sacrifice or works.'[2] Appasamy intentionally sought a deep interaction with *bhakti* spirituality, carrying the exploration farther than anyone before or since. Strategically, he recognized that *bhakti* has been immensely influential in India, and he asserted that the majority of the Hindu population follows the path of devotion (*bhakti marga*). Since this movement has left its mark in such a lasting and profound manner, the elucidation of a Christian approach to *bhakti* is theologically essential.

The purpose of this essay is to explore how A. J. Appasamy, through creative interaction with the rich tradition of *bhakti*, articulated the concept of 'salvation in Christ' to an Indian audience in his theological writings. First, a brief biographical sketch of the life of Appasamy will be provided. Second, the nature of Appasamy's appreciation of the *bhakti* movement and its emphases will be described. Third, the theological methodology and key themes of his indigenous Christian *bhakti* theology will be discussed.

Biography

Aiyadurai Jesudasan (A. J.) Appasamy was reared in a devout Christian family. His father, A. S. Appasamy, was a convert from Shaivism who was affected by the Christian *bhakti* poetry of H. A. Krishna Pillai; he immersed himself in the ancient Tamil and Sanskrit writings, studied meditation, and conversed with Hindu scholars and *yogic* practitioners to enhance his Christian religiosity. A .S . Appasamy's positive evaluation of some aspects of Indian spirituality would make a deep impression on his son.

A. J. Appasamy studied philosophy and religion at Harvard University; he then received the degree of Doctor of Philosophy from Oxford University in 1922. His dissertation was entitled *The Mysticism of Hindu Bhakti Literature Especially in its Relation to the Mysticism of the Fourth Gospel.* He encountered Sadhu Sundar Singh during his time at Oxford and was impressed by the latter's Christo-centric mysticism.

Appasamy served as an editor in the Christian Literature Society publishing company for 9 years (1923–1931). He then took a post in Bishop's College, Calcutta, as professor of History and Philosophy of Religion from 1932–1936. Appasamy was a minister in the Anglican Church of India, and later the Church of South India, for over 20 years. He became Bishop of Coimbatore, Tamil Nadu from 1950–1958.

Appasamy authored nearly twenty books. His most important theological works are considered to be *Christianity as Bhakti Marga, What is Moksha?,*

The Gospel and India's Heritage and *What Shall We Believe?* He also wrote a biography of Sadhu Sundar Singh and compiled a collection of representative *bhakti* poems in a work entitled *Temple Bells*.

Appasamy, V. Chakkarai and P. Chenchiah were known as the 'Madras Trio'. Chakkarai and Chenchiah, personal friends of Appasamy, were leaders of the 'Rethinking Group', which made efforts to promote more indigenous expressions of Christianity. This stimulating group of thinkers published the landmark book *Rethinking Christianity in India*; the volume was a response to Hendrik Kraemer's negative assessment of Indian religion in *The Christian Message in a Non-Christian World*. *Rethinking Christianity in India* was published just before the 1938 International Missionary Council's World Conference at Tambaram, near Madras (or modern-day Chennai), and proved to be very influential and provocative. The Rethinking Group was convinced that for Christianity to flourish and grow in south Asia, it must be like a seed sown in the fertile context of the Indian cultural climate.

Theological appreciation of *bhakti*

Appasamy made clear that 'there cannot be two Christian theologies for India, one for Christians and one for Hindus'. Indigenous theology must reflect the 'point of view, the mode of approach, and the note of emphasis' that has been emphasized throughout south Asian religious history.[3] When this type of reconstruction is faithfully carried out, the resulting theology will be useful for seeing Christ in fresh perspective and for allowing the faith truly to take root in its native context. With such concerns in mind, Appasamy desired to explore the relation between the devotionalism cultivated by the Hindu spirit and the essence of biblical faith. He believed that he found an important overlap between the two in the awareness and practice of mystical union with God. He wrote:

> We would do well to note that at its very sources Christianity is mystical. Our Lord's life showed a perfect balance between its inner and outer aspect. St. Paul's central experience was that of living in Christ. St. John brooded upon the words of our Lord until they yielded a new meaning to him. Coming down the ages we find such great saints as St. Augustine, St. Francis of Assissi, Thomas à Kempis, St. Theresa and others who had real mystical experiences.[4]

Appasamy noted that personalist *bhakti* is similar in many respects to the inner dynamic of Christianity. There is religious compatibility, because the emphasis in both traditions centres on union with God and joy in the love-relationship with the divine. Also, there is metaphysical similarity, since *bhakti* and Christian theology both advocate a basic distinction between the divine and finite personalities. Appasamy was convinced that Christianity in south Asia must place great significance upon mystical experience, for the Indian mind has a natural predilection for and capability in this form of religiosity. Appasamy's main suggestion for attaining an indigenized Christianity was very straightforward: 'To make their Christian religion living and fresh and deep, Indian Christians must relate it to the mystical experiences which have for centuries been the dominant note of religious life in India.'[5]

There are several aspects of *bhakti* mysticism that Appasamy found compelling for his task of theological reflection. First, the adoration of God was a primary concern for many *bhaktas*. Appasamy noted that

> the history of *bhakti* thought shows us that the driving impulse with some of the finest religious men in India has been the passion for God. The infinite grandeur, the alluring beauty, the abundant mercy and the unlimited love of God have captured the heart and soul of India.[6]

Second, the *bhaktas* saw prayer and meditation essentially as communion with God. Their concern for fellowship with the divine outweighed their desire to receive any temporal benefits from their association with God. Third, Appasamy suggested:

> The Hindu *bhaktas* speak again and again of God as dwelling in the depths of their souls. He is closer to them than their life. He is hidden in their innermost being. Like the juice which flows in the sugarcane, He lives in the devotee's soul. God is not thought of as only external to the soul; He is most vitally connected with the deepest parts of man's being.[7]

Fourth, practitioners of *bhakti* find themselves overwhelmed with joy and rapture from the wondrous experience of union with God. Exuberance is a central feature of religion, not simply duty and legalism.

Yet, Appasamy was also aware of the excesses that affected some aspects of the mystical *bhakti* movement. He rejected the flirtation with monism, the obsession with *karma* and the reverence of images that at times were features of the tradition. Thus, he was not blindly accepting *bhakti* ideology wholesale; rather, he sought a responsible critique of *bhakti* that is guided by solid Christian discernment. Appasamy's rejection of the association of *karma* with *bhakti* is an example of his discrimination:

> The full acceptance of the doctrine of *karma* has somehow given to the *bhakti* doctrine of the love of God an air of unreality. A son is continually kept in shackles by his father. (Yet) he keeps on declaring that his father is filled with love for him. . . . In the same way there is a real inconsistency between the *bhakti* doctrine of the love of God and the doctrine of *karma*. It is impossible

to see how a God who is full of love could permit in the world a system which works out so relentlessly and mercilessly.[8]

Appasamy was disappointed that there were so many Indian Christians who had not cultivated a mystical approach to their faith. This was proof to him that believers had accepted theological formulae from 'outside' sources that had little relevance to Indian ways of thinking. They were allowing their personal experiences to be moulded by these foreign interpretations. He felt that there would be a certain shallowness and inauthenticity to the Indian Church until the mystical bent of the people was brought into the service and adoration of Christ.

Methodology and key themes

Importance of the Johannine vision of spirituality

Given that Appasamy wanted to develop the mystical features of Christianity in his theology, he expended much effort discussing the Gospel of John, which he felt presents the concept of union with God in Christ most captivatingly in the New Testament. The language of the fourth Gospel becomes the basis for a lucid presentation of Christianity as a supremely mystical religion. Appasamy noted that many Hindu readers of the New Testament are instinctively drawn to the Gospel of John. The idea of the life-giving Christ dwelling in the soul of individual Christians, providing joy and peace, is immensely appealing to those steeped in the *bhakti* tradition.

While John's Gospel communicates a spiritual vision that is in agreement with the overall theology of the other canonical Gospels, the way that John expresses his perspective resonates with the contemplative seeker. Making John's Gospel the foundation of an articulation of Indian Christianity is strategic and quite justifiable in light of the Indian civilization's temperament and tastes. Appasamy posed a question:

> Is it right to concentrate attention thus on one book of the Bible, important as it is? Our answer is twofold. The gospel of John is of one piece with the rest of the Bible, agreeing with it in all its fundamental doctrines. Also it is quite justifiable for us to strike deep down into a well from which fresh water flows abundantly. A farmer may own a hundred acres. But he sinks his wells only where he knows he will get the water he needs and as much as he needs.[9]

Appasamy believed that the fourth Gospel gives wonderful guidance to those devotees who have attributed the utmost importance to achieving communion with God.

The nature of Christianity as *bhakti marga*

Appasamy adopted key themes in the Hindu tradition for creative theological articulation. Appasamy's basic paradigm was that Christianity is primarily *bhakti marga*, a life of complete devotion to Christ and longing for fellowship with God. The goal of life is *moksha*, which is actualized by cultivating a relationship of faith-union with Christ. It is important to note that in Vaishnava *bhakti*, the term *moksha* does not only depict, negatively, the release of the soul from bondage, but it also has a more positive nuance of joyous mystical connection with the divine in intimate relationship. Such an indigenous concept is ideal for communicating the nature of 'salvation in Christ' that is described in Johannine literature. Just as John's theological category of 'eternal life' includes both the future state of heavenly bliss with God and the present enjoyment of His fellowship, the term *moksha* might be used by Christians to indicate that the believer can commune with the life-giving God even now and can experience the Beatific Vision, or apprehension of the divine presence, on earth.

The notion of 'abiding' in Christ and his love developed at length in the fourth Gospel best captures the dynamic of devoted unity with God that Appasamy hoped to convey by his description of Christianity as *bhakti marga*. This path of 'abiding' demands much of the devotee, calling for the entire surrender of will, emotion and intellect to Christ; however, the end result is the constant reception of divine vitality. Appasamy wrote:

> It has been well pointed out that 'abide in' represents John's doctrine about the highest and ultimate relation of the believer to God, that relation which we are describing as the mystical relation. Those who believe in Christ are not to remain separate from him, functioning as best as they can, but are to be organically connected with him. Just as the stem of a vine is intimately related to its branches, its sap and energy flowing into them, so is he closely connected with us in order that through such organic relation his life and energy may flow into us.[10]

As the Hindu conception of *bhakti marga* allows for the pursuit of both knowledge and works within the greater framework of devotion, Johannine theology asserts that love for Christ will lead to salvific, relational knowledge of God and a desire to obey Him. A life of *moksha*-union with the divine inevitably results in a sense of peace and joy that is like a 'stream of steady flowing oil', to use the words of the *bhakti* philosopher Ramanuja.

The *moksha*-union of Christ, God, and *bhakta*

The discussion of Christianity as *bhakti marga* relates to the nature of the union that exists between Christ, his Father and the *bhakta*. Appasamy devoted much attention to the phrase in John's Gospel where Jesus claims that 'I and the Father are One' (Jn 10.30). He was concerned that Hindus might misunderstand the intent of Christ's words and think that the statement echoes the *advaitic* (non-dualist) assertion 'I am Brahman'. Jesus' point was not to claim that he and the Absolute were one undifferentiated essence. Appasamy asserted that a thorough reading of the fourth Gospel rules out such an interpretation, for it goes against the main features of Johannine theology. Christ's constant reference to God as his Father is evidence that the connection between the two is relational and not an impersonal ontological identification. Appasamy suggested:

> We can, therefore, say that 'I and the Father are one' did not refer to any oneness or identity in the real nature of God and Jesus. The relation between God and Jesus was a personal one. God was his Father and Jesus was His Son. He loved his Father; he realized his entire dependence on Him. The oneness of Jesus with God was a moral identity.[11]

Appasamy meant by this terminology of 'moral identity' that Jesus was entirely submissive to the Father's will, loving what the Father loved, and working to carry out the Father's desires. Indeed, Christ asserts that 'the Father is greater than I' (Jn 14.28). Jesus communed and abided with the Father in such an intimate fashion and with such devotion that he brought his will completely in line with the Father's will. Not only was there a unity of volition between the Father and Christ, but there was a oneness of feeling. Jesus took great delight in performing his Father's works, and thus there was an attachment of the emotions that was firm and gripping.

Since the 'oneness' that exists between the Father and Christ is also said to characterize the relationship between Christ and his devotees and between the *bhaktas* themselves (Jn 17.20–23), Appasamy felt that the statement 'I and the Father are one' (Jn 10.30) cannot be referring to the deity of Jesus; otherwise, the logical inference would be that the disciples of Jesus are also divine. Appasamy, in an effort to avoid a monistic interpretation, asserted:

> The union between God and Christ is said to be the pattern of the union which should prevail among the followers of Christ. . . . There should prevail among Christians such a spirit of love and fellowship as exists between Christ and God. This makes it clear that the union between God and Christ which is spoken of in the fourth Gospel is a union in love and work and not an identity in their essential nature.[12]

Thus, the *bhakta* should examine the response of Christ to the Father in order to envisage what a moral union of will and purpose and love looks like. Christ is the perfect *bhakta* whom the believer should emulate. The relation of believer to Christ and to other *bhaktas* should be of the same quality and intensity as was the union of Jesus to his Father. To Appasamy, statements of Christ such as 'in that day you shall know that I am in my Father and you are in me and I in you' (Jn 14.20) and his petition that 'they may all be one; even as you, Father, are in me, and I in you, that they also may be in us' (Jn 17.21) indicate that the *bhakti marga* of Christianity exudes an interpersonal dynamic. Fellowship between humanity and the divine, between the persons of the Godhead, and between *bhaktas* should be so intimate that the interactions could be characterized as 'oneness' of feeling and will. There is the ongoing potentiality for present mystical union between *bhaktas*, the Father and Christ. Appasamy wrote:

> From the Gospels we know how inward and close and deep the intimacy was which existed between the Father and Christ. We are filled with hope and courage as we meditate upon the fact that in some way our own relation to Christ and God is going to have somewhat of this strength and intimacy. Into what a realm of wonderful possibilities do we enter with this thought! That the mystic union which we can attain here and hereafter can possibly approximate to the warm, unbroken, close fellowship between the Father and Christ is indeed a moving and inspiring thought.[13]

The notions of unity and dependence upon God are not antithetical but come together in harmony in the *bhakti* relationship. Christ the *bhakta* submitted his will to the Father over and over again in his life. Christ's statement that the Father was greater than him is meant to show his complete surrender (*prapatti*) to the Father. The attitude of dependence and submission was not automatic on the part of Jesus but represented a real choice, as the struggle in the garden of Gethsemane displayed. The mystical intimacy was achieved through the disciplined decisions and attitudes of Christ. Appasamy depicted the surrender of Christ in the garden as 'the rich response of a loving and obedient soul to the gracious biddings of the Eternal . . . There is joy only when, because of the urge of a deeply rooted love, two personalities come together, seeking deliberately oneness in the highest things of life.'[14] The unity between Christ and *bhakta* can only be cultivated in the same way. A *bhakta* follows in the path of the historical Jesus, practising obedient, selfless love that leads to personal suffering; in this way, the human heart aligns itself with the heart of Christ and abides in him.

The identification of Christ with the Father did not preclude the desperate feeling of desertion that Jesus experienced on the cross. *Bhaktas* should not be disturbed by emotions of separation from God that sometimes arise in their hearts. Indeed, 'a life of fellowship implies the possibility of separation.'[15] While the *bhakti* relationship involves wonderful feelings of joy and closeness, the aspect of *viraha*, the sense of isolation from the divine, can be a reality for devotees of Christ. The cry from the cross of 'my God, my God, why have you 'forsaken me?' illustrates that the nearness of God cannot always be perceived. Yet, the Gospel of John makes clear that regardless of the feelings experienced, God is still present and willing to comfort and sustain His *bhaktas*.

Appasamy summarized his teaching on the unity between God and the *bhakta* in this way:

> Oneness with God consists in the continuous orientation of the human personality towards the divine so that floods of God's love and power keep running into man's soul. . . . Thus, there is a perpetual flux of life from God into man and then again from man into God.[16]

Christ as *antaryamin* and *avatara*

Appasamy drew out the implications of Jesus' identification with the Father in terms of relationality: 'He was with God,' according to John's Gospel. However, Christ's full identity transcends that of an ordinary human *bhakta*: 'He was God' (Jn 1.1). The notions of *antaryamin* and *avatara*, vital features of *bhakti* ideology, are useful for describing the true nature of Christ.

The *bhakti* movement has always relished the appreciation of God's nearness, all the while affirming His distinctness from the individual soul. The doctrine of *antaryamin*, where the Lord immanently indwells the person, preserves both these emphases adequately. God as the 'inner ruler' is not distant and detached in an unapproachable, transcendent state. He is intimately associated with the world and is accessible, dwelling in the core of humans' souls. Appasamy explained the mystical significance of belief in *antaryamin*:

> To write in the vein of the Hindu *bhaktas*: We are the temple; He is the God within. We are the fruit; He is its juice. We are the milk; He is its cream. We are the sugar; He is its sweetness.[17]

Appasamy used the Hindu term *antaryamin* with great flexibility in his writings, believing that the concept points to a wide range of theological realities, such as the pre-incarnate and the indwelling Christ. Appasamy developed an exposition of the prologue of John through the lens of Christ the *antaryamin* whose immanent presence is continually being manifested. John makes clear that the *Logos-antaryamin* always existed and is sustaining the created order from moment to moment. He perpetually resides within humankind, working in their innermost persons to motivate them to moral living and to uplift the weary heart. Appasamy asserted:

> He abides in everything – the flower blossoms because of his bidding; the sea roars because he has willed it so. . . . He is present in the heart of man, stirring

him to new life, beckoning him with glowing ideals, endowing him with large measures of moral strength. He reveals the truth to us, shows us what we should believe in and how we should act. He does not do all this in a distant or remote way. He dwells in our inmost heart and works from there. He is bound up with our very heart and soul.[18]

Appasamy spent a great deal of time analysing the following affirmation: 'There was the true light, even the light which lighteth every man coming into the world. He was in the world and the world was made by him and the world knew him not' (Jn 1.9–10). Appasamy contended that the *antaryamin* has been illumining the inner selves of all people since his creation of the world. The statement 'he was in the world' does not, to Appasamy's mind, refer to the enfleshment of the Logos; rather it refers to the Logos in the pre-incarnated state. The primary activity of the pre-incarnated Logos was to provide spiritual luminescence through his intimate presence in the contingent realm.

The statement 'the world knew him not' is surprising, for surely created beings would recognize the divine creator and inner light of the world. Appasamy wrote, 'Every man, though indwelt by God, has to relate himself to God. They that are His own are expected to receive Him.'[19] The *antaryamin*'s abiding in the soul does not negate the responsibility of individuals to make their apprehension of the indwelling reality more profound; such a heightened perception can be attained through a wholehearted response of love. In Appasamy's view, God can be present in one individual's soul to a greater degree than He is in another's. For instance, the moral and spiritual state of a person's heart will affect the degree to which the divine immanence will be realized.

The prologue makes clear that humanity was much too ignorant to appreciate fully the light of Christ as *antaryamin*, and they neither recognized nor received him (Jn 1.11). Amazingly, according to the fourth Gospel, this close association of the *antaryamin* did not exhaust the depth of the revelation of the Logos. He who had been present in the created realm from the beginning came into the world in an unprecedented manner in the form of the *avatara* (descent) Jesus, so that humankind would be provided with a fuller understanding of God. In the *bhakti* tradition, there is the ongoing possibility that the Lord can descend to earth as an *avatara*. Appasamy asserted that the Logos became enfleshed as an *avatara* in order that all might be more cognizant of his reality (Jn 1.14). The Logos-*avatara* is a more powerful demonstration of the nature and nearness of God than the mere immanence of the *Logos-antaryamin*. The wonder of the *bhakti marga* is that the Lord does not remain distant from finite humanity, but graciously condescends to allow individuals to have contact with Him, to provide release for His devotees and to allow them to take refuge in Him.

God descended and was incarnated in the physical body of the person of Jesus. The *avataric* descent was glorious, for it was an unrivalled display of the tenderness, concern and goodness of God; nowhere was this epiphany more evident than during the death of Christ. Appasamy asserted:

> Jesus was crucified and endured untold agony and shame. The manifestation of God's love became absolutely clear on the cross. God endured the utmost suffering in order to demonstrate His love for us and to win our love and fellowship in return.[20]

The enfleshment of God in Christ was a momentous indication of the desire of the Lord for communion with humanity. The *avatara*, especially in his suffering on the cross, revealed the indescribable grace of God, as well as His desire for the responsive love of humankind. Appasamy summarized the Christian interpretation of *antaryamin* and *avatara* in this way:

> God is in all men energizing and illumining them. He is their life as well as their light. . . . His indwelling in men, though meant to give them a vivid perception of Himself, may not always be clear and distinct. . . . So this Light chose to shine fully and with all its glory and effulgence through a perfect medium – Jesus – by beholding whom we behold God perfectly.[21]

Conclusion

Appasamy focused upon Johannine theology and its relation to *bhakti* mysticism in his indigenous theology. He explored John's vision of union with Christ and compared its salient features with key themes in Hindu *bhakti* spirituality; he discovered that there are many shared mystical similarities. Therefore, Appasamy used concepts and terms from the *bhakti* tradition to communicate the Christian message in a distinctively Indian fashion. He hoped that such an indigenous theology would help Christianity take root in its contextual south Asian setting and blossom into authentic vitality.

Appasamy believed that God awakens the desire for union with Himself in the soul of every person, and *bhakti* is the devoted response to God's inner prompting. Christ as pre-existent *antaryamin* was immanent within the world and within humanity even before the incarnation, but his enfleshment as *avatara* was meant definitively to portray God before individuals who had not previously responded to his indwelling presence. *Bhakti*-devotion to Christ includes the entirety of the will and emotions, resulting in mystical fellowship (*moksha*) with the divine. Genuine love for God will spill over into concrete acts of love for others and will not hesitate to express itself by following Christ obediently down the path of suffering; then, the human heart will draw closer to the heart of Jesus.

Notes

[1] My reflections on Appasamy have been influenced by the writings of Dr Robin Boyd and by conversations with Dr Timothy Tennent. For further analysis of Appasamy's themes, see Robin Boyd's chapter on him in *An Introduction to Indian Christian Theology* (Delhi: ISPCK, 2000).

[2] A. J. Appasamy, *The Theology of Hindu Bhakti* (Madras: Christian Literature Society, 1970), p. 1.

[3] A. J. Appasamy, *What is Moksha? A Study in the Johannine Doctrine of Love* (Madras: Christian Literature Society, 1931),p. 9.

[4] Appasamy, *The Theology of Hindu Bhakti*, p. 124.

[5] Gurukul Theological Research Group, *A Christian Theological Approach to Hinduism* (Madras: Christian Literature Society, 1956), p. 5.

[6] Appasamy, *The Theology of Hindu Bhakti*, p. 127.

[7] *Ibid.*, p. 129.

[8] *Ibid.*, p. 123.

[9] A. J. Appasamy, *The Christian Bhakti of A. J. Appasamy*, ed. T. Dayanandan Francis (Madras: Christian Literature Society, 1992), p. 149.

[10] A. J. Appasamy, *Christianity as Bhakti Marga: A Study of the Johannine Doctrine of Love* (Madras: Christian Literature Society, 1930), pp. 58–59.

[11] A. J. Appasamy, *The Gospel and India's Heritage* (London: International Society for the Publication of Christian Knowledge, 1942), p. 36.

[12] *Ibid.*, 38.

[13] Appasamy, *What is Moksha?*, p. 47.

[14] *Ibid.*, 66.

[15] *Ibid.*

[16] *Ibid.*, 68.

[17] A. J. Appasamy, *Christ in the Indian Church* (Madras: Christian Literature Society, 1935), p. 54.

[18] Appasamy, *Christ in the Indian Church*, p. 11.

[19] Appasamy, *Christianity as Bhakti Marga*, p. 46.

[20] Appasamy, *The Gospel and India's Heritage*, p. 207.

[21] Appasamy, *Christianity as Bhakti Marga*, p. 54.

Chapter 14

'And the Word Became Flesh': The Journey of Incarnation in the Prelature of Infanta[1]

Sophia Marriage

Introduction

Since Vatican II, Roman Catholic theologians from the Third World[2] have been articulating their own indigenous or local theologies. Traditionally these theologies have tended to take one of two forms, liberation or inculturation. The first concentrates on a political or economic analysis of society and addresses it with the biblical message of freedom from oppression; the second considers the 'colonialism of the mind', re-interpreting the Christianity dressed in Western clothes into the framework of local cultures and religions. Both forms of theology emphasize the importance of grassroots Christians owning and determining the local manifestation of the church.

In the mid-1990s, sociological fieldwork[3] was carried out in the Prelature of Infanta on the east side of the island of Luzon in the Philippines, to draw a picture of how a local church[4] under the guidance of a theologian-bishop was wrestling with these issues. The case study explored how the local church was taking the opportunities presented by Vatican II and by the increased theological activity in the Third World. The research investigated to what extent inculturation and liberation had occurred in a specific situation, suggesting that the old division between inculturation and liberation was no longer valid in real-life circumstances. In place of this dualism, which could be seen as a further legacy of Western colonialism, the research suggested that inculturation and liberation are part of the same process, and can be expressed by Vatican II's understanding of 'Incarnation Theology'. This refers not only to a past event but interprets incarnation as an ongoing process which gives a new understanding and value to history. In this essay we will briefly describe the church in Infanta at a particular moment in time and then draw on their experiences to further our understanding of the incarnation of the Gospel in different situations.

Philippine context

The Philippines were colonized by the Spanish in the sixteenth century, and then from 1898 by the United States of America, who retained control until 1946.

From 1964, President Ferdinand Marcos waged a low intensity war on his people to maintain his power. Martial law was imposed and human rights abuses, murders and kidnappings were common. These were often directed against the more progressive sections of the church.

The Catholic Church represents 80–90 per cent of the population of the Philippines,[5] and religious symbolism permeates much of everyday life. Historically the Church in the Philippines has been the church of the wealthy and middle class. The church buildings are often built in ornate Spanish style; Manila Cathedral, for example, is coated in gilt and air-conditioned. Novelists[6] and historians from the turn of the century show the kudos in attending church and the social status gained. In the villages, recent research has shown how there was sometimes a revolutionary undercurrent in Christian practice and ritual,[7] but that on the whole there was a positive acceptance that the reason for religion was fulfilment in the next life. During much of the 1970s–1990s the Church was split between a progressive and conservative Church, with many priests joining the underground war effort against Marcos in the 1980s. In 1986, a combined effort from parts of the military and the Church, especially Cardinal Sin, the Archbishop of Manila, led to the collapse of the Marcos regime.

In 1992, the Catholic Church of the Philippines held the Second Plenary Council (PCPII). This was to the Philippine Church what Vatican II was to the worldwide Church. Here, the Church officially opted to become 'the Church of the Poor'. The Church of the Poor aims at 'integral evangelisation,' an evangelization which affects the whole of life, restoring the integrity of humanity and creation, and conscientizing people to transform the unjust structures of society. This will by necessity bring about a new way of being church, a transformation from the old style Christendom model, to one that takes all creation and humanity into consideration. It is a theology which necessitates an engagement with world issues, with macro-structures and trade imbalances and seeks for the whole Church to respond to the situation affecting the world today.

Some saw PCP II to be an attempt to co-opt the more radical fringes of the Church into the main fold to prevent them becoming too radical;[8] others believed it to be a genuine response to the situation of poverty in their country.[9] It had the potential to bring together the two strands of church, the traditional and the progressive, or as one writer has put it, the Redemption (already achieved) and the Passion (struggling to achieve) churches.[10]

The Prelature of Infanta

In the 1990s, the Prelature of Infanta was isolated from the rest of the country by appalling roads over the mountains to the west and the Pacific Ocean on the east. The area is split across the middle by a range of mountains, and the only route from the north to the south is via Manila. It is poor, mostly subsistence farmers and fishermen, with tribal groups in the mountains. During the martial law days of President Marcos, the mountains were also used for the underground resistance, which led to a relatively high degree of social awareness in parts of the diocese and also to a heavy military presence.

The Prelature had been orientated to the Church of the Poor for 25 years prior to PCP II. Its theology had been dominated by the bishop, Julio Labayen OCD,[11] who took seriously the concept of Church of the Poor, both from Vatican II and from conferences of Asian bishops, and attempted to put these into practice in the local church. This model of church goes further than the preferential option *for* the poor, advocated by Latin American theologians. The Church of the Poor is composed *of* the poor, being poor alongside the marginalized of society. Labayen's book *Revolution and the Church of the Poor* published in 1995 puts forward his ideas in the clearest fashion, advocating that a change of heart is needed within society to ensure that it can work for the poor and needy. It aims to make all people the authors of their own history. In common with much of the church in the Philippines, traditionally the church in Infanta has been led and attended by the middle class and educated. The bishop's orientation has forced the church to reorientate their faith and lives to their poorer neighbours and those on the fringes of society.

This orientation to the poor and disadvantaged has shaped the bishop's life work. Now in retirement, he continues in his theology and inspiration of the work of the diocese. His convictions permeate how he approaches those who come to church, so that it is the poor fisherfolk and farmers who feel welcome in the cathedral, talking to him and visiting him at home. He has encouraged this change of mind-set throughout the diocese, so that the traditional gap between the priest and the laity has begun to break down in some parishes, with a general acceptance of the humanity of the priest, with his strengths and weaknesses. At meetings of leaders in the church, all were equal and people with little formal education had the courage and language to question the formal teaching of both their priests and the worldwide Catholic Church.[12]

FIGURE 14.1   'Hope in Struggle' (photo courtesy of the author)

FIGURE 14.2   'Hope in Struggle' mural interpretation.

Labayen's perspective and theology can be best summed up in a picture painted on the wall of his church for his Silver Jubilee in 1991 called Hope in Struggle.

The backdrop to the painting is the dark night of St John, recalling Labayen's Carmelite roots, and yet behind the dark clouds the sun continues to shine, breaking through scattered openings. On the horizon, the light breaks through, dark yielding to light, death succumbing to life. On the right is a crowing cock, the symbol of the Pontifical Council of Justice and Peace, announcing the dawn of the hoped-for day. In the centre, barely visible, are two doves flying towards the light. They symbolize the lasting peace that is born of the reign of justice in the hearts of people and in the way they organize their life in community and society. They fly towards a rainbow, the symbol of the New Covenant and a symbol close to the hearts of the people of Infanta. Disappearing into the rainbow is a track of footprints in the sand, the footprints of the Lord who walks with humanity, the living God of, and in, human history. His footsteps will lead to the Promised Land. The man in the top centre of the mural blows a horn (the *tambuli*), traditionally used to mobilize self-defence against a common enemy, and calls the community to join in a common task. The people surrounding him represent a cross-section of the people of Infanta, particularly those the Prelature has helped to organize: fishermen, tribal people, young people, teachers, religious, workers, mothers, women and farmers. At the left hand edge are those who have been killed as victims of the violence. In this mural all the parts of the Church of the Poor are recognized, 'a church in pilgrimage struggling against the idols of this world – prestige, wealth and power'.[13] The Filipino beast of burden, the caribou, is in the middle working with the community.

At the centre bottom of the mural is Bishop Labayen dressed in the shirt and trousers of a worker, pointing towards the light, 'the realisation of our Father's Dream'. He is the Prophet who announces '*Dominus est!*' proclaiming that the risen Lord walks with his pilgrim people. He announces the Good News of God's Kingdom and points to the Dream of the Father 'that the universe, all in heaven and on earth, might be brought into a unity in Christ' (Eph. 1.9–10). Labayen explains how the bishop

> thinks and feels with the living Church that he may lead and guide the Prelature of Infanta in the ways of the Spirit of Jesus who is the giver of life to the living church and the assurance that 'the powers of death shall not prevail against her.'[14]

He sees himself anointed and sent to build the Church of the Poor by being its servant,[15] standing with the people, seeing the world from their perspective.[16]

The name of the painting, *Hope in Struggle* emphasizes what Labayen feels the church is called to be: struggling in history with the hope of God. Here in the picture we see a Servant Bishop, one whose task is to help transform the local situation and church and to stand with the people in their struggles.

Bishop Labayen has tried to use this theology to turn the local church in the Prelature of Infanta around in the last 30 years. His vision of the church is one that is

> decentralized, open, respectful of the autonomy of the secular and the laity's competence, a servant church, but one with a clear and uncluttered view of what its task in the world is: evangelization of the whole of life – economic, political, social, cultural.[17]

The church's role can be best summed up in his own words: 'While the church may be historically conditioned and shaped by history, the same church was founded by Jesus Christ to shape history.'[18] Labayen's mission has been to enable and struggle with his people to turn the church from the Christendom model to that of the Church of the Poor.

Labayen is thus calling people as the church to a conversion of outlook, to enable them to preach the kingdom. He understands preaching the kingdom today to be to work for total human development.

Theology put into practice

Central to the working and orientation of the Prelature is the formation programme first run in 1975. It is a programme which is aimed at the whole church including the bishop, religious, priests and the laity and covers experience, faith, the church, community and God. This programme is called *Yapak ng Panginoon*, or footsteps of the Lord, often shortened to *Yapak*. The meaning of the phrase is multi-layered; it refers to God's intervention in human history, in the history of salvation, denoting action with God to co-create history. However, it is also used as the name of the formation programme. Hence, it is both the orientation of the Prelature and one of the chief ways of implementing that orientation.

Yapak[19] starts with where people are, building on their experiences of life, history and who they are. It looks at the Church and its history, and aims to enhance a life based on prayer. One of the main modules is exposure in the community, which stems from the bishop's conviction that unless you have experienced the poverty of the poor you cannot stand alongside them. Thus, people live for a few days with another family, one more representative of the poverty of the area than is traditionally found in the church, to experience life there; their experiences are then 'processed' afterwards.

The aim of *Yapak* was to build up leaders who would establish Basic Christian Communities in their own parishes. However, the early 1980s were turbulent times in the Philippines, with militarization on the increase. The parish of General Nakar near to the bishop's town of Infanta became famous during this time for the presence of the New People's Army, the communist underground movement. Rumours and black propaganda led to much suspicion in the area. In 1983, this came to a head at a *Yapak* seminar, where priests who were concerned about the decrease of their influence in the emerging new church, joined with people who were nervous about the rumoured communist infiltration and walked out of the seminar. Labayen sees this as the dark night of the Prelature, when his own personal faith was bitterly tested.

Research was carried out by the diocese and the Asian Social Institute, to discover the roots of the problem and the following year the mission statement, or *Pahayag*, was formed. It was discovered that although some people were undertaking the *Yapak* formation, there was no clear understanding of the orientation of the church across the Prelature. The *Pahayag* sought to remedy that. It presented a unified vision throughout the diocese, emphasizing the key points of the Church of the Poor. This was revised in 1995 to include the changes in the situation of the previous 12 years. The *Pahayag* concentrates on the God of History with whom all of humanity walks and in the words of Labayen, 'It mirrors the prelature's historical pilgrimage as a community of believers whose faith in Jesus of Nazareth brought the prelature to recognize and accept its responsibility for and in the world.'[20]

In 1989 there was a complete overhaul of the *Yapak* programme and during the early 1990s it slowly gained strength. By this point, political affiliation was not a matter of life and death and the revised programmes started from the positions and experiences of the participants rather than from either the biblical tradition or political analysis. Through the programme the students look at the relationships between God, Nature, Community and Society and humanity's quest to be fully human. Those who have done the 28-day full programme initiate shorter 3 day programmes to spread the orientation further.

During interviews with *Yapak* graduates, experience of the programme was often seen as the beginning of their activity in the church. Through it they could discover who they were and address their own shortcomings. One claimed 'it was the best thing that has happened to me.' People spoke of how they understood that the Prelature's vision was in step with that of the history of the universal Church and that treating all people as God's children is an important part of being a Christian.

Such a radical change in emphasis of a church is not easy to implement. Participation in *Yapak* is a time consuming commitment and therefore only a relatively small number of people have undergone the programme. There is also little follow up which means that people get swallowed up in the system when they return to their parish. At *Yapak* seminars, as in many of the other teaching seminars held in the Prelature, creative liturgy is encouraged, however, when people return to their parishes, this is used only at fiesta time. Although many in leadership are committed to the Church of the Poor, in outlying areas villagers rarely see a priest and often have very little notion of any church other than a traditional Spanish one. Popular religiosity is common, but the Prelature's aim is to incorporate its adherents into the main church, to slowly alter the expressions and to restore a more progressive view of the church. Some priests are also hesitant about the changes to lay leadership and the Church of the Poor, which means that *Yapak* is not consistently available throughout the area.

Labayen sees education as an integral part of his job. This has been worked out in practice since the 1960s when he and some of his priests expounded the documents emerging from Vatican II during their sermons and workshops. Today, priests conduct their own workshops into different aspects of church life; catechists and lay workers are brought together for nourishment at regular intervals; and on a Prelature-wide level, workers are educating the people about the large multi-national and governmental plans[21] which will affect the livelihood of the people. In this way an integral part of the church's existence is the campaigning for the rights of the people and the conscientization of people to fight for those rights.

To this end, those who have undertaken the programme were expected to become lay workers and catechists in their local areas and to set up *Munting Sambayanan Kristiyano* (MSKs) or Basic Christian Communities. These were seen by the Prelature to be the way forward for the church and there was therefore a concerted effort by religious leaders of the Prelature to encourage the communities to meet together once a month, regardless of whether a priest or sister was present.

In the mid-1990s these communities were in a very early stage and there was no uniformity across the area. In the south of the Prelature, Basic Christian Communities had been strong during the 1970s but, with the increased militarization and communist propaganda, they had stopped during the early 1980s. They had been restarted by different members of the church in 1989 when *Yapak* resumed. In 1996, the community was still synonymous with the *barangay* (roughly a quarter of a village) rather than a smaller unit and were mainly concerned with awareness building, health education and forming liturgies for church and fiestas. It was clear that they were fulfilling a need and people were beginning to feel closer to the church through the community. In the north, MSKs were more developed in terms of their size and there were 3–5 in a *barangay*. They tended to be more spiritually based, but were often not particularly successful when the religious sisters were not present. There were attempts to standardize the experiences of MSKs throughout the Prelature and to encourage a system of tithing, or regular giving, however small, rather than paying for individual sacraments, which would precipitate a further change of mind-set in the church.

People in all positions in the Church were encouraged to undertake the *Yapak* programme and religious communities, often a more conservative wing of the Church, have also been changed by it. The enclosed Carmelites were invited to the Prelature in the early 1980s, and having undertaken orientation and training, have changed their ethos and living conditions to echo the Church of the Poor; and an indigenous religious group called the Apostles in Contemporary Times, who were established in 1972 with the express desire to be led by the Holy Spirit, rather than by traditional church rules, came to the Prelature in the early 1980s. They were responsible for some school education, as well as for lay formation.

Labayen's ideas have become popular. People from outside the area ask to come to the Prelature for exposure and for teaching from Labayen and other leaders, and the Prelature could be seen as leading the Philippine Church forward. It is a church which is involved with the people, it aims to educate them about government plans which threaten their livelihood and stands with the people in their struggles. It is not concerned with traditional doctrinal standpoints, seeing itself as working to ensure everyone can be fully human in their chosen life. It does not seek to convert to Christianity but to a desire for justice and humanity.

Artwork

The presence of indigenous artwork in a church could be seen as a superficial side to inculturation. It is interesting to note that in Infanta there were very few non-Western images in the churches. One is the symbol of *Yapak* which shows the footsteps of the Lord leading to a *bahay kubo*, a traditional Filipino house. A traditional horn calling people towards a common goal and struggle is in the foreground and the rainbow, a symbol of Filipino hope as well as an Old Testament image, arches over the picture. It depicts the calling to walk with the Lord among all people and surrounded by God's hope.

We have already looked at the mural which summarizes Labayen's thinking and the Church of the Poor. The other influential picture in the Prelature is one of the Virgin Mary. The Virgin Mary is a traditional icon in Roman Catholic theology, but in Infanta the iconography emphasizes the orientation of the Prelature.

FIGURE 14.3   'The Virgin Mary in Philippino Context' (photo courtesy the author)

Labayen is a Carmelite and is firmly devoted to Mary; the Prelature was dedicated to her in 1995. She is referred to as the Mother of the Church of the Poor.

The *Yapak* programme encourages a radical change in the people's understanding of Mary. Before people undertake *Yapak*, Mary is commonly seen as a woman with an aquiline nose who is touched with one's handkerchief or as a queen on a throne. She is also revered as a mother who gives help, is affectionate, good and someone to whom they can run in times of need. After *Yapak*, Mary is understood to be a woman who struggles for the rights of people and has an important role in salvation.[22]

This radical understanding of Mary is portrayed in a mural in the church in the town of Infanta.

It depicts a woman dressed as a peasant, who has clearly been working in the fields. She cradles a selection of people in her arms, people identifiable as a farmer, a tribal person, a woman and children. She crushes a crocodile, the Filipino symbol of greed, avarice and selfishness with her feet, which instead of peacefully dying, fights back. The scenery is a Filipino landscape, which is parched and has been blighted by logging. Mary stands at the intersection of two rivers, one depicting divine history and one human history. This is the moment she agrees to become the Mother of Christ. As she consents the traditional symbols of church authority and power, such as thrones, gold and crowns, seen around the edge of the picture, are cracked and destroyed.

The image was put on the 1996 prelatural calendar so that this image of the Virgin Mary would hang in houses, churches, schools and offices throughout the Prelature. All interviewees were consciously beginning to see Mary as a Filipina.

The Marian prayer written to accompany this picture talks of humanity's weakness and unjust society. It asks for Mary's help to purify society and the Church, to help the Church integrate with all people especially the poor, and to build a world that is for all humanity, for the country and for God. This prayer is said at most services and has a unifying effect on the Prelature.

What this study teaches us about the incarnation process

It is beyond the scope of this essay to fully describe the changes in mind-set and programmes that have been taken along the road by the church in Infanta. Here we can simply provide a cursory glimpse at the journey they had started by the mid-1990s.[23] The research was undertaken to consider what lessons could be gleaned for the process by which a church of the Roman Catholic tradition moved from being 'an extension of the local church of Rome' to become 'a truly local church in communion with Rome'.[24] The advantage of a case-study approach to theology is that we can see theories in practice.

In Infanta, I believe we see many aspects associated with both inculturation and liberation, both terms which may not be consciously at the forefront of this church model. The Church of the Poor is born out of the situation of poverty, it responds to people where they are, challenging them to campaign for their rights (e.g. against illegal logging, dynamite fishing, or the government's development plans). It teaches people to analyse society, to work out what is going wrong, advocating the integration of humanity and nature (a theme from the tribal religions), and finding points of reference with Buddhism, a traditionally Asian religion, in the Prelature's links with Buddhist monks in Thailand.

This list is a mixture of ideas normally associated with both inculturation and liberation. Thus I see the Prelature hesitantly moving towards the idea of inculturation and liberation combined. The two theologies are intertwined as the church responds to the situation; both are intrinsically part of the process. In the Prelature there is an attempt to inculturate the structures of the church rather than the external superficialities of vestments, art and liturgy. However, once the structures have changed, it is hoped that a new creativity will be inspired in other parts of church life. In its journey to be a truly local church in its situation, the church in Infanta is naturally and unselfconsciously inculturating and liberating the Gospel message.

Drawing on work from other theologians,[25] this case study[26] highlights three important themes in the process of incarnation.

The place of history in faith

Christianity is firmly rooted in a critical–historical understanding. The tradition is centred on the history of God's people and the action of God within history, most especially recorded in the Old and New Testaments, where the exhortation to 'remember' the covenant with God is repeated time and again. Clearly the word *Incarnation* has historical connotations, not only for the past in the Christ-event, but also in the present as faith is lived in different circumstances, and in the future as Christians strive for a future made possible in Christ.

Vatican II opened the gates for Catholics to take history seriously. *Gaudium et Spes* required Catholics to read 'the signs of the times', thus recognizing human events in the contemporary world to be worthy of note for Christians and theology. In this way '[Vatican II] reconstituted a *recognition* of history – that every historical moment has a dynamic of its own which is of value and is a place where the imminent presence of the kingdom of God may be perceived'.[27] *Dei Verbum* went further to reaffirm the dual nature of revelation as both the Word of God through Scripture and the deeds of God in history;[28] only by reading the Bible and the signs of the times (the history of Israel and the history of our people) can the Word become flesh in each concrete situation (incarnation).[29]

'[T]heology aims to recover, slowly and painfully, the past which has been suppressed by the oppressor, specifically as a tool to build hope in a liberated faith'[30] and, without a history, people have no sense of their identity.[31] History has three interlinking parts: the past, the present and the future. Any attempt to bring past history, or a past culture into conversation with the church with no reference to present day realities, risks an inculturation into a culture no longer relevant to the people. Any attempt to concentrate only on present realities and the immediate short-term future of political goals, risks a liberation which flounders when political realities change, or which does not speak to the soul of the people. Understandings of future history can be used either to pacify people with the belief that rewards in the next life will follow present hardships, or can encourage people to join with God as co-creators of history.

Theology and faith in the Prelature is seen as a process. *Yapak ng Panginoon* conjures up movement as it denotes the footsteps of God, and the programme aims to recognize God acting within history and to give people the responsibility to work with God to bring about a new creation. History creates culture, which in turn creates us, and we need to be in charge of that process as actors not as victims. The first few days of the *Yapak* programme orientates participants to their own history, to know themselves, and to trace the history of the Bible, of their country and of the church. Through their own history and an honest understanding of the history of their people, a faith in the Living God of History can be nurtured.

This understanding of God acting in history is symbolized in the picture of the Virgin Mary mentioned above. Mary is seen standing firmly in the present history of the Philippines, surrounded by the logging and parched earth. But she also stands at the point where divine and human history meet when she says 'yes' to God's plan. Divine and human history are now merged; they are intertwined with the same goal in mind.

Such a dynamic view of history means that the culture in which the church is placed plays a crucial role in the articulation of faith, and a faith which sees God acting in history and wanting fullness of life for all, requires and encourages Christians to get involved in political struggles – the will to change society becomes a central part of being a Christian. The 1983 mission statement is called *Hope in Struggle . . . its historical expression.* The title acknowledges the central role of hope in the expression of our faith,[32] the struggle in life and the fact that 'hope in struggle', the essence of faith, has to have its own historical expression. This struggle of faith is depicted in the picture *Hope in Struggle* which we looked at earlier.

As Labayen himself has written:

[T]he shaping of the Church of the Poor, as a new historical model is in itself the outcome of historical processes and conditioning within the context of revolutionary change and people's struggles. This new historical model is, in a way, a historical revolution vis-à-vis the old traditional model: the Christendom model of church, which emerged from a Euro-centred Christianity during the era of Euro-cultural imperialism and colonialism.[33]

Some inculturation theologies have looked to the distant past, often denouncing colonial history as irrelevant. The incarnation of the Gospel is a holistic process for both the church as a whole and for individual Christians, and therefore its component parts, inculturation and liberation, must address the relationship of Christianity to the past (past culture and colonialism), present (structures and political ideas) and future history of the country and humanity (the dream of where the political process might be taken and the promise of eternity). The phrase 'Incarnation' thus joins all three parts of history as integral to the liberation–inculturation process.

Liturgy of life and the liturgy of the Church

The phrase 'Incarnation' also includes the understanding of theology becoming reality, becoming flesh in daily life; this is theological reflection becoming lived in the liturgy of life. Aloysius Pieris[34] has written extensively about the need for theological reflection to be centred in 'the liturgy of life', a phrase which he contrasts with the liturgy of the church. It is a holistic approach which centres faith firmly in the political, social, economic, cultural and religious aspects of daily life. He argues that unless the liturgy of life changes, any changes to worship are superficial and merely acculturating.

In Infanta, the church has concentrated more on how faith is lived in daily life than in changes to liturgical rituals in the church. It is hoped that the changes in lay participation and understanding will lead to creative liturgies, but that was not the focus in the mid-1990s. This may have been partly because at the time, the Vatican was still withholding permission for a Filipino mass setting that had been submitted in 1989. However, the more informal approach to services, with the Christian communities leading parts of the services, and priests and laity seen as partners in the work of the church, led to a certain informality and a light adaptation in each situation, so that the liturgy of the church was beginning to speak from the situation of the people.

Interviews with key church workers in the Prelature made it clear that many had moved away from believing that attendance at mass was the most important aspect of being a Christian. They saw it as their role to encourage different people to be part of the service, but also to live a life of liberation and community, one which sought to enhance the human in everyone. Under such an understanding, rules about who could receive communion and who was excluded were not followed and the church of the poor lived happily alongside more folk religiosity especially at fiesta time.

Basic Christian Communities have not spearheaded the changes in the Prelature,[35] since they were still at an early stage, but an awareness of the liturgy of life, rather than an over-concentration on the liturgy of the church first and foremost, has allowed the paradigm shift in the church to emerge and has prevented superficial inculturation or liberation. In this way the new model of church is based on a new orientation of the Prelature and it is hoped will eventually be 'owned' by all in the church.

Local versus universal models of church

Thirty years after Vatican II's rediscovery of the local church,[36] this research considered one particular local church to see whether it was realizing its potential and whether through the local church, rather than through meta-theology, academic theologians could understand further the inter-relationship of inculturation and liberation. In Infanta, incarnation of the Gospel was happening through a change in the model of church which was propagated by all levels of the hierarchy and all formation programmes.

Gutierrez has argued that 'the primary task of the Church [...] is to celebrate with joy the salvific action of the Lord in history'.[37] The discussion above suggests that a rediscovery of the whole of history will lead a church to examine the image it has of itself, and how it embodies the past, struggles for the present and prepares for the future. This happens within the universal Church. It is the Church which celebrates the great historical remembrance of the eucharist and it is within the Church that Christians who interact with present history and society in their daily lives come together. The Church is a sign of the incarnation which is a never ending process, since the faith needs to be sown afresh in every new generation. Incarnation is a journey which is never completed while Christians seek to work with God to bring the Kingdom of God on earth.

This involves a different attitude to church, the difference between a Passion and a Redemption Church,[38] where the first model sees itself in a continual struggle in life and the second upholds a church which has already arrived at Redemption. In Infanta, the church model, although spearheaded and strongly influenced by the bishop and the religious, is based on the participation and importance of the laity and understands itself as a community which works for justice, giving guidance and dynamism to society and social transformation.[39] They were encouraged to 'own' the new model of church, the Church of the Poor and to look for ways to put it into practice. It is a rediscovery of church as a movement rather than an institution,[40] which is prepared to take risks and cross boundaries,[41] a church which moves in passion and struggles for humanity rather than seeing itself as the perfect redeemed society.

The church in Infanta has a strong sense that it is a local church and most of the people interviewed during this research saw the church's identity located in the local area rather than in its catholicity and links with Rome – reference was made to the church or the bishop rather than to the Roman Church. Rome is considered far away and largely irrelevant to the national people, so that encyclicals and other documents have to be 'translated' in concept as well as language and may end up being sidelined by the local church.

Infanta theology emphasizes the unity of the bishop and the people, including those not traditionally associated with the church. The bishop is well known by lay workers and priests. It is a conscious local church, which uses insights from other local churches and sees Rome as a unifying, but ultimately other, local church. Some in the Prelature recognized that the church can become too local, and parishes can become separate from others if there is not the same understanding of church throughout the diocese. If this happens a local church (the diocese) risks division which would actually negate its position as a local church (a diocese under one bishop). In Infanta, the bishop saw his own links to the rest of the Catholic Church and to the rest of Asia as vital to his own thinking and to the work of the church in the locality. Perhaps the only way to become a truly unified local church (not dividing into parishes) is to maintain links to the universal Church. The church risks moving from being a local church to becoming a sect if links with a wider church community are not nurtured and maintained, but also risks fossilization and irrelevance if it tries to emulate the universal Church rather than discover what it is called to do as a local church. Links to the universal Church enable churches to become truly local churches, rather than mini-kingdoms with priests working in isolation. After all, Christianity is a communal religion and an understanding of the universal Church maintains the communion between the many local churches around the world, all different models of church depending on their own situation.

Conclusion

This essay has given a brief synopsis of the main findings of a larger project which looked at the way in which the local church was operating in the Prelature of Infanta. It shows how the ideas of a bishop theologian have been translated into reality in a specific situation. It shows how diversity enters into the local church when it is struggling with the context in which it lives.

There are differences between the individual parishes in the Prelature, with some taking the ideas from the Church of the Poor to a greater extent than others and in places there was a gap between the articulated vision and the reality, but these are the issues with which all local churches must struggle. Bishop Labayen has been crucial to the changes which have occurred and some could accuse it of being a 'top-down' approach. However, the nature of the Roman Catholic Church requires that space be created in which reform and innovation can arise, and Labayen has facilitated and encouraged the empowerment of the people, has been challenged by them and has been in tune with their hopes and fears.

This research has shown that it is often difficult to differentiate between inculturation and liberation when they are the result of a church theology trying to become relevant and live among the people. Some may argue that it has achieved inculturation without the acculturation (modification of images, liturgies etc) which is often seen as the precursor of inculturation. It has brought about liberation without having an established Basic Christian Community network first. It works through a holistic church programme, which encourages the community to take an interest in political, economic, social and religious issues. It is an incarnation of the Gospel into a specific time and place.

The new way of being church is involved in the people, working to ensure everyone can be fully human in their chosen life. It inspires the people to see the intertwining of life and faith and has created programmes and activities to change the direction of the church. This Catholic Church is discovering a new way of being church, one which gives the laity the leading role with the clergy becoming facilitators and sacrament givers. The church struggles with the people in their trials, informing and educating them of threats from governmental plans and standing with them to affirm life.

Throughout many areas of the Third World, a paradigm shift is taking place in the Catholic Church, as people take the promises of Vatican II seriously, questioning the old ways of church, and the old understanding of universality. Here in Infanta, we can see that inculturation and liberation are not clearly defined separate processes, but that in becoming a local church, there is a need to incorporate all of life, holistically, allowing each people to redefine their own ways of doing things. Through the study of a particular local church we have explored one way in which this process happens.

Through the local study which listens to the people we have come to a greater understanding of the complex process of becoming a local church. The methodology allows the theologian to see how an articulated vision is lived in reality and allows the pitfalls and successes of such a living to influence the direction of the church – a never ending cycle. Thus, local study is a useful tool for the study of theology, since it can lead to new insights as to how theologies interplay in the reality of the church setting. This may diminish the tension between elite and grassroots theology.

There is no one blueprint for how a church realizes its calling to become a local church. This work has identified certain changes in mind-set which could move the church along the journey – a holistic re-examination of history, an embracing of the liturgy of life rather than simply the liturgy of the church and a balance between maintaining links with the wider church community and fostering an understanding of autonomy at the local level. Such theories offer hints for the incarnation process, but the outworking of these issues would be very different in each situation. Together they may help local churches to realize their own potential to allow the Gospel of Christ to become truly incarnated in every culture and generation, while maintaining communion between the many local churches throughout the world.

Notes

1   This essay emerges from a PhD thesis: S. Marriage, *The Local Church and Incarnation Theology: The Convergence of Inculturation and Liberation in two Roman Catholic Dioceses – Zomba (Malawi) and Infanta (the Philippines)*, University of Edinburgh, UK (1998) and is also dependent on S. Marriage, 'The Place of the Local Church in the Liberation/Inculturation Debate: the Infanta Prelature Experience' in *East Asian Pastoral Review*, 37(2000).
2   Although there has been concern about the use of the phrase 'Third World', many theologians from the southern hemisphere continue to use it in preference to politically correct alternatives since it denotes the third rate citizenship they

feel. This is institutionalized in the formation of the Ecumenical Association of Third World Theologians (EATWOT), founded in Dar es Salaam in 1976.

[3] This was carried out by the author for 3 months, 50 interviews were conducted, among a mixture of educated and uneducated, men and women, old and young, lay and clergy, vernacular and English speakers, alone and in groups. Local documents were consulted. Evidence from participant observation was used to complement this material to build up a picture of the Church.

[4] In the Roman Catholic Church, a local church is a diocese under one pastor, the bishop, rather than a local parish or congregation: David Bosch, *Transforming Mission: Paradigm Shifts in Theology of Mission* (Maryknoll, NY: Orbis Books, 1991), note p. 531.

[5] It is very difficult to accurately estimate the Catholic population. P. T. Giordano put it at 85 per cent Catholic. See *Awakening to Mission – the Philippine Catholic Church*, 1965–1981 (Quezon City, 1988), p. 1.

[6] For example, *Noli Me Tangere* by Jose Rizal (first published in 1886, translated by Leon M. A. Guerrero, published Manila 1995).

[7] R. C. Ileto, *Pasyon and Revolution: Popular Movements in the Philippines*, 1840–1910 (Quezon City and Manila: Ateneo De Manila University Press, 1979).

[8] From a private conversation with eminent Filipino theologian Karl Gaspar.

[9] A. A. Linsangan (ed.), *Catholic Bishops' Conference of the Philippines*, 1945–1995, Manila.

[10] M. Verlet, 'Passion and Redemption: Political Stakes of Religion in the Roman Catholic Sphere of the Philippines' in *International Intercommunications Part 61:26–33(A) and Part 62:19–24(B)*, 1992: 24. This division refers to the ethos of the church, whether it considers the church to be the realized perfect society or whether it struggles with the people to realize the kingdom of God; and at a practical level, whether the church, while voicing concerns for human justice, actually identifies itself with the powerful and rich of society, or with those on the fringes.

[11] Julio Labayen was appointed Apostolic Administrator in 1961, in 1966 he was installed as bishop and he retired in 2004.

[12] Most clearly seen when a group of lay catechists looked at the recently published Roman Catholic Catechism. They came to the conclusion that its phraseology and concepts were fine for the Church in Rome but had little bearing on the Church in the Philippines.

[13] Julio Labayen, *The Bishop, Builder-Servant of the Church of the Poor* (Manila, 1991), p. 2.

[14] *Ibid.*, p. 3.

[15] *Hope in Struggle – its historical expression, The Pahayag of the Prelature of Infanta,* the mission statement of the Prelature of Infanta (Infanta, 1992), pp. 41–43.

[16] From conversations with Bishop Labayen.

[17] J. X. Labayen, 'Vatican II in Asia and the Philippines' in Ecumenical Review, 38, (1985): 276.

[18] J. X. Labayen, *Revolution and the Church of the Poor*, (Manila, 1995), p. 60.

[19] The Yapak programme has gone through many revisions in the past forty years. The full programme is residential and 28 days long. Participants are expected to run 3–7 day mini-Yapak in their own parishes afterwards.

[20] *Hope in Struggle*, p. 2.
[21] This includes large scale development for tourism, logging and illegal fishing. Labayen and the church were also at the forefront of the aid efforts in the wake of disastrous mud slides and flooding in General Nakar in the Prelature in December 2004.
[22] Z. Narito, 'Report on Yapak in the Prelature of Infanta' (SPI unpublished, Manila, 1995).
[23] For a full description of the Prelature of Infanta, see Marriage, 1998.
[24] A. Pieris 'Inculturation: Some Critical Reflections' in *Jahrbuch für Kontextuelle Theologien* 93 (1993):136.
[25] See for example: F. J. Verstraelen, *An African Church in Transition: from Missionary Dependence to Mutuality in Mission: A Case-study on the Roman-Catholic Church in Zambia* (Leiden, 1975); A. Pieris, *An Asian Theology of Liberation* (New York, 1988); K. Gaspar, *How Long?: Prison Reflections from the Philippines* (ed.) H. Graham and B. Noonan (New York, 1984).
[26] And a similar case-study conducted in the dioceses of Zomba, Malawi – see Marriage 1998.
[27] P. Sheldrake, *Spirituality and History* (London, 1991), p. 29.
[28] *Gaudium and Spes* No 2, Vatican II documents.
[29] See Pieris, 'Inculturation', p. 140.
[30] M. Grey, 'Liberation Theology and the Bearers of Dangerous Memory' in *New Blackfriars* (1994), p. 512.
[31] S. Rayan, 'Reconceiving Theology in the Asian Context' in *Doing Theology in a Divided World* ed. V. Fabella and S. Torres (New York, 1985), p. 129.
[32] J. B. Metz, Faith in *History and Society: Toward a Practical Fundamental Theology* (London, 1980), p. 3: 'Any Christian theology [. . .] can be defined, at least in its task and intention, as a defence of hope. . . . [T]he solidarity of hope in the God of the living and the dead, who calls all [. . .] to be his subjects. In our defence of this hope, we are concerned not with a conflict between ideas unrelated to any subject, but rather with the concrete historical and social situation in which subjects are placed, with their experiences, sufferings, struggles and contradictions.
[33] Labayen, *Revolution and the Church of the Poor*, pp. 13–14.
[34] For a good discussion of Pieris' concept see Pieris, *An Asian Theology of Liberation*, pp. 4–8.
[35] As is often considered to be vital – see for example, Pieris, *An Asian Theology of Liberation*, A. Shorter, *Toward a Theology of Inculturation* (Maryknoll, NY: Orbis Books, 1988), J. Marins, *The Church from the Roots: Basica Ecclesial Communities* (London, 1989), among others.
[36] See *The Decree of Missionary Activity of the Church (Ad Gentes)*, especially chapter 3.
[37] G. Gutierrez, *A Theology of Liberation* (New York, 1988), p. 160.
[38] Verlet, 'Passion and Redemption'.
[39] Narito, 'Report on Yapak in the Prelature of Infanta'.
[40] See Bosch, *Transforming Mission*, pp. 50–51.
[41] Such as welcoming those of other denominations and even other faiths to fully worship alongside them.

Chapter 15

A Chinese Theology of Suffering and Social Responsibility: The Essays of Liu Hsia

Maurie Sween

Introduction

This essay examining the theology inherent in the essays of Liu Hsia (劉俠, 1942–2003) was compiled under the tutelage of David Kerr. After being presented with an account of Liu's writings, Professor Kerr was able to quickly and succinctly correlate the essayist's thinking to patterns in Chinese philosophy that established the contextual nature of Liu's arguments. This essay is included as a testament to Professor Kerr's command of world theologies, which extends to familiarity with Chinese philosophy. It is also offered with admiration for the courage Professor Kerr exhibited as he faced a debilitating illness. Professor Kerr was truly a Christian *gentleman* (*jwen dz*, 君子).

Liu Hsia and the question of suffering

Constraints of space allow for only an abbreviated introduction to the theology of the Chinese essayist and social activist Liu Hsia. A more complete presentation of the author herself, her genre and the importance of her contributions can be found in this researcher's PhD thesis.[1] At this point it is sufficient to note that suffering is a pervasive theme throughout Liu Hsia's writings, and that she is an individual who is intimate to the subject. Liu was diagnosed with atrophic arthritis at the age of 12. Her disease brought her a lifetime of severe and constant physical pain. It also gave her experience with the emotional and social stresses that accompany disability in Taiwan.

Nevertheless Liu's essays reflect an optimistic personality. She opens one collection with a piece extolling the glory of nature. A world made over long periods of time and with such wisdom, she concludes, demonstrates that God is love. That humans are created in such a way as to be able to enjoy this beauty further proves her point. People are meant to take pleasure in life.[2] Liu criticizes an artist who bought a house with a view, yet complained the interior was not as large as he hoped. She argues that the whole vista was his. In fact the whole world belongs to all humanity and is a gift given for their delight.[3]

Liu, who is published under the pen-name Xing Lin Zi (杏林子), writes to advise her readers on how to find the happiness they are meant to enjoy in a world where suffering can be intense. Yet collections of Liu's essays systematically examine neither joy nor pain. Rather they predominantly contain pieces written over a particular period of time. A wide variety of issues related to environmental, social and individual problems can be discussed in any one volume. A careful reading of these, however, reveals that the response Liu encourages is consistent. The reader is to seek both emotional and physical health. In this case, 'physical' is used in the widest possible sense including both the body and the environment.

Emotional health

Liu relates the means by which she attained emotional health in an essay that begins by describing the hopeless feeling she had when she first became sick. She had been an active child. With the advent of her painful illness, however, she was forced to drop out of school and was confined to home and hospital. She felt she could find few reasons to live and considered suicide.[4] But after she became a Christian, there was a very real change in her life.[5] Liu's faith led her to accept the classic conundrum that God is simultaneously all-powerful, benevolent and lets good people suffer.[6] A process was begun that ended in Liu being convinced that life is good and has a rational meaning.[7]

This conviction naturally led Liu to explore possible explanations for suffering. She most often concludes that suffering is related to education. Liu typically presents her theories by means of vivid illustrations. Boatmen stabilize their vessels to face high seas by filling the hull of their ships with stones.[8] Straight and fast highways are the most dangerous. People get sleepy and accidents are common. Winding and hilly roads, however, make one alert.[9] Military recruits do tasks that they do not understand. The result is disciplined and well-trained soldiers.[10] Flowers bloom best after being trimmed.[11] The rushing river makes sharp but fragile rocks smooth and hard.[12] In each of these examples difficulties lead to an improved character.

Liu is conscious that in attempting to find the good in suffering she is countering the anxiety that accompanies pain. She credits Abraham Lincoln as expressing that the best way to defeat an enemy is to make him your friend and applies this principle to suffering.[13] Though there is often nothing that can be done to change one's circumstances, one is able to develop an attitude that rises above the difficulties. She has succeeded to the point of being able to write that her illness has awakened her to the many blessings she has and has also helped her develop courage. She declares, 'Life is a school and suffering is a class I'm glad I took.'[14]

This is not to say that Liu believes suffering itself is good. It is an enemy. Though suffering can bring good Liu insists that it is not a gift from God. However, God allows it for special purposes.[15] Illness has brought good to Liu, but it is not a friend. She does not try to make light of suffering or provide answers for all the pain people experience. When writing of a woman who lost everything, her whole family and all her possessions in a devastating earthquake, Liu does not suggest the blessings that might come to the woman in her loss. She clearly describes the horror and simply teaches that sometimes all one can do is not give in.[16]

One cannot always understand the reason for suffering. Yet one's emotional state can make a great difference.[17] Liu argues that even with severe limitations one can find real joy. One of Liu's fables relates a conversation between a bird and a flower. The bird boasts that he can fly. The flower says that he can too. The bird wonders how, as the flower is anchored to the ground. The flower replies, 'You use your wings to fly. I use my heart to fly.'[18] Liu rejects the idea that one must wait until the next life to find happiness. She believes that the peace and joy of heaven can be experienced here, and that all individuals should make an effort to acquire these while they are still alive.[19] To this end Liu advises both active and passive responses to suffering.

Active and passive responses

Liu's message is important in a country where, she informs us, many with disabilities feel certain they are useless and thus have no ambition.[20] The feeling is often enhanced by the popular belief in fate. People are certain their luck is bad and there is little they can do to change their condition.[21] Fortune-tellers often confirm the prognosis. When Liu herself was very young a relative who practised fortune telling predicted she would be a failure.[22] Liu strongly opposes the notion and argues that the things some people call good luck, like health and wealth, do not necessarily bring happiness.[23] One can be both joyful and productive with what some would call 'bad luck'.

Liu counsels those with 'bad luck' to think of the term in new ways, to overlook the ignorance of others, and to work hard to have a productive life.[24] Liu herself learned of the individual's power over emotions when she was young. In Taiwan one's personality is believed to be linked to one's type of blood. A friend who knew her guessed she had type 'O' blood because she seemed emotionally strong. The friend guessed correctly and Liu consciously changed her personality by acting brave when she felt weak. She now sees the episode as a sort of training that affected her future life.[25]

Liu believes in self-determination.[26] Yet, she also believes in fate of a certain type; events are under the control of a divine power. Liu's belief that this power is friendly gives further impetus for encouraging a positive attitude. One should live aware of the many blessings that have already been given.[27] Furthermore, one can experience divine comfort in present difficulties and anticipate help in future endeavours.[28] Life itself is a gift from God and those to whom it is given are valuable and have dignity.[29] This is a novel message in a society where the majority not only believes in 'bad luck,' but also in a cosmology that teaches suffering is related to punishment.[30]

Liu tells several fables that elucidate her ideas regarding the attitude that an individual who suffers should maintain. In one she presents a flower who complains on sunny days because the weather is too hot and on rainy days because the humidity makes it uncomfortable.[31] In another tale a flower complains to the Creator that people smell its fragrance, delight in its beauty and eat its stem. 'What else do you want from me?' questions the agitated flower. The Creator responds, 'I want you to stop complaining!'[32] These transparent stories of blessed flowers are especially enlightening when one sets them beside two of Liu's fables about weeds. A weed that, unlike the flowers faces serious problems, has struggled to live despite being beaten down by wind and rain. It uses its dying breath to assert, 'You have taken my life but I keep my dignity!'[33] A story that follows immediately after tells that in the spring the weed returns, amazing those who had tried to kill it the previous year.[34]

Here one sees parallel thoughts about coping with suffering. One should live contentedly, whatever the circumstances. Yet the individual must also struggle to overcome. One must be determined and oppose false meanings imposed by society; yet should also refuse to entertain the anxiety that can arise when facing difficult circumstances. One must open oneself to the goodness that surrounds and receive the blessings that Liu testifies have transformed her life.[35]

Liu presents the concept in a different way when writing for a strictly Christian audience. Writing a humorous parody of the kind of martial arts' novels that young Chinese teenagers like to read, Liu teaches four explicitly Christian kung-fu moves, or lessons, that can help one 'blow away troubles as the wind blows away dry leaves'.[36] The first two of these apply to the internal life of the individual facing difficulties.

Lesson one is obedience. Obedience means accepting God's will even when it is difficult. Jesus suffered to complete God's plan. Paul knew his 'thorn in the flesh' was from Satan, but after praying three times for it to be removed, this man of faith found God's blessing could be even more greatly seen in his weakness and submitted himself to God's purpose.[37] Liu, with less faith than Paul, took longer to learn the same lesson. She has finally stopped praying for healing and now focuses on obeying God even when she doesn't understand God's purpose.[38] Liu concludes, 'God wants us to obey, not to surrender, feel self-pity, be hopeless, be bitter, or give up. Since we believe in the love of God we must have faith in God's plan in our lives and God's work through us.'[39]

The second Christian martial arts lesson involves offering oneself to God. When praying for a sick person, for example, it is better to offer the patient to God than to ask for healing. The same should be done regarding one's own burdens. This implies complete trust in a God who has a plan and is able and willing to help the individual who suffers.[40]

Lesson one corresponds to Liu's ideas regarding self-determination. An individual can decide to accept and obey God's will, however difficult. This requires effort and may lead one into an interpretation of experiences that is in opposition to the status quo. Lesson two relates to the acceptance of God's divine and friendly power and leads to a sort of release. One can enjoy the many blessings that are given.

In a fable entitled 'Eden on Earth', Liu describes a conversation between a bird and a fish over the polluted environment in which they live. Each would enjoy life more if the air and the water were clean. They ask when heaven will come. The Creator tells them that heaven is in their hearts.[41] Liu believes that individuals are empowered with an ability to overcome negative experiences. When facing problems people should not resign themselves to the predicament but adjust their attitudes so as to live full and joyful lives.[42]

Physical health

The response to suffering that Liu recommends involves not only seeking emotional health, but also physical wellness. That one should not give up but continue to struggle against illness is an important part of Liu's message. She criticizes a woman for valuing a scholarship to study in the United States of America over her health when she disregarded doctor's orders to remain in a Taiwan hospital.[43] She is also upset with a man who had a disease that was similar to hers. Because of his pessimistic attitude he isolated himself from all activities. This resulted in total physical paralysis about which Liu had warned him.[44] Thus when there are possibilities to improve one's physical health one should make every effort to do so.

When writing about physical well-being, however, Liu most often asks the reader to be responsive to the needs of others. She would have her readers work to improve social and environmental ills.[45] An essay in which Liu tells about her feelings after meeting wounded soldiers helps explain her attitude. She considered the soldiers to be heroes for sacrificing themselves to repel an attack from the People's Republic of China. She argues that, like these soldiers, her readers can be heroes. In many ways life is a war. One should fight for what is right.[46] Liu writes:

> I suddenly discovered that I also could be a hero; not just me, every person can – for life, for environment, for ideals. We can contribute our blood and

tears and never give up. We can fight to the end. We can become our own hero in the battles in our life. To be a hero doesn't mean not having any moments of fear, it involves not being conquered by fear. To be a hero doesn't mean there is no time of failure, it means never to be defeated by failure. . . . Life is process of challenges. We don't ask that the sufferings go away, but that we can overcome suffering. It's not important whether we win or lose but that there is a heart willing to fight.[47]

In this short paragraph the two fronts on which one must struggle are apparent. Internal, emotional, battles related to anxiety, cynicism and hopelessness can be won. External, physical, battles must also be fought. One should struggle for the welfare of others. Liu believes that heaven starts in the heart. But she also encourages her readers to exert themselves to make the world a 'garden of joy'.[48]

Social objectives

In urging her readers to struggle for the well-being of others Liu is careful to explain her objectives. Certainly not every group agrees as to the composition of the ideal society. In one essay she describes a friend who believes it is better to die rather than live with a serious disability like cerebral palsy. In this way one will not be a burden to others. Liu rejects the idea arguing that a world that supported such a concept would quickly develop into an abysmal place with increasingly demanding standards regarding who has the right to live. Once people under a certain IQ score would be eliminated, for example, a new low would be determined and there would be a need to dispose of still others.[49]

The healthy society that Liu envisions involves not culling but serving the disadvantaged. It entails sacrificing oneself for the good of others. Liu is unhappy that many give up on Taiwan and immigrate to the West.[50] She urges them to remain and work for the good of society.[51] Liu's ideology has led to her using her own expertise to care for people suffering disabilities. In so doing much of her energy is spent on advocating a proper social response to the needs of this specific group.[52]

Liu's patronage goes beyond requesting acts of charity so that the disadvantaged receive proper physical care. She urges communities to allow them to participate in social life and be treated as equal citizens.[53] Liu has successfully lobbied for the employment rights of those suffering disabilities.[54] Yet, in demanding equal treatment, Liu commends those who justly hold persons with disabilities responsible, praising one employer for dismissing a disabled woman because he both gave her an opportunity and held her accountable.[55] Thus in Liu's model, both those who help the disadvantaged and those who are being served have responsibilities to each other.

One of Liu's fables describes an encounter between a kangaroo and a beggar. The kangaroo apologizes for not being able to offer money, as he is equally poor. The beggar shook the kangaroo's hand and said, 'Thank you'. The Creator explains to the confused kangaroo that the kangaroo had given the most valuable gift: fellowship and dignity.[56] In another piece she commends the slogan that the Seven-Eleven convenience store chain adopted to raise money for her foundation: 'Lead You, Be with You, Go Forward Together' is much better than giving out of pity as it entails building a relationship with the disadvantaged.[57]

Developing meaningful relationships in modern Taiwan, however, is not easy. Liu believes that urbanization has made the process especially difficult. Urban dwellers tend to be afraid of strangers and, image conscious, reticent about revealing their weaknesses. Yet Liu asserts that if an individual is willing to enter into an honest reciprocal relationship, helping and being helped, many blessings will follow.[58]

In one of her essays Liu shares a letter written to her by a woman who was pretty, had a good education, had enough money and was happily married with healthy children. However the woman felt that something was missing in her life. What she is missing, Liu confidently asserts, is service. Liu advised her to open her heart and leave her safe world. If she would 'rejoice with those who rejoice and weep with those who weep'[59] in an imperfect world, her life would become meaningful.[60]

Liu encourages involvement by recounting the blessings she has received through her service. On one occasion she visited a girl with disabilities who taught Liu about joy in trials.[61] In two different essays Liu explains how she was moved by the concern of a young man with developmental disabilities whom a foundation she established had helped with vocational training. After getting a job at a McDonalds restaurant he tried to offer his salary to Liu's organization. At another time, seeing how tired she was, he asked her to rest and innocently offered to take over leading the charity until she recovered her strength.[62] Liu also describes the enjoyment she had in fellowship with blind students who would seriously ask her questions like the colour of the wind.[63]

It is significant that in this case Liu uses herself in examples of the blessings that come to those who serve others. Liu asks those who suffer to serve. Christian martial arts' lessons one and two, introduced above, apply to a person's internal life. When Liu introduces lessons three and four she focus on externals. Number three teaches that the reader is to witness and number four that the individual is to glorify God. One should live a life that both positively impacts the community and brings glory to God.[64] Liu expounds upon what she means by 'witness' with a short poem:

If we call God light, but walk in darkness;
If we call God the way, but are far from righteous way;

If we call God love, but are selfish and envious;
If we call God fair, but cheat and act craftily;
If we say, 'Peace and joy,' but have a downcast face;
If we say, 'God gives encouragement and power, but hesitate and doubt;
If we say, 'God is all powerful,' but don't have full faith in God;
If we do these things, how can we show others to help them trust in God?[65]

It is important to note that Liu's poem was not written to a general audience of Christians, but specifically to those who are suffering. The first segment of each line touches upon what the Christian believes. This is immediately followed by a corresponding action that would negate the faith. Stated in positive terms, the Christian who suffers should walk in light, live righteously, focus on the needs of others, be generous, smile, act with courage and confidence and live in hope.

Essays written for audiences that do not share the faith indicate that Liu encourages much the same response from them.[66] Thinking perhaps of the Chinese concept that one who receives a gift is obliged to give something in return, Liu argues that love comes to those who suffer from family, friends and society. Those who receive are also obliged to give.[67] The contribution one is able to make to others varies greatly according to one's condition. Liu tells the disabled that what one has to offer is not so important as what one does with what one has.[68]

Liu encourages her readers to exert themselves for a healthy society. In regard to those who suffer her objective involves improving society by offering not charity but relationships between the healthy and the disadvantaged. She is concerned that many in her culture have misplaced values, writing that babies laugh and cry for themselves but her readers should laugh and cry for others.[69] In one case she censures popular culture by describing her youthful delight in finding a beautiful butterfly. On being told it was actually a moth she threw it away. Her childhood prejudices are then compared with those who judge others by their appearance and position.[70] Liu finds no value in the struggle to achieve an elevated social status. She warns her readers that life is short and one can take nothing to the other side.[71]

One can, however, leave something behind. Liu compares the Buddha and Jesus to the many powerful figures in history and notices that the powerful leave only ruins while the Buddha and Jesus have left something significant that lasts to the present day. The difference, Liu contends, was that the two had love.[72] In one of her fables, Liu tells of a conversation between river water and rocks. The water asks the rocks why they are in the way. The rocks respond, 'To make you beautiful. To make your life feel exhilarating and vibrant.'[73]

This story suggests that one of the reasons for suffering may be for the good of society. Problems bring people together.[74] The negative effects of urbanization, for example, can be overcome when people enter into meaningful fellowship with others.[75] Thus a proper response to a need achieves Liu's ends of both improving the environment and the emotional health of activists. When this happens Liu's martial arts' lesson number four is achieved. God is glorified.[76]

A Chinese theology

The message that Liu offers sets the human reality of suffering, based in her own experience, within a belief in the omnipotence and essential goodness of God. Suffering is not good in itself and may be experienced as the enemy of well-being, but she does not allow the reality of suffering to distort her essentially optimistic view of life. Even one who suffers intensely can enjoy a life that is full and meaningful. To this end Liu encourages her readers to emotional and physical well-being. These can be achieved through a combination of passive acceptance of suffering and active overcoming of its impediments. Her passive acceptance is not a negative resignation but a positive embracing of God's will in suffering, a will that Liu tries to explain but essentially remains a mystery. Activity involves endeavouring to carry out what is known about the will of God. To this end Liu defines society as it should be, a society in which the healthy and suffering serve each other, thereby creating a healthy physical and emotional environment.

To a trained theologian Liu's ideas may seem threadbare. The fundamental starting points for discussions of theodicy are affirmed in Liu's writing. God is omnipotent and good. Evil is a real force in conflict with these affirmations.[77] Yet Liu does not grapple with the paradox. She merely affirms that suffering is an enemy that one is to actively overcome and also that suffering be understood as *permitted* by God for good ends. Liu simply does not seek to explain suffering in origin and nature.

To dismiss Liu's theology as superficial, however, would be to fail to interpret Liu in context. She writes as a Chinese author to a Chinese audience, assuming a common worldview. As the theologian C. S. Song emphasizes, hers is 'a society dominated by Confucian culture'.[78] When one examines Liu's theology in terms of Confucian thought it becomes apparent that there is a corresponding relationship. On the subject of suffering Liu appears to have appropriated Confucian culture and extended it to incorporate her Christian understanding.

Suffering in Chinese philosophy

Throughout Chinese history there have been differing theories regarding the question of suffering. Some philosophies, like that found in the *Shu Ching* (書經),[79] have stressed self-determination, associating one's condition with merit.[80] Other teachings, like those found in the Taoist classic *Tao Te Ching* (道德經),[81]

propound forms of fatalism in which behaviour is inconsequential to circumstances.[82] Confucius (孔子, 551–479 B.C.E.), avoiding extremes, incorporated both self-determinism and fate into his philosophy. He believed in a heaven (天) that is both powerful and good.[83] Heaven is also personal. According to Julia Ching, a Chinese Christian scholar who compares Confucianism with Christianity, the classic Confucian texts portray heaven in a way that 'resembles the Christian God'.[84] Yet heaven was not particularly close to any individual, save the emperor. The emperor was divinely ordained to carry out heaven's work in the human sphere and was the only person permitted to worship.[85]

Ordinary people had a much more tenuous relationship with the divine. On the question of suffering, when a seemingly innocent individual experienced a problem that seemed unjust there was no direct recourse to heaven. Confucius allowed prayers and offerings to be made to the ancestors and even to the evil spirits that were believed to be behind natural disasters.[86] It came to be believed that these could intercede for the petitioner or provide some level of assistance.[87] Yet Confucius himself refused to speculate about the ability of spiritual beings to help an individual. His focus was firmly on human relationships and he approved of ceremonies for the deceased primarily because they reflected proper social values. Confucius gave his full attention to earthy matters and would not conjecture about the spiritual, saying, 'To foster right among the people; to honour ghosts and spirits and yet keep aloof from them, may be called wisdom.'[88]

Confucius seems not to have questioned that suffering can indeed come upon an innocent individual. In such cases the sufferer was encouraged to bear with pain in a virtuous way, with courage and without complaint.[89] When Confucius was himself in difficulties a disciple questioned why the sage must suffer so. Confucius answered, 'A gentleman can withstand hardships; it is only the small man who, when submitted to them, is swept off his feet.'[90] Again, when Confucius and his followers were short of food a disciple asked why he seemed happy. He answered: 'I have tried to avoid being reduced to such a strait for a long time; and that I have not escaped shows that it was so appointed for me.'[91] Confucius' ability to cope comes from a belief in fate. This positive fatalism is possible because of a belief in a just heaven.

Confucius believed in a just heaven, but seems not to have developed a theology pertaining to the question of innocent suffering. Mencius (孟子, 371–289 B.C.E.), who refined Confucian thought,[92] did take steps in this direction, suggesting that heaven may allow suffering as a discipline to develop character. He wrote:

> For God, when about to charge a man with a great trust, will try his soul with bitterness, subject his bones and sinews to toil and his body to hunger, reduce him to nakedness and want, and bring his enterprises to naught. Thus his mind is made active, his character tempered, and his weakness made good.[93]

Sageliness

However it was clear to Confucius that heaven desired just rule on earth and he focused his efforts on teaching earthly rather than heavenly ethics. The focus of human endeavour was sageliness (*sheng*, 聖), which Julia Ching defines as the 'Chinese equivalent to the English word holiness'.[94] Evil arises when the individual is not acting in accord with the harmonious universe.[95] One should transcend this evil.[96] This can be accomplished by cultivating the seed of sageliness that Confucians came to believe lies in every human. One should endeavour to become a sage.[97] As Confucian thought developed Confucius himself, and other remarkable individuals, were held out as examples to verify it was possible to become a sage.[98]

Confucius, however, did not consider himself a sage. A sage was an exalted title indeed. The more common virtuous individual was a gentleman (*jwen dz*, 君子).[99] The *Analects* of Confucius use the term 107 times. Wing-tsit Chan summarizes the attributes of the gentleman presented in the *Analects* as follows:

> . . . one who is wise, loving, courageous; who studies the Way and loves people; who stands in awe of heaven; who understands the mandate of heaven . . . who does not seek to gratify his appetite or seek comfort in his dwelling place but is earnest in deeds and careful in speech; who is not a 'utensil' that is useful only for a specific function; who does not set his mind for or against anything but follows only what is right; who practices respect, reverence, generosity and righteousness; who studies extensively but restrains himself with ceremonies; who meets with friends on the basis of culture and helps himself with their friendship.[100]

Confucius summed up all these virtues in one word, *jen* (仁). *The Dictionary of World Religions* calls this Confucius' central doctrine and translates the term as 'goodness', 'benevolence' and 'human-heartedness'.[101] The sage has *jen*. The gentleman pursues *jen*.[102]

Active and passive responses

It is important to note that the individual who cultivates the seed of sageliness, who seeks *jen*, does not strive for his own benefit but for others.[103] As Confucian ideas developed, adherents often censured Buddhists for their monastic way of life.[104] One must not neglect social responsibility. There were three types of sages: kings, ministers and hermits.[105] The meaning of sage in all three examples relates to social service. Hermits were individuals who renounced their positions for reasons related to the good of society, not to escape from social responsibility.[106] According to Julia Ching, their best efforts resulted in

> a dynamic discovery of the worth of the human person, of the possibilities of moral greatness and even sagehood, of one's fundamental relationship to

others in a society based on ethical values, of an interpretation of reality and a metaphysics of the self that remain open to the transcendent.[107]

As regards suffering, the disciples of Confucius dealt with the problem in two ways. Emotionally, the will of heaven was to be courageously accepted. Physically, every effort was to be made to bring about the well-being of society.[108] By means of proper passive and active responses the sage would conduct himself in a cultivated manner. The reward of such service was not based in a belief in the afterlife, but in living in harmony with nature.[109] Julia Ching describes the motivation as follows:

> The Confucian finds his joy in his harmony with nature, and in his own humanity. . . . He does not seek to abound in good works in this life to save himself in the next. He has rather a realized view of eschatology. Here on earth, the future life is not his primary concern. It will take care of itself. [110]

Liu Hsia: An extension of Confucian principles

It is quite clear that Liu's writing resonates with Confucian thought. Rather than developing a new system to explain her faith, Liu seems to explain suffering in essentially Confucian terms. The difference between Liu's ideas and those of Confucian thinkers seems to be one of extension. Liu extends basic Confucian thought to include principles developed in relation to the contemporary culture of Taiwan and her Christian faith.

As Confucius' teachings are based in a belief in the will of heaven, so Liu's starting-point is her understanding of that will. Liu extends the thought of an omnipotent and good God to include a God who is in relationship not just with the emperor, but also every individual. God is personal. God allows suffering. God also comforts. Liu applies this to herself, a woman with disabilities.

Liu's view of the value of women and those with disabilities is different from that of Confucius, who wrote, 'Only women and common persons are difficult to care for. Be familiar with them, and they lose their modesty; avoid them, and they become resentful.'[111] Women certainly did not have an esteemed position in Confucius' social model.[112] Yet Confucius' ideas are purported to have led to 'a dynamic discovery of the worth of the human person.'[113] Liu extends this view to women and those with disabilities.

The advice Liu offers her readers is essentially the same as that of Confucian teaching. One should not complain, but seek emotional health by courageously accepting the will of heaven. Suffering may actually be God's blessing. One should passively (not pessimistically) accept that will. Liu writes,

> The obedience that God wants is not a 'submission' that entails feeling sorry or wronged with no recourse. . . . It's that we believe in God's love, in his plan for us, and the work he is going to achieve for us.[114]

In accordance with Confucian philosophy one should also be active, working for the well-being of others. That Liu applies this advice to herself and includes those suffering disabilities is significant. All, even women and those who traditionally have no place in society, are to pursue *jen*. Each person is to cultivate the seed of sageliness that is in their souls.

Liu uses herself as an example of the emotional health and social consequences that can come when one cultivates oneself.[115] However, the humble tone with which she writes proves she does not consider herself to have attained the status of a sage. Yet, like the Confucian writers, she indicates it is possible by pointing to Jesus. Jesus is Liu's sage. In Liu's writings Jesus is not so much portrayed as a Savior from sin, but as an example that should be emulated. He suffered well, accepting the will of heaven. He lived well, devoting himself to the well-being of others.

When Liu wrote about obedience in her article on *kung-fu* she used Jesus as her example. Though it was extremely difficult for Jesus to submit himself to God's will and suffer in a completely unjust way, he was willing to do so.[116] The fact that Jesus also suffered unjustly gives encouragement to those who themselves suffer. Liu writes, 'When we are stuck in our dark deep pit and cannot pull ourselves up out of despair . . . we know someone (Jesus) has been through it.'[117] The depth of Confucian *jen* can clearly be seen in the ends for which Jesus suffered. When arguing against culling those with disabilities Liu points to Jesus as the sagely example, writing:

> Jesus Christ, in order to be close to the poor, was born into a poor carpenter's home. In order to be close to lonely, helpless, blind, lame, worried and tormented souls he was willing to be driven away, persecuted, humiliated and live in a homeless state without even a pillow.[118]

Conclusion

Liu extends the teaching of Confucius by arguing for a relationship between God and each person, insisting that women and those with disabilities are part of the sagely calling and presenting Jesus as a sage to be emulated. Moreover, when Liu instructs her readers to passively accept the will of heaven while at the same time actively serving the disadvantaged she is reiterating basic Confucian teaching. Liu is also in harmony with Confucian thinking in that she does not believe service should come out of a desire for a better afterlife. One should endeavour simply to live in accord with the will of a benevolent heaven.[119]

Liu works out her theology in much the same way as Confucius, keeping the same tension between fate and self-determination and presenting a way that results in both the emotional and physical well-being of the self and society. In doing this it is doubtful that Liu has made a conscious attempt at inculturation.

She has not formally studied theology. Her writings neither mention theologians nor discuss the theological issues considered central to questions of theodicy. This essay has portrayed Liu as one whose writings 'tend to flow from life to the Bible rather than vice-versa'. This being the case it appears that Liu simply writes as a Chinese Christian who works out her faith in terms of her own culture.

If Liu's message results in less than a theological explanation of the nature of suffering, its value lies in generating a system that responds to the culture and needs in Taiwan. It takes seriously the anxiety and even the corresponding socio-political problems in which the distress is rooted. Specifically, it enables the disadvantaged to take a positive approach to life and their contribution to society and at the same time challenges healthy people to treat those who suffer on a basis of equality.

Liu applies her theology to her own life and testifies:

> I have already conquered this illness. . . . Nobody knows if I can be cured or if I will get worse. This is not important to me. It is important that I know life, and know the Lord who created life. I will live, and live vibrantly and with strength.[120]

Liu did live well. Sadly in February 2003 a domestic assistant suffered a psychotic episode and pulled Liu from her bed, resulting in her death.[121] For the 2 years prior to her death she served as a formal advisor to President Chen Shui-bian.[122] At her memorial service President Chen eulogized her as the force behind government initiatives such as creating barrier free environments.[123] At the same service one of Liu's friends read a piece of her writing that included the words, 'When I pass away, please don't bury me with tears. I have departed for a mysterious meeting. How I wish you could be joyous just as I am.'[124] Her brother recalls that she wanted to share her faith experience, the source of her ability to endure, even to be joyful, in severe difficulties.[125] This she did, in a manner that in her context proved most effective.

Notes

[1] Maurie Sween, 'Chinese Protestant Theologies of Social Ministry in Nationalist Taiwan, with Special Emphasis on the Eden Social Welfare Foundation and Liu Hsia' (PhD thesis, University of Edinburgh, 2006).

[2] Xing Lin Zi, 'The World of Love' in *Sing the Song of Life* (Taipei: Chiu-Ko Publishing, 1995), p. 10; Xing Lin Zi, 'Contentment' in *Watch Your Soul* (Taipei: Chiu-Ko Publishing, 1997), pp. 76–77; Xing Lin Zi, 'Walking with Grace and Ease' in *Thinking of You* (Taipei: Chiu-Ko Publishing, 1993), p. 81.

[3] Xing Lin Zi, 'Everything You See is Yours' in *The Song of Life* (Taipei: Eurasian Press, 1997), pp. 123–124.

4 Xing Lin Zi, 'Surviving the Catastrophe' in *The First Family in the North Pole* (Taipei: Crown, 1995), p. 105; Xing Lin Zi, 'Breaking Through the Difficulties of Life' in *The Song of Life* (Taipei: Eurasian Press, 1997), 326–327; Xing Lin Zi, 'Cherish Life' in *Why I Didn't Kill Myself?* (Taipei: Chien-Hsing Publishing, 2000), pp. 7–8.

5 Xing Lin Zi, 'The Parent's Heart' in *The First Family in the North Pole* (Taipei: Crown, 1995), p. 10.

6 Xing Lin Zi, 'The Four Spiritual Moves' in *Victory Song Series* (Taipei: China Christian Mission, 1983), pp. 161–162; David Van Biema, 'When God Hides His Face' *Time Magazine*, 13 August 2001, pp. 56–58; D. W. Amundson, 'Suffering' in *New Dictionary of Theology*, ed. Sinclair B. Ferguson and David F. Wright (Leicester: Intervarsity Press, 1988), p. 667.

7 Xing Lin Zi, 'Knowing Life' in *Sing the Song of Life* (Taipei: Chiu-Ko Publishing, 1995), p. 145.

8 Xing Lin Zi, 'Burdens' in *Sing the Song of Life* (Taipei: Chiu-Ko Publishing, 1995), p. 152.

9 Xing Lin Zi, 'Road' in *Sing the Song of Life* (Taipei: Chiu-Ko Publishing, 1995), p. 195.

10 Xing Lin Zi, 'Training and Discipline' in *Psalm of Life* (Taipei: Chiu-Ko Publishing, 1995), p. 21; Xing Lin Zi, 'Looking at Life from a Different Angle' in *The Song of Life* (Taipei: Eurasian Press, 1997), p. 92.

11 Xing Lin Zi, 'New Life' in *Sing the Song of Life* (Taipei: Chiu-Ko Publishing,1995), p. 167.

12 Xing Lin Zi, 'Li Wu River Stones' in *The Song of Life* (Taipei: Eurasian Press, 1997), p. 129.

13 Xing Lin Zi, 'The Best Way to Annihilate an Enemy' in *The Song of Life* (Taipei: Eurasian Press, 1997), p. 348.

14 Xing Lin Zi, 'Fortunately' in *Always Joyful* (Taipei: Chinese Sunday School Association, 1976), p. 14.

15 Xing Lin Zi, 'Spiritual Moves', p. 162.

16 Xing Lin Zi, 'The River Li after the Disaster' in *The Song of Life* (Taipei: Eurasian Press, 1997), pp. 35–37.

17 Xing Lin Zi, 'Choice' in *Apricot Forest Essays* (Taipei: Chiu-Ko Publishing, 1979), pp. 77–78.

18 Xing Lin Zi, 'Able to Fly' in *Fables of Our Time* (Taipei: Chiu-Ko Publishing, 1994), p. 26.

19 Xing Lin Zi, 'Eternal Eden' in *The Song of Life* (Taipei: Eurasian Press, 1997), p. 324.

20 Xing Lin Zi, 'The Limit of Life' in *Psalm of Life* (Taipei: Chiu-Ko Publishing, 1995), p. 51.

21 Xing Lin Zi, 'Spiritual Moves', p. 163.

22 Xing Lin Zi, 'Fortune Telling' in *Watch Your Soul* (Taipei: Chiu-Ko Publishing, 1997), p. 196.

23 Xing Lin Zi, 'Fate – Fate' in *Psalm of Life* (Taipei: Chiu-Ko Publishing, 1995), pp. 160–161.

24 Xing Lin Zi, 'Distributing Pears and Sending Books' in *The Song of Life* (Taipei: Eurasian Press, 1997), pp. 256–257; Xing Lin Zi, 'The Unlucky Crow' in *Fables of*

Our Time (Taipei: Chiu-Ko Publishing, 1994), p. 28; Xing Lin Zi, 'Fashion' in *Fables of Our Time* (Taipei: Chiu-Ko Publishing, 1994), p. 17.

[25] Xing Lin Zi, '"O" Blood-type Personality' in *Apricot Forest Essays* (Taipei: Chiu-Ko Publishing, 1979), pp. 38–39.

[26] Xing Lin Zi illustrates her belief that God wants humans to actively overcome negative emotions in, Xing Lin Zi, 'Is the Moon Full?' in *Fables of Our Time* (Taipei: Chiu-Ko Publishing, 1994), p. 126.

[27] Xing Lin Zi, 'Unexpected Meeting' in *Thinking of You* (Taipei: Chiu-Ko Publishing, 1993), pp. 10–11, 25.

[28] Xing Lin Zi, 'The Long Night' in *Psalm of Life* (Taipei: Chiu-Ko Publishing, 1995), p. 47; Xing Lin Zi, 'I Want to Live' in *Always Joyful* (Taipei: Chinese Sunday School Association, 1976), p. 121; Xing Lin Zi, 'Bad Horse' in *Always Joyful* (Taipei: Chinese Sunday School Association, 1976), p. 36.

[29] Xing Lin Zi, 'Want to Live' pp. 122–123.

[30] Xing Lin Zi, 'Great Enlightenment Great Compassion' *Thinking of You* (Taipei: Chiu-Ko Publishing, 1993), p. 89; Arthur P. Wolf, 'Gods, Ghosts, and Ancestors' in *Studies in Chinese Society,* ed. by Arthur P. Wolf (Stanford: Stanford University Press, 1978), p. 153; Stevan Harrell, *Ploughshare Village: Culture and Context in Taiwan* (Seattle: University of Washington Press, 1982), p. 205.

[31] Xing Lin Zi, 'Neither Clear nor Rainy Days are Fun' in *Fables of Our Time* (Taipei: Chiu-Ko Publishing, 1994), pp. 102–103.

[32] Xing Lin Zi, 'No Complaining' in *Fables of Our Time* (Taipei: Chiu-Ko Publishing, 1994), p. 30.

[33] Xing Lin Zi, 'The Weed That Will Not Surrender' in *Fables of Our Time* (Taipei: Chiu-Ko Publishing, 1994), p. 44.

[34] Xing Lin Zi, 'The Weed's Life' in *Fables of Our Time* (Taipei: Chiu-Ko Publishing, 1994), p. 45.

[35] Xing Lin 'Want to Live,' p. 124.

[36] Xing Lin Zi, 'Spiritual Moves' p. 171.

[37] 2 Corinthians 12.7–10.

[38] Xing Lin Zi, 'Spiritual Moves', p. 163.

[39] *Ibid.*

[40] *Ibid.*, pp. 164–166.

[41] Xing Lin Zi, 'The Garden of Eden on Earth' in *Fables of Our Time* (Taipei: Chiu-Ko Publishing, 1994), p. 147.

[42] Xing Lin Zi, 'Directionless' in Xing Lin Zi, *Victory Song Series* (Taipei: China Christian Mission, 1983), pp. 88–89.

[43] Xing Lin Zi, 'Life and the World' in *Apricot Forest Essays* (Taipei: Chiu-Ko Publishing, 1979), pp. 102.

[44] Xing Lin Zi, 'Human Effort can Achieve Everything' in *Psalm of Life* (Taipei: Chiu-Ko Publishing, 1995), pp. 62–63.

[45] Xing Lin Zi, 'Hold Up the Light' in *Sing the Song of Life* (Taipei: Chiu-Ko Publishing, 1995), p. 204.

[46] Xing Lin Zi, 'Hero' *Sing the Song of Life* (Taipei: Chiu-Ko Publishing, 1995), pp. 205–206.

[47] *Ibid.*, p. 206.

[48] Xing Lin Zi, 'Eden' in *Watch Your Soul* (Taipei: Chiu-Ko Publishing, 1997), p. 64.

49 Xing Lin Zi, 'Walking Willingly on this Path' in *The Song of Life* (Taipei: Eurasian Press, 1997), p. 181.

50 Xing Lin Zi, 'The Love that Never Gives Up' in *Watch Your Soul* (Taipei: Chiu-Ko Publishing, 1997), p. 46–47.

51 Xing Lin Zi, 'This Piece of Land' in *Watch Your Soul* (Taipei: Chiu-Ko Publishing, 1997), p. 147; Xing Lin Zi, ' Addendum' in *Meet You at the Harbor of Life* (Taipei: Chiu-Ko Publishing, 1999), p. 207.

52 Xing Lin Zi, 'It is Beautiful to Live Splendidly' in *Give Thanks to the Thorny Rose* (Taipei: Chiu-Ko Publishing, 1989), p. 63.

53 Xing Lin Zi, 'Angel Without Legs' in *Meet You at the Harbor of Life* (Taipei: Chiu-Ko Publishing, 1999), p. 177.

54 Xing Lin Zi, 'Equality' in *Watch Your Soul* (Taipei: Chiu-Ko Publishing, 1997), p. 168.

55 Xing Lin Zi, 'Martial Artist Tsai Jr-Jong' in *Meet You at the Harbor of Life* (Taipei: Chiu-Ko Publishing, 1999), p. 35–41.

56 Xing Lin Zi, 'The Kangaroo and the Beggar' in *Fables of Our Time* (Taipei: Chiu-Ko Publishing, 1994), pp. 140–141.

57 Xing Lin Zi, 'Lead You, Be with You, Go Forward Together' in *True Love is a Life-long Promise* (Taipei: Eurasian Press, 2000), p. 128.

58 Xing Lin Zi, 'Knocking at the Door' in *Watch Your Soul* (Taipei: Chiu-Ko Publishing, 1997), pp. 50–51.

59 Romans 12.15 NASB; Xing Lin Zi, 'Defect is the Only Way to Bring Love Out' in *The Song of Life* (Taipei: Eurasian Press, 1997), p. 230.

60 Xing Lin Zi, 'Defect' pp. 227–231.

61 Xing Lin Zi, 'Strong Person' in *Always Joyful* (Taipei: Chinese Sunday School Association, 1976), p. 8–11.

62 ing Lin Zi, ' Angel in Disguise' in *Watch Your Soul* (Taipei: Chiu-Ko Publishing, 1997), p. 66; Xing Lin Zi, 'General Wang Ru-Kai' in *Meet You at the Harbor of Life* (Taipei: Chiu-Ko Publishing, 1999), pp. 81–81.

63 Xing Lin Zi, 'There is Still Blue Sky out the Window' in *The Song of Life* (Taipei: Eurasian Press, 1997), pp. 315–317.

64 Xing Lin Zi, 'Spiritual Moves', pp. 166–171.

65 *Ibid.*, p. 168.

66 Xing Lin Zi, 'Christ's Messengers' *Sing the Song of Life* (Taipei: Chiu-Ko Publishing, 1995), p. 117; Xing Lin Zi, 'Lamp,' 20; Xing Lin Zi, 'The Melody of Life' in *The Song of Life* (Taipei: Eurasian Press, 1997), p. 395.

67 Xing Lin Zi, 'The Treasure of Life' in *Watch Your Soul* (Taipei: Chiu-Ko Publishing, 1997), pp. 22–23.

68 Xing Lin Zi, 'Knowing Life', p. 145.

69 Xing Lin Zi, 'Tears and Laughter' in *Watch Your Soul* (Taipei: Chiu-Ko Publishing, 1997), pp. 92–92.

70 Xing Lin Zi, 'Looking Down on People' in *The Song of Life* (Taipei: Eurasian Press, 1997), pp. 135–137.

71 Xing Lin Zi, 'The Camel is Sick' in *Fables of Our Time* (Taipei: Chiu-Ko Publishing, 1994), p. 148; Xing Lin Zi, 'Don't Rub Salt in Someone's Wound' in *The Song of Life* (Taipei: Eurasian Press, 1997), p. 207; Xing Lin Zi, 'The History of the Changing World' in *Thinking of You* (Taipei: Chiu-Ko Publishing, 1993), pp. 90–98.

[72] Xing Lin Zi, 'Everlasting Love' in *Watch Your Soul* (Taipei: Chiu-Ko Publishing, 1997), p. 27.

[73] Xing Lin Zi, 'The Stream and the Hidden Stones' in *Fables of Our Time* (Taipei: Chiu-Ko Publishing, 1994), p. 158.

[74] Xing Lin Zi, 'The Weak Help Each Other' in *The Song of Life* (Taipei: Eurasian Press, 1997), p. 111.

[75] Xing Lin Zi, 'Reading the List of Donors' in *True Love is a Lifelong Promise* (Taipei: Eurasian Press, 2000), p. 68; Xing Lin Zi, 'Beautiful to Live' p. 63; Xing Lin Zi, 'The Long Road' in *Sing the Song of Life* (Taipei: Chiu-Ko Publishing, 1995), p. 15.

[76] Xing Lin Zi, 'Spiritual Moves', p. 170.

[77] Harold A. Netland, 'The Problem of Evil in Mission' in *The Evangelical Dictionary of World Mission*, ed. A. Scott Moreau (Grand Rapids, MI: Baker Books, 2000), p. 789.

[78] C. S. Song, *Jesus in the Power of the Spirit* (Minneapolis: Fortress Press, 1994), pp. 72–73.

[79] The *Shu Ching*, or Book of History, is the oldest of the five classics of Chinese antiquity. The majority of material contained therein is pre-fourth century B.C.E. It is a foundational book for subsequent Chinese philosophy and would have been known to Confucius. *The New Encyclopaedia Britannica*, 1991 ed., s.v. 'Shu Ching'; Clae Waltham, *Shu Ching, Book of History: A Modernized Edition of the Translations of James Legge* (London: George Allen & Unwin, 1972), p. x; 'Chinese Cultural Studies: The Mandate of Heaven, Selections from the Shu Jing,' Brooklyn College of the City University of New York, n.d., http://acc6.its.brooklyn.cuny.edu/~phalsall/texts/shu-jing.html (5 September 2001).

[80] H. H. Rowley, *Submission in Suffering and Other Essays on Eastern Thought* (Cardiff: University of Wales Press, 1951), pp. 4–5.

[81] Translated the 'Classic of the Way of Power.' Scholarly opinions place the composition of the book between the eighth and third centuries B.C.E. 'Tao-te Ching,' *Encyclopaedia Britannica* http://www.britannica.com/eb/article?eu=73071&tocid=0&query=tao%20te%20ching (5 September 2001).

[82] Rowley, pp. 40–45.

[83] Julia Ching, *Confucianism and Christianity: A Comparative Study* (Tokyo: Kodansha International, 1977), 10, 77–78; Karl Ludvig Reichelt, *Religion in Chinese Garment*, trans. by Joseph Tetlie (London: Lutterworth Press, 1951), p. 44.

[84] Ching, *Confucianism and Christianity*, p. 10.

[85] *Ibid.*, pp. 9, 84; Reichelt, p. 44.

[86] Reichelt, pp. 47-48.

[87] Evelyn S. Rawski, 'A Historians Approach to Death Ritual' in *Death Ritual in Late Imperial and Modern China*, ed. James Watson and Evelyn S. Rawski (Los Angeles: University of California Press, 1988), p. 23; Emily M. Ahern, *The Cult of the Dead in a Chinese Village* (Stanford, CA: Stanford University Press, 1973), p. 91; James L. Watson, 'The Structure of Chinese Funerary Rites: Elementary Forms, Ritual Sequence, and the Primacy of Performance' in *Death Ritual in Late Imperial and Modern China*, ed. James Watson and Evelyn S. Rawski (Los Angeles: University of California Press, 1988), p. 9; Stuart E. Thompson, 'Death, Food, and Fertility' in *Death Ritual in Late Imperial and Modern China*, ed. James L. Watson and Evelyn S. Rawski (Berkeley: University of California Press, 1988), p. 73; Jordan, p. 92.

226   *World Christianity in Local Context*

Rowley, 93; Confucius (孔子), *Analects 6.20*, trans. Leonard A. Lyall, *The Sayings of Confucius* (London: Longmans, Green & Company, 1935), p. 25.

[89] *Ibid.*, p. 36–37.

[90] Rowley, 35; Confucius, *Analects 15:1*, trans. Arthur Waley, *The Analects of Confucius* (London: George Allen & Unwin Ltd., 1949), p. 192.

[91] Rowley, 38; Chuang-tzu (莊子), *The Writings of Kwang-zze:* XVII, ii. p. 9, trans. James Legge, *Sacred Books of the East*, Vol. 39 (Oxford: Clarendon Press, 1891), p. 386.

[92] Chung-ying Chen, 'Mencius (Mengzi, Mengtzu)' in *The Encyclopedia of Chinese Philosophy*, Antonio S. Cua (London: Routledge, 2003), p. 440; 'Confucianism' in *The Encyclopedia of Eastern Philosophy and Religion*, ed. Stephen Schumacher and Gert Woermer (Boston: Shambhala, 1989), p. 79.

[93] Mencius (孟子). *Book Six*, trans. Lionel Giles, *The Book of Mencius* (London: John Murray, 1942), p. 106.

[94] Ching, *Confucianism and Christianity*, p. 80.

[95] *Ibid.*, pp. 10, 73–75, 77–78, 88, 103.

[96] *Ibid.*, p. 79; 'Sages' in *Oxford Dictionary of World Religions*, ed. John Bowker (Oxford: Oxford University Press, 1997), p. 836.

[97] Ching, *Confucianism and Christianity*, p. 10.

[98] *Ibid.*, p. 88.

[99] *Ibid.*, pp. 79–81.

[100] Wing-tsit Chan, 'Confucian Thought' in *The Encyclopedia of Religion*, ed. Mircea Eliade (New York: MacMillan Publishing Company, 1987), p. 107.

[101] 'Confucius' in *The Oxford Dictionary of World Religions*, ed. John Bowker (Oxford: Oxford University Press, 1997), p. 233.

[102] Ching, Confucianism and Christianity, p. 94.

[103] *Ibid.*, p. 88.

[104] *Ibid.*, p. 77.

[105] *Ibid.*, p. 80.

[106] *Ibid.*

[107] Ching, 'Confucianism: Ethical Humanism and Religion' in *Christianity and Chinese Religions* Hans Küng and Julia Ching (London: Doubleday, 1988), p. 90.

[108] Ching, *Confucianism and Christianity*, p. 87.

[109] *Ibid.*, pp. 87–88.

[110] *Ibid.*, p. 10.

[111] Confucius, *Analects 17.25*, ed. John B. Khu and others, *The Confucian Bible*. (Philippines: Granhill Corporation, 1991), p. 290.

[112] James Legge, *Christianity and Confucianism Compared for Their Teaching on the Whole Duty of Man* (London: Religious Tract Society, n.d.), 29; Hans Küng, 'Confucianism: Ethical Humanism and Religion' in *Christianity and Chinese Religions* Hans Küng and Julia Ching (London: Doubleday, 1988), p. 121.

[113] Ching, 'Confucianism: Ethical Humanism and Religion', p. 90.

[114] Xing Lin Zi, 'Spiritual Moves', p. 163.

[115] Xing Lin Zi, 'Live Well, Die Well', p. 44.

[116] Xing Lin Zi, 'Spiritual Moves', p. 162.

[117] Xing Lin Zi, 'Give Thanks to the Thorny Rose' in *Give Thanks to the Thorny Rose* (Taipei: Chiu-Ko Publishing, 1989), pp. 69–70.

[118] Xing Lin Zi, 'Walking Willingly', p. 186.

[119] Xing Lin Zi, 'Live Well, Die Well', p. 46.

[120] Xing Lin Zi, 'Want to Live', p. 124.

[121] 'Top Taiwanese Author Liu Hsia Dies at 61 after Alleged Assault by Maid' in *Yehey! Corporation*, 8 February 2003 http://www.yehey.com/lifestyle/jpeople.aspx?artid=836 (11 April 2005).

[122] China Post, 'President Appoints New Team of Advisors,' *Taiwan Government Information Office*, 21 May 2001 http://th.gio.gov.tw/show.cfm?news_id=8756 (11 April 2005).

[123] Melody Chen, 'President Promises Disabled Pension Help at Activist's Memorial Service' *Taipei Times*, 23 February 2003, http://www.taipeitimes.com/News/Taiwan/archives/2003/02/23/195596 (11 April 2005).

[124] *Ibid.*; 'Top Taiwanese Author Liu Hsia Dies at 61 after Alleged Assault by Maid'. *Yehey! Corporation*, 8 February 2003 < http://www.yehey.com/lifestyle/jpeople.aspx?artid=836>. Accessed 11 April 2005.

[125] Liu Kan, interview by author, tape recording, Pingtung Taiwan, 27 July 2000.

Index

Scriptural Index

Biblical References

Genesis 3.20	96, n. 86
Genesis 9.18–27	95, n. 57
Genesis 10.1–14	95, n. 56
Genesis 16.12	55, n. 16
Genesis 17.7–8	55, n. 15
Genesis 33	104
2 Samuel 12.1–14	101
2 Samuel 24.11–17	101
1 Chronicles 1.8–16	95, n. 56
Psalm 87	54, n. 10
Isaiah 19.23–24	54, n. 10
Hosea 1.4	101
Hosea 4.4–11	101
Amos 7.17	101
Micah 4.5	54, n. 10
Micah 6.8	54, n. 10
Malachi 2.1–9	101
Matthew 7.18–23	102
Matthew 8.28	31, n. 2
Matthew 25.31–46	173
Matthew 28.18–20	29
Mark 5.1–20	25
Mark 7.6	101
Mark 14.65	101
Luke 1.67	101
Luke 4.18–19	173
John 1.1–18	186, 187 (4x)
John 4.19	101
John 10.30	184 (2x)
John 14.20	185
John 14.28	184
John 17.20–23	184, 185
John 20	109
Acts 2	174
Acts 2.4	101
Acts 2.16–21	101
Acts 4.31	101
Acts 9.4–5	105
Acts 10.46–47	102
Acts 11.28	101
Acts 13.8	102
Acts 17.22–31	15
Acts 21.9	102
Romans 4.20–24	55, n. 14
Romans 5.11	104
1 Corinthians 11.4–5	101
1 Corinthians 14.3, 31	102
2 Corinthians 5.11–21	104, 105, 109, 110
Galatians 3.28	141
Ephesians 1.9–10	194
Ephesians 2.12–16	104
Ephesians 4.11–16	102
Ephesians 5.22	96, n. 88
1 Timothy 1.15–16	109
1 Timothy 2.8–15	96, n. 88
2 Timothy 4.7	127
Hebrews 1.3	62
Revelation 2.20	102

Qur'anic References

S. 3:68	55, n. 18
S. 3:110	38
S. 5.4	38

Lightning Source UK Ltd.
Milton Keynes UK
UKOW06f0730260716

279238UK00005B/205/P